Teacher
TV

Studies in the
Postmodern Theory of Education

Joe L. Kincheloe and Shirley R. Steinberg
General Editors

Vol. 320

PETER LANG
New York • Washington, D.C./Baltimore • Bern
Frankfurt am Main • Berlin • Brussels • Vienna • Oxford

Mary M. Dalton
Laura R. Linder

Teacher
TV

Sixty Years of Teachers on Television

PETER LANG
New York • Washington, D.C./Baltimore • Bern
Frankfurt am Main • Berlin • Brussels • Vienna • Oxford

Library of Congress Cataloging-in-Publication Data

Dalton, Mary M.
Teacher TV: sixty years of teachers on television / Mary M. Dalton, Laura R. Linder.
p. cm.— (Counterpoints; v. 320)
Includes bibliographical references and index.
1. Teachers on television. I. Linder, Laura R.
II. Title. III. Title: Teacher television.
PN1992.8.T3D35   371.33—dc22   2008025247
ISBN 978-0-8204-9715-0
ISSN 1058-1634

Bibliographic information published by **Die Deutsche Bibliothek**.
Die Deutsche Bibliothek lists this publication in the "Deutsche
Nationalbibliografie"; detailed bibliographic data is available
on the Internet at http://dnb.ddb.de/.

Cover photos courtesy of Photofest
Cover design by Joni Holst

The paper in this book meets the guidelines for permanence and durability
of the Committee on Production Guidelines for Book Longevity
of the Council of Library Resources.

© 2008 Peter Lang Publishing, Inc., New York
29 Broadway, 18th floor, New York, NY 10006
www.peterlang.com

Printed in the United States of America

For my son, Dalton Smoot, and my niece, Melanie Joyner

For my father, James B. Linder, my friend and teacher

Contents

Acknowledgments

We wish to acknowledge the support of our friends and colleagues at Marist College and Wake Forest University. We are grateful for the Z. Smith Reynolds Foundation Research Leave awarded to Mary Dalton from Wake Forest University and the special consideration given to Laura Linder from Marist College to work on this project. The staff of the James A. Cannavino Library at Marist College was especially helpful during the early stages of research. It has also been a pleasure to work with the editors and staff at Peter Lang. The team at The Paley Center for Media in New York were especially helpful and allowed us to remain in our cubicle watching episodes until we were bleary eyed. For all their help in securing photos, we thank all the folks at Photofest. The multiple readings and careful editing by Gary Kenton were immeasurably helpful at every stage of the process.

We are grateful to the following students who helped with ideas about series and episodes: Matt Anderson, Sally Brock, Lesley Burkert, Cassie Dorris, Olivia Fisher, Ben Ginn, Emily Goldman, Kevin Hon, Maggie Horne, Katie Kitchin, Jon Kolnoski, Jenna Loeb, Emily Mathews, Laura Riddle, Alex Saks, Stephanie Schmitt, and Chris Sutton. We must extend a special thanks to

Laura Riddle for allowing us to cite a passage from her class journal.

Special teachers who have mentored us along the way are John R. Bittner, Kathleen Casey, Julian C. Burroughs, John Lee Jellicorse, Maggie Mileski, Svi Shapiro, Bynum Shaw, and Robert W. Spires.

To our family and friends outside of our academic circles who have nurtured us and, by extension, this work, every step of the way, we cannot thank you enough. All those long hours, days, and months of work would have been much harder without your love and understanding.

Finally, to all our students throughout the years who have allowed us to be their teachers and to learn from them, we are grateful for the privilege of sharing our knowledge and experiences in the classroom. As teachers on television demonstrate so ably, the best learning process is always reciprocal.

Overview

Why TV? Why Teachers?

This book offers an examination of some of the most influential educator characters presented on primetime television from the earliest sitcoms to contemporary dramas and comedies. Both topical and chronological, the book follows a general course across decades and focuses on dominant themes and representations within each time period. Although the chapters present an overview of the compendium of teachers on television for each decade, the focus of each chapter is a thesis that links some of the most popular shows of the era to larger cultural themes. *Teacher TV: Sixty Years of Teachers on Television* is an extension of the authors' earlier work and melds explorations of the cultural and curricular implications of how teachers are represented in *The Hollywood Curriculum: Teachers in the Movies* and an examination of critical questions of culture and genre taken up in the anthology *The Sitcom Reader: America Viewed and Skewed*.

Why TV?

Robert C. Allen poses the question in the introduction to *Channels of Discourse*

Reassembled. "Why study television? For starters, because it's undeniably, unavoidably 'there.' And, it seems, everywhere" (1). Todd Gitlin is talking about more than television in *Media Unlimited* when he argues that the "main truth" about media is that it "slips through our fingers" (4), and it would be difficult for anyone to refute the importance of analyzing television texts and their larger contexts when considering something else Gitlin goes on to say: "The obvious but hard-to-grasp truth is that living with the media is today one of the main things Americans and many other human beings do" (5). The very obviousness of this condition is precisely what causes people to take television and other media for granted. Gitlin maintains that the reason we spend so much time engaging media is not for information but for "satisfaction, the feeling of feelings" (5–6). We believe the result is not mere stimulation but—intended or not—inculcation from the repetition of specific patterns of representation across time and, in some cases, across media. Our purpose here is to look critically at patterns of representation of teachers that many people "know" but fail to consider carefully and to make connections among these television shows, relevant historical topics, and ideologies.

Visual texts with moving images have become the dominant textual forms of contemporary global culture. Liberal education today must include developing the ability to decode and interrogate visual texts and, optimally, learning to produce them as a means of empowering students. Critical viewing is necessary for consumers of popular culture, but the power to produce goes further and is democratizing. We begin in this book with what is necessary, viewing critically, and introduce a few concepts here that will serve as useful tools for explicating the television shows that feature teacher characters: intertextuality, competing messages, and genre and the popular.

Intertextuality

We know that media—and our particular focus here, television—is ubiquitous but so, very nearly, is schooling. One might point to the growing number of students who are home-schooled and not exposed to professional teachers, but even these students likely have occasion to encounter teachers on television and know about group classrooms if only through narratives shared by others. Most of us, in fact, will encounter more teacher characters over time in mediated classrooms than actual teachers in our own classrooms, and there are certain lessons we learn from these fictional educators. This is also the case for teacher education students (and for actual classroom teachers). In the article "Culture and Pedagogy in Teacher Education," Ronald Soetaert, Andre Mottart, and

Ive Verdoodt discuss exercises they use in a teacher education program to help reveal "literacy myths" in popular texts:

> One of the possible ways to make students aware of the politics of representation is to confront them with the ways—for example—in which "teachers" are represented in literature, movies, advertising, television, and so on. In our teacher training course we invite students to collect material from different media in which teachers and literacy practices and events are represented. (163)

Others, including Dierdre Glenn Paul, have written about their choices to use popular teacher films in teacher education programs for similar reasons. While Henry A. Giroux is framing an argument about the value of studying films when he notes that their "popularity and widespread appeal" are precisely what "warrants an extended analysis"(147), we believe that premise applies equally to television for the same reasons. We see media and culture as indistinct constructs swirling together and sometimes merging as we, individually and collectively, draw on the narratives we encounter as "scripts" filled with both limitations and possibilities for our lives, scripts that provide patterns we draw upon in creating our identities and world views.

We know that media texts never exist separately from contexts, including a reader's own lived experience, and that lived experience is similarly informed by many other media texts and personal narratives. The texts under consideration here, television shows featuring educators, are incorporated into the reader's everyday life at the same time the reader's everyday life becomes part of the construction of the text. John Fiske writes in *Understanding Popular Culture*:

> Because of their incompleteness, all popular texts have leaky boundaries; they flow into each other, they flow into everyday life. Distinctions among texts are as invalid as the distinctions between text and life. Popular culture can be studied only intertextually, for it exists only in this intertextual circulation. The interrelationships between primary and secondary texts cross all boundaries between them; equally, those between tertiary and other texts cross the boundaries between text and life. (p. 126)

To begin to understand ourselves, we must look at the stories that make us who we are and consider the implications of those leaky boundaries.

Competing Messages

The critical tools we will use to contextualize television programs featuring teacher characters are not new to this process. We owe intellectual debts to the critical theorists of the Frankfurt School, researchers at the Centre for Contemporary Cultural Studies in Birmingham in the 1960s and 1970s, feminist media scholars, historiographers, and practitioners of cultural studies, especially Stuart Hall, John Fiske, and Doug Kellner. Their work encourages a multi-layered questioning of media texts[1] within a larger cultural context. This is what we want to do, all the while realizing that our critique may lead to more questions than it answers because meaning in media is dynamic and not particular across time or among readers. The most important point here is to generate an understanding that media texts do not have singular and consistent meanings but can be read critically to encourage a fuller understanding of the competing messages readers can uncover. An example of this type of textual analysis can be found in the analysis of the sitcom *Our Miss Brooks* in Chapter Two. While critics and scholars can argue over preferred readings and interpretations of mass media texts such as television shows and films—and there is an important place for discourses that promote persuasive readings—the fact is that interpretations and meanings of texts will never be monolithic; there can never be a consensus reading, because the lived experiences of audiences (including the training and practice of the readers) will never be completely uniform. Far from making this a discouraging condition, the dynamic and ubiquitous status of media makes its consideration crucial to understanding connections media share with the larger culture. The more time audiences spend with mass media texts, the more important it is for them to begin to question the patterns of representation they see in moving images, to think about the systems that create those images, and to look for links among those images and other sites in their lived experience, including pockets of resistance to dominant depictions.

Genre and the Popular

Although there is no clear consensus among scholars about whether or not genres actually exist let alone what constitutes them, we believe the Good Teacher texts exhibit distinct and identifiable characteristics, or conventions, and that these patterns constitute agency and are significant because they are replicated over time and seen by audiences repeatedly.[2] We are looking for connections between this group of television shows and larger cultural and political concerns. Scholars such as Jane Feuer have noted some usefulness but also some limits of genres in television studies because the medium has a "greater tendency to recombine across genre lines" than film or literature (158). The formal and structural concerns of earlier scholars are of interest to us only in the sense that they may help deepen our textual readings as we look beyond this genre of media texts to a larger social context. Our thinking on this question of genre is much closer to Jason Mittell's in "A Cultural Approach to Television

Genre Theory." He writes, "The goal of most cultural media scholarship is not to understand the media in and of themselves, but rather to look at the workings of media as a component of social contexts and power relations" (178). If our interest in genre studies is qualified, our enthusiasm for taking popular forms seriously is unbridled.

In a new introduction to the 2003 edition of *Reading Television*, John Hartley makes a case for the importance of television studies: "It seeks to make the tacit, implicit knowledge that everyone has as part of the audience, and their general curiosity about contemporary media, into explicit, formal knowledge" (Fiske and Hartley). Allen cites the anthropological tradition of taking something familiar and making it "strange" so that a situation or condition can be considered from a new perspective and suggests the importance of making television strange to encourage new insights into the medium and its cultural influence (3). This is what we propose to do with *Teacher TV*: to elicit a wider understanding of links among history, culture, education, media, and how these sites influence the construction of various identities.

Why Teachers?

How we characterize teachers directly reflects the collective opinion about the larger enterprise of formal education. In the last 10–15 years, academic conferences, papers, and books analyzing the depiction of teachers in popular culture have appeared in a steady stream. The work reflects different traditions and approaches from the sociological (such as Robert C. Bulman's *Hollywood Goes to High School: Cinema, Schools, and American Culture*) to the predominately psychological (such as Jo Keroes' *Tales Out of School: Gender, Longing, and the Teacher in Fiction and Film*) to the autoethnographic (such as Dierdre Glenn Paul's "The Blackboard Jungle: Critically Interrogating Hollywood's Vision of the Urban Classroom") to critical pedagogy and cultural studies (such as Henry A. Giroux's *Breaking in to the Movies: Film and the Culture of Politics*). Most of these studies have focused on teachers in the movies, but the relevance of studying teacher characters certainly transcends media. Furthermore, the overarching themes expressed by these scholars provide a useful background for some of the themes and contexts addressed in this book.

In this section, we'll take a brief look at the most general category of representation for teacher characters then provide a quick overview of the literature linking race and representation to movie teachers and linking eroticism in the classroom to motion pictures. Several scholars have noted the tendency of Hollywood films to depict classroom teachers in a heroic light. Adam Farhi focuses on the "superteacher myth" (157); Rob Edelman dichotomizes idealized teachers into two camps, the "single-mindedly devoted teachers" and the cynics who "persist despite frustration and heartbreak" (28); and William Ayers, who bases his essay on five films, reduces teachers in the movies to "slugs" and "saints" (201). Some of the analyses are more specialized. Lisa Weems links popular culture narratives with lived experiences of teachers and educational policy and identifies three dominant images of substitute teachers in films and television programs—the incompetent, unqualified teacher; the deviant outsider; and the guerrilla superhero—and connects these categories to observations made by professional teachers and to "real life" issues in education such as the teacher shortage, educational reform, and public policy. The problem, however, is that Weems identifies only the 1996 film *The Substitute* and the television shows *My So-Called Life*, *King of the Hill*, and *South Park* as examples of media texts that inform her analysis (she does use some other examples not related to popular culture). Weems is right when she argues that "unpacking these representations with regards to the images and assumptions about teaching that they present might shed insight into the contemporary disjunction in models of teaching that abound in popular culture, classroom practice, and institutional reform" (264), but she does not do enough herself to unpack those very representations. Similarly, Charles A. Duncan, Joe Nolan, and Ralph Wood start an investigation of the negative portrayals of physical education teachers and identify some general thematic patterns that emerge with these characters that merit further study. Some of these essays are interesting and even useful as a starting place for looking at teacher characters, but most of them are reductive in their construction of categorization schemes and do not allow for competing messages in the media texts they consider. Films, like television series, have layers of meaning that include contradictions, even in the stories that seem the most simplistic.

Giroux has written extensively about the links between education and popular culture. His book *Breaking into the Movies: Film and the Culture of Politics* is autobiographical in relating his experience of films from multiple perspectives over time—as a child who loves the movies, as a young high school teacher showing documentaries in class, and as an academic who writes about them as "public pedagogy" (1–6). Among the essays included in this volume, Giroux critiques *Looking for Mr. Goodbar*, *Dead Poets Society*, *Dangerous Minds*, and *187*. While his passion for movies has not wavered, the context in which he sees them has expanded over time. "Films do more than entertain, they offer up subject positions, mobilize desires, influence us unconsciously, and help to construct the landscape of American culture" (2). Certainly, part of that cultural landscape includes race and sexuality, and scholars writing about teachers in the movies have been attentive to these constructs.

In his book *Hollywood Films About Schools: Where Race, Politics, and Education Intersect*, Ronald E. Chennault looks primarily at films that focus on teachers and principals that were released between 1980–2000 and were widely seen by audiences either in theatrical release or on cable and home video. Like others writing about race and representation in teacher movies, Chennault is particularly interested in *Dangerous Minds*, which he cites for its "regressive and demeaning" racial representations (118) and its attempts to "reestablish white supremacy" as part of the natural order of things (121). Robert Lowe also identifies *Dangerous Minds* as a "blatantly racist film" (212), and Giroux writes that the film "attempts to represent 'whiteness' as the archetype of rationality, authority, and cultural standards" (46). In her book *Tales Out of School: Gender, Longing, and the Teacher in Fiction and Film*, Jo Keroes writes primarily about sexuality, but she also notes that "teacher narratives have trouble with race" (71). Keroes does an excellent job detailing two of the common problems:

> When the teacher belongs to a minority group, he must, despite his "difference," uphold conventional mainstream values; when the students are members of minorities, they appear to represent the liberal vision of an oppressed group waiting to be rescued, usually by a white teacher-knight, while they remind us of the fears such groups engender. They must be tamed. (71)

Television depictions of race in the classroom were initially nonexistent, then careful, and now sometimes surprisingly complex. It is, perhaps, intuitive to believe that films would offer a more progressive set of depictions than television, but the lower production costs of some series compared to major motion pictures and, more importantly, the episodic nature of the television narrative without the constraint of a self-contained narrative arc limited to roughly two hours of running time creates a set of possibilities for television and cable series that is not shared by commercial Hollywood films.

In "Indecent Proposals: Teachers in the Movies," Dale M. Bauer argues that teaching, as depicted once in the movies as a "profound calling" has become a "sexual proposition" (302), but the intriguing critiques given to some films in the essay do not develop overarching themes needed for a convincing meta-analysis of the genre. Keroes provides a more expansive and compelling view. With an overarching argument that "teacher texts are fundamentally about love" (66), she argues that as a microcosm of the larger culture, the classroom—with the teacher as an authority figure—presents gender and power relations and expresses "a connection between teaching and sexual politics" (9). Later Keroes' argument, based on typical narrative patterns in teacher films, is developed further:

> When the teacher is male, he brings the force of public masculine power and all that it entails into the relatively confined psychic and social space of the classroom, where it may be subject to potential challenges but is almost always reconfirmed. When the teacher is a woman, she generates conflict between unleashed maternal (female) power and the alluring solace of domestic space. (15)

Of course, as Keroes notes, men regularly "succumb to the erotic temptations teaching affords" (15) while the "erotic impulses of women teachers are usually suppressed, disguised, or demonized" (16). As with representations of race and teaching, television has begun to offer a modestly wider range of acceptable expressions of sexuality for women teachers than cinematic depictions. While the bulk of scholarly writing about representations of teacher characters in popular culture has focused on film, some interesting and surprising developments have been taking place on television.[3] The answer to the question "Why Teachers?" posed at the beginning of this section relates to the recent rush of interest in academic writing about teachers in popular culture. It is at least partly due to the fact that the writers themselves are often teachers. The ruptures between what happens in our own classrooms and those depicted in films and television programs are sometimes glaring but also revealing. Understanding the patterns perpetuated in popular culture is an important enterprise for teachers and students alike because of the role film and television play in establishing our expectations and shaping our identities. Before turning our attention to television for the remainder of the book, however, it is useful to look at one more analysis of teacher characters in films and to make connections between how Hollywood has constructed the celebrated Good Teacher character in the movies and how that character has emerged on television.

The Hollywood Model

In Dalton's *The Hollywood Curriculum: Teachers in the Movies*, a study of over 115 popular films released in the United States over a period of 75 years, distinct patterns of representation for teachers and principals emerge. Because virtually all of the teachers in starring roles on television fall into the Good Teacher category of representation, it is useful to take a look at the "The Hollywood Model" of the good teacher outlined in *The Hollywood Curriculum* to first draw parallels, and identify divergences, in portrayals of educators. Movie depictions of dedicated (and even heroic) teachers have been remarkably consistent over time to the degree that the patterns and conventions suggest a genre of Good Teacher movies. Although there are earlier films, *Goodbye, Mr. Chips* (1939) is a good example of the primitive cycle of the Good Teacher movie when the conventions of the genre are first taking shape. *Blackboard Jungle* (1955) codifies the conventions of the form and launches the classical cycle of these films. As the genre matures, it spawns the parody *High School High* (1996) that reinforces the readily identifiable conventions of the genre by spoofing them (parodic cycle). The final generic cycle to emerge is revisionism. Although there have been revisionist elements in some Good Teacher movies over time, the boldest and fully revisionist films have emerged more recently: *Election* (1999) and *Half Nelson* (2006).

Television representations of teachers, beginning in the early 1950s, follow the Hollywood Model closely for several decades before developing, perhaps surprisingly, a more progressive and expansive portrayal of Good Teachers, especially with regard to women teachers and gay teachers beginning in the 1990s before cinema's revisionist teachers emerge onscreen. Although genres are more problematic constructions for television than for film, a topic to be addressed later, most of the conventional traits given to Good Teachers in the movies are transferred, at least in some degree, to teachers on television. The defining characteristics of cinema's Good Teachers are as follows: they are outsiders of one type of another; they become involved with their students on a personal level; they learn important lessons from their students; they often have problems with administrators; they personalize the curriculum; and, many of them have a ready sense of humor, especially the males.

Outsider

Invariably, good teachers in the movies are positioned as outsiders of one sort or another in their schools, either by virtue of their social class, race or ethnicity, nationality, political ideology, sexual orientation, the fact that they have trained for a profession other than teaching, or some combination of these traits. There are compelling reasons for screenwriters to construct their characters this way (even in the popular teacher biopics, which are based on or inspired by events in real teachers' lives or memoirs[4]). Hollywood films are rife with iconic individualist characters who stand up to authority and fight the good fight—from rugged cowboys to hard-boiled reporters to mysterious detectives to heroic teachers. Casting these stock types as outsiders up against the oppressive system raises the stakes by ratcheting up the narrative conflicts and also engages viewers in the drama.

Because of the episodic nature of television series, teachers on TV are differentiated from their peers in one way or another, and certainly elevated by their starring status when they are eponymous characters or part of a featured cohort, but their outsider status is tempered if it is left intact. Television has a tendency to smooth out some of the rough edges in character and story to appeal to the broadest possible audience and, especially before Federal Communications Commission (FCC) deregulation during the Reagan administration, there were guidelines in place that limited just how far television could go, even in primetime, to explore controversial topics and present complex characters if that complexity suggested a deviation from the perceived "norm." For most of its short history, television has made safe programming choices, and the broadcast stations have shown little resistance to FCC programming rules.[5] It is fair to say that Good Teachers on television have been positioned as outsiders in subtle ways that are discernible either by deep readings of television series that encourage alternate interpretations, or readings "against the grain," or distinguished by making these featured teachers "more" and "better" than their colleagues. For example, Miss Brooks' acerbic wit is indelible on *Our Miss Brooks*, Gabe Kotter is cooler and funnier than anyone else on *Welcome Back, Kotter*, and Mr. Cooper was a professional basketball player before becoming a teacher on *Hangin' with Mr. Cooper*. They do not have the outsider status that is conferred on teachers in the movies because that dramatic tension could not be sustained easily or credibly on episodic television over a long period of time.

Personally Involved with Students

The second characteristic of the Hollywood Model of good teachers is also evident in many of the television series we studied, especially the sitcoms. These good teachers are frequently more closely aligned with their students than with anyone else in the school, which links them to young people rather than their peers. Because of the dramatic possibilities presented by films, this alliance between teacher and student often involves some incarnation of "breaking the rules" in the service of justice or student empowerment, and the types of activities range from relatively benign to quite serious. A typical manifestation of this story element is the teacher's repeated attempts to connect with the most difficult or distant student in the class, a connection that is finally forged either in the climax or resolution of the film. While not all Good Teachers fit this paradigm—after all, Professor Kingsfield in *The Paper Chase* is a distant taskmaster who emerges as a gruff mentor rather than a friend—it is easy to recall other teachers and counselors who do—from laid back, aging hippie Charlie Moore on *Head of the Class* to English teacher Richard Katimski on *My So-Called Life* who lets a homeless student live with him to counselor Tami Taylor on *Friday Night Lights* who is concerned about the totality of her students' lives.

Learns from Students

One generic convention of the Good Teacher movie is that the teacher must become the student; at least once over the course of these films, usually when the teacher has become tired and discouraged somewhere past the halfway mark in the story, the Good Teacher makes some sort of breakthrough in reaching the most difficult or elusive student or in some other way learns a lesson that keeps her or him going in order to tackle another obstacle and teach another day. Usually, the lessons these teachers learn could be reframed as prosaic, but perhaps comforting, platitudes, something like the following: "Quitters never win, and winners never quit." The narrative structure of television being what it is, there are many more opportunities over the course of a season for TV teachers to learn from students, and often they do. Chet Kincaid has his eyes opened about discrimination in an episode of *The Bill Cosby Show*, Edna Garrett learns to stand up for what she believes in, and Gabe Kotter discovers that his students learn because they feel accepted and secure in his classroom. The importance of this narrative device is not limited to the actual lessons that the Good Teachers learn from students, but the greater significance is the promotion of a progressive idea of reciprocal education in which the authority figures—the teachers—do not possess all of the knowledge and the power that goes along with deciding what constitutes knowledge and how it will be disseminated.

Problems with Administrators

Their outsider status contributes to the problems teachers in the movies have with administrators, and there is usually a storyline in these films related to their conflicts. These administrators, who are often department chairs jealous of the new teacher, range from outright villains dripping with malicious intent to uninterested paper pushers who don't want to be bothered, to former idealists, who are just too beaten down to care much anymore. Their role in these films is to provide one more obstacle for the Good Teacher to overcome to connect with her or his students and make a positive difference in their lives. Notably, Good Teachers usually win a symbolic but hollow victory in teacher movies, and the feel-good effect of that victory masks the fact that the system never really changes in Good Teacher movies. Audiences have the pleasure of watching progressive teachers go up against the system (and helping individual students but not succeeding in mustering collective action) and the dubious comfort of stability when the status quo is intact at the end of the film. Television shows have a bounty of administrators, mostly principals and vice principals, who are less than enthusiastic and encouraging. In his survey of thirty-five television programs and films from 1950 to 1996, Jeffrey Glanz identifies three patterns of representation of principals: first, an authoritarian principal with an autocratic management style; second, the principal-as-bureaucrat, who puts paper above people; and third, the principal-as-numbskull, whose dimness is exaggerated (4–5). It is easy to see how these three dominant representations would put television principals in conflict with dedicated teachers. How could it be otherwise? In a footnote, Glanz observes that not all administrators are portrayed negatively but argues that even good principals like Mr. Kaufman "when portrayed positively in shows such as *Room 222*, grapple with bureaucratic and autocratic tendencies" (23). His major example of the principal-as-numbskull is the often maligned character on *Welcome Back, Kotter*, Mr. Woodman, a memorable object of ridicule on virtually every episode.

Personalizes the Curriculum

Teachers in the movies, when they are the protagonists, are shown in the classroom actually teaching more than their television counterparts because the films are usually plotted around conflicts related to the teaching process while the television programs usually feature a series of storylines focused on various interpersonal situations. When teachers in the movies personalize the curriculum to meet everyday needs in their students' lives, pedagogical strategies are employed to "reach" students or otherwise engage them in learning with the goal of making the experience transformative. In television, the curriculum is usually personalized as a plot device or a punchline. In an episode of *Mister Peepers*, for example, Robinson Peepers invites his students to bring their pets to science class, and he is forced to try to hide a cow when the superintendent decides to make an unannounced inspection of the school that day. This is a far cry from James Leeds using the vibrations of rock music to encourage his deaf students to sing in *Children of a Lesser God*, but both curricula are personalized nonetheless.

Sense of Humor

This final characteristic is not a standard trait of the Good Teacher in The Hollywood Model, though commonplace enough that it was noted in *The Hollywood Curriculum*, and a ready sense of humor is even more likely to be a trait ascribed to television teachers on sitcoms. Gabe Kaplan's character on *Welcome Back, Kotter* arises from his stand-up routine, and Bill Cosby was a successful stand-up comedian before he became the teacher/coach Chet Kincaid on *The Bill Cosby Show*. Eve Arden is known for her humorous portrayals from droll to wisecracking, and she hits every comedic note in between throughout her career playing characters in motion pictures, radio, and television, but she is best known as Miss Brooks, a spinster English teacher with a sense of humor marked by a hard edge. Given the nature of the sitcom, most teacher characters in starring roles get more than their share of punchlines.

Many of the teachers on television are demonstrably good teachers. They encompass some or all of the characteristics of a Good Teacher as noted above. They are outsiders like Edna Garrett and Charlie Moore. They become involved with and learn from their students, like Chet Kincaid and Gabe Kaplan. They personalize the curriculum. Most display an independence that puts them at odds with administrators. And, as mentioned above, nearly all of them possess a sense of humor capable of defusing any situation—and smoothing over potential controversies. Teacher characters abound on television, and their portrayals seep into our consciousness. Through examination and deconstruction of these characters and their contexts, we gain a better understanding of how the Good Teacher archetype influences us.

Upcoming Chapters

Subsequent chapters will trace the evolution of portrayals of teachers on television chronologically and topically. Chapter Two, "1950s Gender Wars: *Mister Peepers* and *Our Miss Brooks*," compares and contrasts the most popular teacher sitcom starring a woman with the only program to offer her a contemporary. Wise-cracking spinster Connie Brooks chases after her oblivious colleague, a science teacher named Mr. Boynton, and she exhibits a strength and independence along with her sense of humor that makes her performance indelible. Mr. Peepers, on the other hand, is a mild-mannered science teacher who appears to fumble through school situations but ultimately prevails over the problems that arise. Although he is single as the show launches, Mr. Peepers eventually marries school nurse Nancy Remington. The contrast between acceptable behavior for men teachers and for women teachers on television offers a context for making links to how gender is socially constructed in popular culture and in society, as well as exploring how media and society simultaneously construct and reflect one another.

The war between the sexes provides explicit tension in the most popular of 1950s TV classrooms, but the racial tensions of the 1960s will take a more implicit form on two series. The iconography of Bill Cosby and the social movements that inform any analysis of this decade are cornerstones of Chapter Three, "1960s Race and Social Relevancy: *The Bill Cosby Show* and *Room 222*." Bill Cosby plays a physical education teacher in the unconventional sitcom (no laugh track, single-camera, and location shoots). The show follows Cosby's historic co-starring role in *I Spy* that marked the reintroduction of a Black character in a major role into primetime for the first time since early 1950s "dialect comedies" such as *Amos 'n' Andy*. *Room 222*, also set in Los Angeles and featuring a male, African American history teacher, is a dramedy (hybrid sitcom/drama) that complements the tone and overall style of *The Bill Cosby Show*. Most episodes of each series are structured around teaching a lesson; usually a general lesson of tolerance designed to have universal appeal. These programs contrast sharply in tone with the better-known social relevancy sitcoms on the horizon, such as *All in the Family*.

Just as the more pointed cultural critiques characterizing social relevancy programs sidestep classroom settings—perhaps because students provide so much impetus to social movements in real life that mainstream television programs were bound to appear bland in comparison—the ideology of the classroom setting in the 1970s becomes implicit as creative teams strive for neutrality in entertainment. In Chapter Four, "1970s Ideology and Social Class: *Welcome Back, Kotter* and *The Paper Chase*," identification of both lower and upper ends of the class spectrum is blunted in favor of storylines that are personal and predictable instead of overtly political. *Welcome Back, Kotter* replicates the inner-city location and vocational approach to education brought to film twenty years before in *Blackboard Jungle* when former student Gabe Kotter returns to teach at his old school, but the television series removes both the threat and the promise of the students along with any compelling representation of their status in the underclass. At the other end of the spectrum, *The Paper Chase* follows a law student at an Ivy League school through his encounters with a brilliant but demanding professor, who is both aloof and certain of his place at the top of the Ivy League. By minimizing the consequences and implications of social class at both ends of the spectrum, these series also minimize the importance of class in America.

The 1980s mark a return to conservatism in American party politics, and two popular television sitcoms reflect the transition by validating educational privileges for elite students. Chapter Five, "1980s Normalizing Meritocracy: *The Facts of Life* and *Head of the Class*," looks at two groups of students and who are accorded special status in the classroom. *The Facts of Life* is set at a girls' boarding school, and *Head of the Class* is set at an urban public school in a special class for academically gifted students. In both cases, the shows suggest that these special students have earned their rightful places of privilege, and their teachers are complicit in perpetuating the meritocracy.

The 1990s mark a time of significant change for teachers on television. In Chapter Six, "Gaining Ground from Margin to Center: *Hangin' with Mr. Cooper* and *My So-Called Life*," the most popular TV teacher of the decade is an African American man and the most surprising depiction of a teacher is of a gay man. In *Hangin' with Mr. Cooper*, an African American teacher (a character who was briefly a professional basketball player no less), assumes the title role, and his cousin, an African American woman, becomes principal of the school where he teaches. Although the ratings for the series were erratic over its five seasons, it still ranks as one of the top five teacher sitcoms of all time. The most provocative depiction of a teacher on television during the decade was not found in a sitcom, however, but in an understated drama that lasted a single season on ABC before gaining cult status in syndication and DVD release. *My So-Called Life* embedded many compelling themes into the everyday lives of a diverse group of high school students, but of prime concern to this project is English teacher Richard Katimski, who is gay and a mentor to Rickie Vasquez, a gay Hispanic fifteen-year-old, who is being raised by a physically abusive uncle. Katimski and his partner eventually become foster parents for Rickie, which is an extraordinary transition for a teacher to make, especially on television.

Chapter Seven pulls together many of the themes expressed previously— gender, race, social class, sexual orientation—and explores them through a new lens in "Embracing Multiculturalism: *Boston Public*." For the first four years of a new century, the drama *Boston Public* broadened the scale of *My So-Called Life* by considering more types of issues but took a similar approach to embedding controversial topics into the everyday lives of teachers and students at a large, diverse high school. The program is radical in at least one regard—women teachers are allowed to express their sexuality without being directly punished for it. (Remarkably, this is a boundary yet to be crossed in cinema.) This chapter will conclude with an overview of the ways in which conventions of teachers on television have remained the same and other ways in which they have evolved over time and the significance of those patterns of representation.

Finally, Chapter Eight will look beyond the TV teachers to explore more fully the world in which they work, including larger issues related to the depictions of students, administrators, and schools. Broadly ideological, "What About Students and Schools?" places teacher characters into the larger landscape of their television series to look more closely at power relationships and the politics of place before looking beyond the small screen to explore the cultural implications of these television narratives.

In of the 2000 edition of *Television: The Critical View*, Horace Newcomb says that there remains one step, a final stage, in the history of television criticism.

> In that stage the serious histories, the detailed analyses, the studies of television reception that now remain, in every sense of the word, "academic" approaches to television, will be shared more widely with all audiences. (9–10)

This wide sharing is what we hope *Teacher TV* will achieve. We hope this book will be of use to the academy, to students in teacher education programs, to classroom teachers, and to the general public.

TWO

1950s Gender Wars

Mister Peepers and *Our Miss Brooks*

Before 1950, the history of television was marked by patent wars, testing plans, and various demonstrations of technology but not a great deal of programming. On July 1, 1941, NBC became the first network to launch a commercially sponsored broadcast; CBS and others followed, but the advent of World War II quickly led the FCC to ban the commercial production of television equipment for the duration of the war. Postwar prosperity and a broad cultural desire for "normalcy" following the Great Depression and World War II created a surge in demand for television. It is estimated that there were fewer than 10,000 sets in 1945, about six million in 1950, and almost 60 million by 1960.[1]

The decade was marked by expansion in programming and technology except for the development of color, which was suspended in 1951 for the duration of the Korean conflict. That same year, *I Love Lucy* (CBS, 1951–61) became the first sitcom filmed in front of a live audience; it's only fitting that *TV Guide* began publication in 1953 with a picture of Desi Arnaz, Jr. and a little insert of Lucille Ball on the cover. The FCC lifted its four-year "freeze" on the construction of new television stations in 1952. Two other developments might have been less heralded at the time but have certainly resonated over time: Robert Adler invented a remote control called the Zenith Space Commander in 1955, and overnight local market ratings were introduced by Nielsen Media Research in New York in 1959.

Early television networks emerged from the successful radio networks, and programming at the beginning of the decade was dominated by the same formats proven on radio. Musical programs, variety shows, and sitcoms were early TV favorites. *I Love Lucy* was a ratings powerhouse, rated third highest show in its first season (1951–52) and ranked first in four of the next five seasons. *Gunsmoke* (CBS, 1955–75) would claim the top spot in the ratings for four consecutive seasons beginning in 1957. Some of the other popular programs of the 1950s were *Arthur Godfrey's Talent Scouts* (CBS, 1948–58), *Dragnet* (NBC, 1952–70), *The $64,000 Question* (CBS, 1955–58), *Alfred Hitchcock Presents* (CBS, 1955–60), *The Danny Thomas Show* (ABC, 1953–57; CBS, 1957–64), *The Real McCoys* (ABC, 1957–62; CBS, 1962–63), *Perry Mason* (CBS, 1957–66), and *Wagon Train* (NBC, 1957–62; ABC, 1962–65). As the decade unfolded, production values for programs rose so that television shows began to look more like low budget movies with more realistic sets, location shoots, and recognizable guest stars than earlier shows that either had the constraints of studio-produced live programming or lacked the larger budgets of top programs like *I Love Lucy*.

It is tempting to think of 1950s television programs as bland, formulaic, and mildly reassuring. That characterization would be as incomplete, however, as suggesting that 1950s culture was as calm as the surface conformity invariably associated with the period. While it is the case that middle class White women who were encouraged to work outside of the home as part of the war effort were displaced by returning GIs and very many of them were dispatched to the suburbs, the idyllic lifestyle promised by that transition, and relentlessly marketed on television (as Gerard Jones notes in *Honey, I'm Home! Sitcoms: Selling the American Dream*), was not seamless and untroubled. As Betty Friedan would document in *The Feminine Mystique*, White middle class women retreated to the suburbs and a life of domesticity, supported by a slew of new labor-saving devices, but the result for many was not unmitigated domestic bliss but rather a sense of unease and loss of identity. Just as television would fail to note this apparently widespread dissatisfaction, the lives of women of color and working class women would be largely ignored on the small screen in the 1950s.

The question isn't whether or not dissatisfaction with gender roles existed in life or in television—after all, gender wars were a regular fixture on sitcoms from the beginning, and seeds of suburban dissent flowered into the consciousness raising and political protests that marked the second wave of the women's movement a decade later. The question that endures in the wake of the second wave is whether viewers have the critical tools to read television texts against the grain. Narratives always include competing messages, but viewers have not always been trained or encouraged to read them. The 1950s might be a rather bland decade of relative prosperity and conformity, but it is also the decade that gave rise to the cold war, McCarthyism, the civil rights movement, the second wave of the women's movement, beatniks, Elvis Presley (who wasn't bland at the time), and art house cinemas screening complex films by international directors. Even the form that might be considered by some the blandest and most formulaic of all—the sitcom—is open to a critical reading. Consider Gerard Jones' commentary on one of the most emblematic family sitcoms of all time: *Leave It to Beaver* (CBS, 1957–58; ABC, 1958–63). Jones argues that "A subtle but constant theme of the show was that the Cleavers were the only functional family around" (127). A simple shift in perspective shines an entirely different light on Mayfield, revealing that Eddie Haskell is an "enemy of authority," that Larry Mondello's compulsive eating and disobedience are related to the fact that his father is always away on business and his mother is an "ineffectual nut," that Lumpy Rutherford is smothered by his father's "preposterous expectations and a projected self-image," and that Whitey Whitney is a "high-strung kid prone to psychosomatic ailments" continually yelled at by his parents (Jones 127). Ward and June Cleaver may seem like nearly perfect parents, and Wally and Beaver are good kids, but looking beyond 211 Pine Street to the rest of the neighborhood offers a more complex and less reassuring view.[2]

Teachers on TV: The 1950s

The same can be said for depictions of teachers on television even from the earliest days. On the surface, teachers offer a comforting reassurance that the world is predictable and everything turns out all right in the end, but reading series against the grain and considering series within a larger and more complex cultural context uncovers competing messages within and between programs. This is especially true of the two most popular and enduring teacher programs of the decade, the sitcoms *Mister Peepers* and *Our Miss Brooks*. Before turning to an in-depth analysis of these two shows in the context of gender politics, it is useful to look briefly at the handful of other programs featuring educators broadcast during the period.

School House (Dumont 1949) is a comedy variety program broadcast for only three months. Set in a school, the "teacher" is played by emcee Kenny

Delmar. A rotating roster of children comprises the student body. One of the youngsters is Wally Cox, who would go on to play general science teacher Robinson Peepers just a few years later on *Mister Peepers*.[3] In the early days of television, older forms often served as inspiration for series, and *School House* is based on a vaudeville routine that had been popular nearly fifty years before. No school teacher has a more unusual profile than the emcee on *Life with Snarky Parker* (CBS, 1950), which features marionettes and ran for eight months. Snarky Parker is a deputy sheriff in an old Western town, and he is in love with the school teacher, the only puppet school teacher to hit primetime television.

Stu Erwin is notable as the eponymous character in *The Stu Erwin Show* (ABC, 1950–55), "perhaps TV's leading bumbling-father series in the 1950s" (Brooks and Marsh 1143). Erwin plays the principal of Hamilton High School rather than a teacher, and most of the activity of the sitcom centers around his life at home rather than at school. *The Sam Levenson Show* (CBS, 1951–52) is a comedy show featuring Levenson, a former school teacher, as the only regular on this series that aired live from New York. His monologues were a notable feature of the program, and many of these humorous pieces were based on his experiences as a teacher.

Mister Peepers (NBC, 1952–55) and *Our Miss Brooks* (CBS, 1952–56), which will be discussed in detail later in the chapter, feature strong actors in indelible roles. *Mister Peepers* is original to television while *Our Miss Brooks* is based on the radio program of the same title that ran from 1948–57. It is difficult to imagine better examples than these two sitcoms for considering the double standard that exists for women teachers on television (and in the movies) when it comes to balancing a personal life off the clock and a professional presence in the classroom.

Three other series of note emerged in the mid-1950s. In the first season, *The Ray Milland Show* (CBS, 1953–55) was titled *Meet Mr. McNutley*, and Milland plays the head of the English department at a women's college. During the second season he returns, with the last name McNulty, as a drama professor at a coeducational university. Many plots in this sitcom revolve around his problems with other faculty members, and even though women colleagues and students find him attractive and charming, his wife remains loving and supportive throughout. An administrator rather than a teacher, Ronald Colman plays Dr. William Todhunter Hall, president of Ivy College, in the sitcom *Halls of Ivy* (CBS, 1954–55). The program is based on the radio program of the same name that ran from 1950–52 on CBS. In the sitcom *Dear Phoebe* (NBC, 1954–56), Peter Lawford plays a former college instructor who has given up teaching to write an advice column in a newspaper under the name Phoebe Goodheart.

Gender Wars: The Double Standard
Outside the Classroom

The double standard for teachers that originates on television in the 1950s—but is not confined to this decade—is illustrated by comparing and contrasting the most popular teacher sitcom in television history starring a woman, *Our Miss Brooks*, with the only program to offer her a male contemporary in that decade, *Mister Peepers*. *Our Miss Brooks* first aired in October 1952, exactly three months after *Mister Peepers*. Robinson Peepers is a mild-mannered science teacher who appears to fumble through school situations but ultimately prevails with kindness and surprising grace. Although he is single as the show launches, Mr. Peepers starts dating school nurse Nancy Remington the first season and eventually marries her. In marked contrast, wise-cracking spinster Connie Brooks chases after her oblivious colleague, a science teacher named Mr. Boynton, but never gets her man. Both characters prevail over annoying or ineffectual administrators, colleagues, and students in situations that arise each episode, but they do so with completely different personal styles. Their differences transcend personal style, however, to offer insights into larger cultural attitudes about gender roles and the public and private spheres. The contrast between acceptable behavior for men and women teachers on television offers a context for making links to how gender is socially constructed in popular culture and in society, as well as exploring how media and society simultaneously construct and reflect one another.

Examining portrayals of teachers on television reveals striking differences in many cases between men and women teachers once they step outside the classroom, a pattern similar to gendered depictions of teachers in motion pictures analyzed in *The Hollywood Curriculum: Teachers in the Movies* (see Chapter Five). In both television shows and movies featuring teachers, it is clear that relatively fewer of these narratives star women than men as the central character, despite the fact that there are nearly three times as many women as men actually teaching in America's public elementary and secondary school classrooms.[4] Aside from the small volume of narratives featuring women, there is a distinct difference in the stories depending on the sex of the teacher character who plays the lead role; in the first decades of television, women teachers are forced into divided lives in which they must privilege their jobs over their lives away from work to be considered Good Teachers, and these characters are not allowed to have satisfying personal lives that include a romantic (no less sexual) component. Ironically, however, both women and men teachers are seldom seen actually teaching in their classrooms in the texts surveyed. Instead, their days are generally spent sparring with administrators, kibitzing with colleagues, or running interference for students. In terms of sexual politics, television has been a more progressive medium than film by expanding our ideas about Good Teachers who are women and/or gay at an earlier date.

While television has enlarged the opportunities available to women outside of the classroom in recent years with shows such as *Boston Public*, movies continue to thwart women teachers' desires for romantic fulfillment or to punish the characters in some way for expressing their sexuality.[5] This pattern was established before teacher characters moved from the big screen to the small screen, and the 1950s television sitcoms considered here reinforce these narrow images of teachers. Both Robinson Peepers and Connie Brooks fit the Hollywood Model of the Good Teacher set forth in Chapter One. Teacher sitcoms draw on the established tradition and conventions of the Good Teacher in the movies and fold that model into the sitcom format, a relatively new television format when *Mister Peepers* and *Our Miss Brooks* were launched but fully established by the time the other most popular or influential of the teacher sitcoms and dramas went on the air beginning in the late 1960s.

Mister Peepers

In films and early television programs, most women teachers are single and childless, or their marital and maternal status is not revealed to the audience. While many of the male teachers portrayed in films and some of those on television are also single, others are not, and the issues are different for men and women teachers. On television, as in the movies, male teachers are allowed to have happy, full lives outside of the classroom *and* to be heroes at school. Consider the main male characters in four of the top five rated teacher sitcoms of all time: Chet Kincaid (Bill Cosby) in *The Bill Cosby Show*; Gabe Kotter (Gabe Kaplan) in *Welcome Back, Kotter*; Charlie Moore (Howard Hesseman) in *Head of the Class*; and Mark Cooper (Mark Curry) in *Hangin' with Mr. Cooper*. All of these characters have some combination of casual dates, love interests, and lasting relationships in their respective series, and Gabe Kotter and his wife, Julie, became the parents of twins during the run of the show. Men teachers are allowed a range of moral latitude that is not open to female teachers. Even a man as seemingly unlikely to attract romantic attention as Robinson Peepers finds a girlfriend almost immediately on *Mister Peepers*, and many of the storylines involve his personal relationship.

Figure 2.1. Patricia Benoit as Nancy Remington and Wally Cox as Robinson Peepers in *Mister Peepers* (NBC, 1952–55). Photo courtesy of Photofest. Used by permission.

Mr. Peepers is infantilized by the school nurse in the pilot episode of the series when she mistakes him for one of the junior high school students sent to her for care and shoves a thermometer in his mouth over his feeble protests. It's no wonder, really, that she makes this mistake. Peepers is slight of stature, his ill-fitting suit jacket makes him look like a boy in his father's coat, he peers shyly at the world from behind oversized glasses, and his soft, high-pitched voice is not unpleasant but sounds as if he might be locked in the midst of puberty. Mr. Peepers typified the common perception of "nerd" before the term entered the lexicon in the 1960s. His articles for the publication "Petal and Stem" send the old ladies of the wildflower group into an appreciative tizzy (07–10–52)[6] and motivate the owner of the Winkler Seed Company to offer Peepers a fabulous salary to sell their products (08–28–52). When his sister comes to town, the lack of contrast between siblings is startling. She looks like her brother; she works at an observatory; she brings him a Geiger counter as a gift, and they talk joyfully about assorted scientific subjects. Gender is the great divide, however. Peepers has gone from being treated like a child by the school nurse in the pilot episode to having his romantic fortunes improve considerably over the season without any adjustment on his part, yet he advises his sister that she will need to play down her intelligence in order to attract a man.

In the third episode of the series (07–31–52), the music appreciation teacher Rayola Dean (Norma Crane) casts her eye on the new science teacher. She knows that Peepers has not yet received his first paycheck and believes that he is not eating well, so she enlists the help of the home economics teacher to prepare him a wonderful meal under the pretext of having him sample some food. Their understated flirtation continues intermittently for several episodes, but an episode focused on the school dance (09–11–52) marks the appearance of Peepers' best friend, history teacher Harvey "Wes" Weskit (Tony Randall) and the reappearance of school nurse Nancy Remington (Patricia Benoit). As the episode opens, Peepers is decorating for the school dance but says he isn't planning to go because he doesn't like to dance. When Weskit goes on about his conquests, Peepers, whom "Wes" tends to call "Rob" or "Robby," talks as if he has had a number of girlfriends, too. About this time, Nancy Remington walks past, smiles at Peepers, and says "Good morning." The sound effect indicating an arrow piercing Peepers' heart lets the audience know that something significant has happened. The shy science teacher asks the school nurse to the dance, and while Weskit is the one who actually takes her out on the dance floor, the new couple enjoys a promising talk about botany on the balcony. Their courtship in subsequent episodes is not without some minor complications, but its tenderness and steady progress to their marriage on the air at the end of the 1953–54 season seem a natural progression for two quiet, gentle characters.

While Peepers is clearly the focus of each episode, there is another teacher who merits special consideration because he illustrates a different but very common portrayal of male teachers. It is a bit odd at first to see Tony Randall, who later became known for his portrayal of the simpering and fastidious Felix Unger on *The Odd Couple*, play a buff and confident ladies man on *Mister Peepers*. Weskit is always giving Peepers advice on how to handle his girlfriend, advice that does not suit Robinson Peepers' quiet persona, but somehow things always turn out all right in the end when Peepers admits his discomfort and shows his characteristic grace. While Peepers' romance with Remington is moving along at a gentle pace, the Christmas episode of the first season (12–21–52) reveals that Weskit is about to marry a rich woman from Chicago and leave Jefferson City to work in his prospective father-in-law's meatpacking firm. Peepers arrives for the bachelor party, and the brother of the bride makes fun of the sensitive intellectual. Weskit, standing up for his friend, takes an early train with Peepers back to Jefferson City where Weskit says he intends to stay and teach. His fiancée shows up on the train and announces that she's going to Jefferson City with Weskit for the holidays and that she will move there when they marry. Given the standard pro-consumerist and anti-intellectual bent of most mass media, Weskit's decision to leave the big bucks and city life behind for his version of the life of the mind is a bit surprising. What is not represented as an anomaly, however, is Weskit's ability to have both personal and professional elements to his life as he moves seamlessly from private to public spheres and from casually dating many women to settling down with one.

Where does teaching fit in the lives of these teachers? For most television teachers, the classroom is just a set (in some cases rarely visited) to launch a conversation or to serve as a transition between scenes. While we see Mr. Peepers in front of the blackboard and hear fragments of some lectures, most of these scenes are truncated and only very rarely are students shown participating. In one episode (08–21–52), Mr. Peepers has students bring their pets to school and deliver oral essays about them with the complication that one student brings a cow on the day the superintendent shows up for an inspection. In another episode (09–18–52), a troubled student wreaks havoc with what should have been a simple experiment, and Mr. Peepers takes it upon himself to go to the boy's house and take him fishing to try to forge a connection with the student. Later in the term (12–07–52), a student gets a crush on Mr. Peepers, and he is at a loss as to how to handle the situation. The plots are standard and the resolutions not surprising, but the genuine kindness, gentle manner, and unexpected sense of humor that inform Robinson Peepers' strong character are not standard fare. He generally fits the Hollywood Model: his youthful appearance makes him a bit of an outsider even though he gets along well with his colleagues; he gets personally involved with his students (even though instances of this interaction are not featured as often as storylines involving his personal life); his sense of humor is a bit unconventional, but it is at the ready and emerges quietly at opportune moments; and there is some limited evidence that Peepers personalizes the curriculum. It is made clear in several episodes that Robinson Peepers loves to teach and is as committed to his students as to his beloved discipline. Much is made of the low pay, but even when he receives an offer for several times the salary to work for the Winkler Seed Company, Peepers will not seriously consider leaving his vocation.

Our Miss Brooks

Eve Arden's acting career spanned five decades and includes over fifty motion pictures, but she is best known for a single role, Madison High School English teacher Connie Brooks. *Our Miss Brooks*, which earned Arden an Emmy in 1953 as Best Female Star of Regular Series, is the only teacher sitcom featuring a woman as the main character to land in the top 30 rated programs during its broadcast.[7] The bifurcation of the public and private worlds available to women—not the condition for male teachers in movies or in television shows—is played out in films and early television series as women teachers are forced to alternately draw upon and deny their femaleness, as when they are asked to nurture but not to mother the children they teach and to maintain a chaste domestic life. The assumption for many middle class women in the 1950s was that they would work until they married, but marriage was their ultimate goal.

The brisk suits and shoulder pads favored by strong women stars of the 1940s such as Barbara Stanwyck, Joan Crawford, and Bette Davis, as well as the women who emulated them, were replaced the following decade in Hollywood and local department stores with a more feminine silhouette of soft shoulders, cinched waists, and flowing skirts. The suits of the 1940s suggested public power, but the twinsets of the 1950s suggest a return to home and hearth. Brooks wears youthful clothes that accent her long and lean figure. It's *almost* as if she could rip off the flopping bowtie she often favors as a silent signifier of her "schoolmarm" status and be ready for a day of domestic chores in the rose-covered cottage she suggests she would like to share with her colleague, Mr. Boynton. This is *almost* the case because even though Miss Brooks talks the talk of a woman who wants to marry and "settle down," Arden's sarcastic delivery of her lines as well as her overall performance suggest that Brooks prefers the independence of making her own money and her own decisions. It does not take much reading against the grain to glean that Miss Brooks is dis-

Figure 2.2. Robert Rockwell as Philip Boynton and Eve Arden as Connie Brooks in *Our Miss Brooks* (CBS, 1952–56). Photo courtesy of Photofest. Used by permission.

ingenuous in her pursuit of the apparently clueless biology teacher (whom she refers to as "frog boy" because his most intimate relationship appears to be with his pet frog). The closest we see Connie Brooks come to domestic bliss is her relationship with her nosy but well-meaning elderly landlady, Mrs. Davis (Jane Morgan), who assists in Miss Brooks' hapless efforts to snare the purported object of her affection. Despite their plots and schemes, Mr. Boynton deflects her rather dispassionate advances with a curious detachment.

Our Miss Brooks follows the pattern of many shows with teacher characters who don't seem to spend much time in any given day teaching; she is almost never depicted in the classroom, and it remains completely up to the viewer to imagine her pedagogical style. While students play larger roles in *Our Miss Brooks* than in *Mister Peepers*, there seem to be only three students enrolled at Madison High School: Harriet Conklin (Gloria McMillan), the principal's daughter; Walter Denton (Richard Crenna), a blundering student who is dating Harriet against her father's wishes and who, when inexplicably picking Brooks up for school each morning, settles into a full breakfast prepared by Brooks' landlady, Mrs. Davis; and, "Stretch" Snodgrass (Leonard Smith), a "dim" athlete whose senselessness in conversation is offset by his amazing pitching arm. Even without direct evidence from inside the classroom, there are numerous references and plot devices that locate Brooks firmly in the classroom space in accordance with the conventions of the Hollywood Model to suggest she is a Good Teacher.

It is less important on television than on film for teachers to be outsiders and have contentious relationships with colleagues because of the episodic nature of series television. Those story elements would become tedious over time, but other elements common to the movies are just as true on television and form a key plot component of most episodes of *Our Miss Brooks*. Audiences readily recognize, for example, that Brooks is engaged in an ongoing battle with her principal, Osgood Conklin (Gale Gordon), the bumbling, self-absorbed, blustery administrator who provides an enduring model for others like him in subsequent decades (such as Mr. Woodman, an especially nasty vice principal on *Welcome Back, Kotter*, and Dr. Samuels, a self-serving principal on *Head of the Class*). Just as the Good Teacher must get involved with students on a personal level, Brooks is constantly running interference between Walter and Mr. Conklin, and she also gets involved with the other two students, such as the time she pretends to be Stretch's sister to try to negotiate a baseball contract with a scout in "The Great Baseball Slide." Usually it is male teachers who present a ready sense of humor, but her dry wit and ostensible self-deprecation are key elements of Connie Brooks' character. Even without seeing Miss Brooks in the classroom, she is firmly established as a Good Teacher, beloved by her students and respected by everyone except her principal.

Gerard Jones notes that a number of new shows were introduced in the early 1950s featuring "cute but dizzy" women in an attempt to replicate the success of *I Love Lucy* (79). Some of these programs may have been ratings hits, but they were generally safe and bland. Bland is certainly not how Jones describes another Desilu endeavor:

> No other TV woman was as combative. Says Walter to her; "I'd say you were in your late twenties or early thirties or—" And says she: "Quit now. Teeth become you." Connie was the only one of those dames of the depression (sic) mold to win a place in TV comedy. In keeping with the times, she worked at a nurturing, surrogate maternal job, and her prime goal was to get married and quit. Yet in her struggles the tension of changing American life was preserved. (85)

That's not all that was preserved; Connie Brooks' inability to get her man—or any man—may have been played broadly for laughs, but it kept her from leaving Madison High School and disappearing into the domestic sphere. It is hard to imagine that Brooks' strength, independence, and individuality would have thrived, or even survived, if she left the workforce.

Consider the possibility that Connie Brooks is really putting one over on the audience, and her popularity and resonance with viewers is enhanced by some level of recognition that there is more complexity in the characters of *Our Miss Brooks* than appears on the surface.[8] Miss Brooks plays the Good Teacher and obeys the rules circumscribing the behavior of a woman in her position, but she also gives lip service to what are supposed to be the primary goals of single women in her era: marriage, a home, and a family. She dresses the part with formfitting, feminine, but not revealing, clothes that typify the 1950s. She wears make-up and has her hair "done" in a way that mimics the schoolmarm bun but includes a feminine fluffiness and some waves framing her face. She circumvents references to her age, which we assume to be late thirties, as in the episode "Here's Your Past" in which she appears on a *This Is Your Life* type show that includes numerous age jokes while references to her actual age are drowned out by a loud horn. She talks incessantly about wanting to marry Mr. Boynton and even alludes to her sexual desire for the "frog boy," but an intractable inaccessibility in her expression contradicts what she says. She is strong, bold, and irrepressible, and this is an image that does not meld with any vision of Miss Connie Brooks as Mrs. Connie Boynton. And it isn't only Philip Boynton who fails to get to first base.

By the final season of the series, Boynton is out of the scene and ardent suitors have appeared. In "Library Quiz," fellow teacher Gene Talbot (Gene Barry) describes himself as a "close, close friend" and is jealous when a distinguished older man brings Brooks home in his limousine from shopping and dinner. The dialogue indicates that Brooks and Talbot have been dating for three months, but she displays a complete disregard for him. She shows a bit more interest in her new suitor solely because she thinks he has money. When the new man comes on to Brooks at his mansion, she physically recoils from his embrace and later replies affirmatively to Mr. Conklin's question about whether or not her suitor is "middle-aged" and adds that he has "young ideas" and is in his "second wolfhood." With Mr. Boynton, Miss Brooks gives lip service to her attraction to him even if her overall performance casts doubt on what she says. With Talbot and her rich suitor, Brooks' disinterest borders on antipathy, a far cry from the gentle courtship of Mr. Peepers and Miss Remington. Is Brooks openly dissembling for the viewer because she knows that women teachers cannot, after all, "have it all," or are her romantic interests elsewhere in a realm that could not be named on television in the 1950s or for decades to come? Not until the mid 1990s would a gay teacher appear in a recurring role. The openness of Miss Brooks' performance invites a multiplicity of textual readings, and it is not just scholars who engage in "reading against the grain."

This excerpt from an undergraduate student's weekly journal (in a course called Culture and the Sitcom) demonstrates that intertextuality and iconography are compelling tools for examining media critically:

> Intertextuality played a role in my interpreting *Our Miss Brooks* because I have seen *Grease*. The 1978 film *Grease* features Eve Arden, the same actress who played Connie Brooks, as a principal of a 1950s high school. *Grease* is a 1970s film set in the 1950s, and the whole film has a feel of lightly poking fun at a simpler time. By allowing Eve Arden to be a principal in the 1950s, I feel that Connie Brooks received the promotion. In a sense, she gets to sit behind the desk and put her feet up like she did in the episode we watched ["Trying to Pick a Fight"]. Eve Arden's Principal McGee seems to provide the answer that *Our Miss Brooks* was pulling one over on the audience; twenty years later in a film that made fun of the 1950s, Eve Arden reappears and satirizes the 1950s Miss Brooks.

In comparing Eve Arden's portrayal of Connie Brooks in *Our Miss Brooks* to her portrayal of Principal McGee in the feature film *Grease* (1978), this student notes that the producers appear to promote Connie Brooks when they cast Arden as the principal. By reprising her earlier iconic, role she is simultaneously evoking nostalgia for and satirizing the 1950s Miss Brooks, reinforcing the idea that *Our Miss Brooks* is a more complicated text than most viewers realize.

Conclusion

Although we often write about the politics of gender, the relationship can be better expressed through a more direct connection: gender *is* politics. Looking at the interstices of the private person and the public teacher, it is clear that Connie Brooks was a character ahead of her time in understanding the boundaries constructed to keep women teachers firmly "in their place," and she pushed against those boundaries to create a niche for herself as the most indelible of television's women teachers. Mr. Peepers is delightful and, like Miss Brooks, fits the Hollywood Model perfectly, but the double standard and its accordant privileges for men teachers strip him of the need to be subversive like Connie Brooks. Mr. Peepers' challenges to the (school) system seem mild as a result, a perfect complement to his usual demeanor and nowhere near as challenging a persona as Miss Brooks provides.

The dominance of these gendered depictions of teachers in film and television is reproduced time and time again and reinforces our expectations of real teachers, which makes these patterns worthy of recognition and consideration. Of course, gender is not the only critical lens that should be applied to television. By the 1960s, race became a consideration on television beyond the evening newscasts that reported on the early years of the civil rights movement. The entertainment programs of the 1950s had largely avoided racial issues (after protests and controversy early in the decade over the television broadcast of *Amos 'n' Andy*) by entering a period where African American characters appeared occasionally as domestic workers or special guests instead of in recurring or starring roles. As the 1960s unfolded, however, this pattern was no longer sustainable as audiences demonstrated a growing appetite for social relevancy.

THREE

1960s Race and Social Relevancy

The Bill Cosby Show and *Room 222*

If the superficial calm of the 1950s obscured underlying tensions, the 1960s were unambiguously distressed as full-pitched military, political, and cultural wars were waged. The decade began quietly enough with the first televised presidential debate in 1960. Even though the majority of people listening to the debate on radio thought that Nixon had the edge, those watching the debate on television were influenced by the visuals—John F. Kennedy's good looks and easy manner contrasted with Richard Nixon's pallid, sweaty countenance, trumping content. Kennedy would go on to win the election, becoming the country's first Catholic president. The Berlin Wall was erected in 1961, and the Cuban Missile Crisis occurred the following year when President Kennedy demanded that the Soviet Union remove its missiles from Cuba. The country was rocked by the assassinations of President Kennedy in 1963, Malcolm X in 1965, and both Martin Luther King, Jr. and Robert Kennedy in 1968. In each instance, the people of the nation turned to their television sets for solace; the aftermath of President Kennedy's assassination and his funeral were telecast non-stop for four days.

The civil rights movement gained momentum with leadership from the Rev. Martin Luther King, Jr. and Malcolm X. Over two hundred thousand people marched for civil rights in Washington, D.C. in 1963. The landmark event culminated with Dr. King's "I Have a Dream Speech" on the Washington Mall and gave millions of African Americans hope for a more just and equitable future. Other marches and acts of civil disobedience nationwide led to the passage of the Civil Rights Act of 1964 and the Voting Rights Act in 1965. Thurgood Marshall was appointed to the U.S. Supreme Court, the first African American to achieve such status. The Vietnam War escalated with huge troop buildups in the second half of the decade, fueling more fervent anti-war demonstrations. The women's movement gained strength, spurred by the publication of Betty Friedan's book, *The Feminine Mystique* in 1963, and the formation of the National Organization for Women. The Stonewall Riots in New York City in 1969 marked the inception of the gay rights movement. The Soviet Union began the Space Race in 1957 when it launched the satellite *Sputnik*, inspiring President Kennedy to issue a call for the U.S. to put a man on the moon before 1970. The quest began in 1961 when Alan Shepherd became the first American in space, followed by John Glenn's orbit around the earth in 1963. Although he didn't live to see it, Kennedy's dream was achieved in 1969 when the world watched on television as Neil Armstrong and Buzz Aldrin walked on the moon.

Tens of millions of baby boomers became teenagers and young adults during the 1960s, sparking a counter culture of hippies and freaks. Students joined the burgeoning civil rights, women's, and anti-war movements, but they also lobbied for their own causes, holding sit-ins across the nation to demand everything from college coed housing to the legalization of marijuana. The music of the decade reflected this growing militancy. The Beatles, introduced to the U.S. on *The Ed Sullivan Show* in 1964, transformed themselves (and their global audience) with every subsequent recording, disseminating new musical, cultural, and political ideas as they evolved. The Woodstock Festival, held on a farm in upstate New York at the end of the decade, marked the apotheosis of the ecstatic, psychedelic, make-love-not-war hippie lifestyle.

The Super Bowl made its debut in 1967, the same year of the first heart transplant (no connection). The Children's Television Workshop, formed in 1967 by a group of women concerned about television's effects on children, created *Sesame Street* in 1969. Yet, primetime television programming remained a reality-free zone. The airwaves were dominated by westerns, variations on detective and lawyer dramas, quiz shows, and variety shows. Some of the most escapist shows on the air during the decade were sitcoms. *Mr. Ed* features a talking horse. In *I Dream of Jeannie*, an astronaut finds a bottle on a beach housing a scantily-clad genie who becomes his slave (and later his wife). On *Bewitched*, a beautiful witch pledges to give up her powers to become a suburban housewife. *My Favorite Martian* and *The Flying Nun* need no explanation.

The Flintstones, a prehistoric cartoon family, and *The Jetsons*, their space-age counterparts, brought animation to the sitcom and foreshadowed *The Simpsons*. By decade's end, some audiences sought more substance in humor and were rewarded, at least for a couple of years, with *Rowan and Martin's Laugh In* and *The Smothers Brothers Comedy Hour*. But, for the most part, conflict and controversy were relegated to the nightly news, and the primetime network schedules remained committed to escapist entertainment.

Teachers on TV: The 1960s

Shows depicting teachers were no exception to this escapism. There were fourteen shows featuring teachers in either starring or recurring roles during this decade, and all portray teachers in varying degrees of remove from the sociopolitical fray. Television has always depicted an idealized view of the world; television shows that offer too much realism rarely find a wide audience. From *East Side, West Side* (1963–64), a gritty portrayal of social workers in New York City, to *Freaks and Geeks* (1999–2000), an authentic depiction of high school students, television's forays into more true-to-life representations have met with cancellations even when the critics favor the shows (as they did in both of the above).

Although *Leave It to Beaver* (CBS, 1957–58; ABC, 1958–63) is remembered as the quintessential 1950s family sitcom, it remained on the air in primetime until 1963. And because it revolves around a family with two school children, some of the episodes involve teachers. The teachers on *Leave It to Beaver*, Miss Canfield (Diane Brewster) and Miss Landers (Sue Randall), are both classic 1950s elementary school teachers—young, unmarried, and dedicated. A few of the later episodes show one of Beaver's middle school teachers, Mrs. Rayburn (Doris Packer), a not-so-young, married, but still dedicated, teacher. Of the 234 episodes, thirty-two feature teachers or principals and in ten of those they are involved in the main story. In the early episode "Beaver's Crush," Beaver (Jerry Mathers) has a crush on Miss Canfield. Later, Beaver learns that his teacher is engaged when he and his friend Whitey Whitney (Stanley Fafara) see Miss Landers talking to a man in "Miss Landers' Fiancé." In several episodes, "Most Interesting Character," "Beaver and Ivanhoe," and "Beaver's Poster," the teachers are shown in the classroom giving assignments. Teachers and parents are shown interacting in "Baby Picture," "The Last Day of School," "Beaver and Kenneth," "Substitute Father," and "Pet Fair." Miss Landers even comes to Beaver's house for dinner in "Teacher Comes to Dinner." And, in "Beaver's Pigeons," Beaver honors his two favorite teachers by naming his pigeons Miss Canfield and Miss Landers.

In *The Many Loves of Dobie Gillis* (CBS, 1959–63), teachers play a peripheral role. Once again, because the show is about teenagers and teenagers go to school, teachers are included occasionally. In keeping with the counter-culture tone of the show, teachers are cynical, tired, and resigned to the grind of teaching bored, smart-alecky students. The most notable teacher on the show is Mr. Leander Pomfritt (William Schallert), Dobie's high school English teacher. Tuesday Weld and Warren Beatty are featured as Dobie and Maynard's classmates Thalia Menninger and Milton Armitage, and Mr. Pomfritt reads "Kubla Khan" to the class in "The Best-Dressed Man." When Dobie and the gang go to college, Mr. Pomfritt begins teaching at the college, and at least two other teachers, Dr. Imogene Burkhart (Jean Byron), a sociology professor, and Coach (Nesdon Booth), the football coach, make several appearances. Although the teachers are secondary characters, there are a few times when they stand out. One is "Goodbye Mister Pomfritt, Hello Mr. Chips" in which Dobie (Dwayne Hickman) and his beatnik compatriot, Maynard G. Krebs (Bob Denver, who went on to expand his fame as Gilligan on *Gilligan's Island* later in the 1960s), try to convince Mr. Pomfritt to stay at Central High. It seems that Mr. Pomfritt has had an effect on his students after all. And in another episode, "Like, Oh Brother," Dobie and Maynard help their sociology professor, Dr. Burkhart, start a center for disadvantaged kids. In "The Day the Teachers Disappeared," the teachers are replaced by parents when all the teachers become sick and are unable to come to work. Except for the episodes listed here, teachers are rarely seen teaching, and when they are shown teaching, it is at the beginning or end of the scene, thereby marginalizing the characters and the practice of teaching.

One of the most popular shows on television during the 1960s was *The Andy Griffith Show* (CBS, 1960–68). This show featured Andy Griffith as Sheriff Andy Taylor, a widower with a young son living in the small, fictional North Carolina town of Mayberry. His son, Opie (Ronny Howard), was tended to by Aunt Bea (Frances Bavier). Deputy Barney Fife (Don Knotts, Ralph Furley from 1979–84 on *Three's Company* ABC, 1977–84) is memorable for his tendency to over-react and his possession of a single bullet, which Sheriff Taylor made him keep in his shirt pocket.[1] Over the course of the show, there are several teachers featured, but none is more popular than Helen Crump (Aneta Corsaut). Originally cast for a single-episode, Crump becomes a recurring character. In her first appearance, "Andy Discovers America," she gives Opie what he considers too much homework and earns the moniker "Old Lady Crump." Opie tells Miss Crump that his "Pa" said history doesn't matter, which infuriates Crump, who then confronts Taylor. Andy realizes that "Old Lady Crump" is no "old lady" but is an attractive young woman.

Figure 3.1. Andy Griffith as Sheriff Andy Taylor, Ron "Ronny" Howard as Opie Taylor, and Aneta Corsaut as Helen Crump in *The Andy Griffith Show* (CBS, 1960–68). Photo courtesy of Photofest. Used by permission.

This begins a long courtship between the two characters that culminates in their wedding at the end of the show. Opie gets a crush on his teacher in "Opie

Loves Helen." Although we rarely see Crump in the classroom, she becomes a major character on the show (appearing in over fifty episodes). In opposition to the Hollywood Model, this is one of the few instances when a female teacher is accorded a personal life. This transgression is due to the fact that Crump serves primarily as a romantic interest for Andy Taylor and only secondarily as Opie's teacher.

Mr. Novak (NBC, 1963–65) is an hour-long drama featuring a young high school English teacher, John Novak (James Franciscus), in his first teaching job. The show is set in a predominantly White high school and features many teachers and students in stories socially relevant for their time—at least for White audiences. Black audiences would be less likely to identify with the characters and situations. Endorsed by the National Education Association, the show was based on research at fifty high schools and advice from a panel of high school teachers because the producers wanted to create a portrait of the ideal teacher ("Naked Classroom"; Brittenham 157). And Novak is quite nearly perfect, his earnestness outshone only by his immaculate good looks. At one point during the first episode, Principal Albert Vane (Dean Jagger) sums up the title character and the Hollywood Model of a teacher: "A born teacher. He knows when to break the rules." This smart and thoughtful show presents teachers (and students) in an optimistic and idealistic fashion befitting the early 1960s. One of the ways *Mr. Novak* relates to socially relevant issues of the day is illustrated by the episode "Death of a Teacher." In this installment, all the characters deal, each in their own way, with the sudden death of one of the teachers. This episode was produced and aired a few weeks after President Kennedy was assassinated and showed a nation that there were many different ways to mourn ("Mr. Novak").

Other episodes deal with civil rights, sex education, anti-Semitism, escape from East Germany, Russian defection, and the rights of the disabled (Watson 74). The idealistic nature of the lead character was stated by the show's creator, E. Jack Neuman, "I hope that because he hates bigotry and prejudice and apathy and indifference others will recognize and hate the same things; I hope that his patriotism and good citizenship and morality will influence people to admire these qualities. . . . I can't think of any better place for that sort of ethical shootout than our television screens" (75). Although Neuman specifically mentions bigotry and prejudice, the show rarely deals with race and barely shows any African American, Asian American, or Hispanic characters. There is an African American teacher, but he is not featured and is rarely seen. One episode does, however, address prejudice and racism head on. "A Single Isolated Incident" concerns an African American student who is terrorized by a few White students who object to her and other Black students attending

Figure 3.2. Dean Jagger as Principal Albert Vane and James Franciscus as John Novak in *Mr. Novak* (NBC, 1963–65). Photo courtesy of Photofest. Used by permission.

"their" school. The characters deal with the prejudice directly by confronting the White culprits and talking with the student body at an assembly (Watson).

Mr. Novak deals with other types of prejudice and bigotry, but except for this notable episode, it generally ignores the elephant in the living room—race and race relations—major social issues at the time.

Mr. Novak exemplifies the socially relevant characterization of a teacher that has occasionally appeared on television. Because the series originally aired 1963–65 at a time when the civil rights movement was underway, yet features little diversity among the characters, it seems retro and dated. The show's failure to relate to its larger cultural context reflects the unwillingness of television to deal directly with the most difficult and divisive social issues. It also shows that the producers paid attention to the fact that *East Side, West Side*, another socially relevant drama, had just been cancelled. Not wanting to have the same fate visited upon them, they tread lightly in this area.

Please Don't Eat the Daisies and *To Rome with Love* were broadcast for two years each, and although they both have teachers as lead characters, both shows focus on the home environment. *Please Don't Eat the Daisies* (NBC, 1965–67) revolves around a suburban married couple Jim and Joan Nash (Mark Miller and Patricia Crowley) and their four children. Jim Nash just happens to be a college English professor. The show was based on Jean Kerr's book and the subsequent movie of the same name, both about her life as a newspaper columnist and suburban housewife. *To Rome with Love* (CBS, 1967–71) centers on a widowed college professor, Michael Endicott (John Forsythe), who moves his three daughters to Rome to take a teaching position at the American Overseas School. Once again, the show centers on familial relationships.

Of the remaining shows featuring teachers that aired during the 1960s, all were on for a season or less, and four were sitcoms. Most of these shows have teacher characters, but usually the focus is not on the classroom. In *The Gertrude Berg Show* (CBS, 1961–62), the main character, Sarah Green (Gertrude Berg), a matronly widow, decides to enroll in college. In *McKeever and the Colonel* (NBC, 1962–63), the focus is on the students, and in *The John Forsythe Show* (NBC, 1965–66), the focus is on the new headmaster, retired Air Force Major John Foster (film star Forsythe), his friend, Ed Robbins (Guy Marks), a retired air force sergeant, and the major's daughters. In an implausible turn during the second half of the first year, the two men become undercover agents for the U.S. government and are sent on assignments around the world. Another show builds on a reversal of *My Fair Lady*, as the richest man in the world, O.K. Crackerby (Burl Ives, winner of the Best Supporting Oscar in 1958 for *The Big Country*, 1957, but most famously known as the singer/narrator of the 1964 television special *Rudolph the Red Nosed Reindeer* still aired every December.), hires an unemployed Harvard graduate, St. John Quincy (Hal Buckley) to tutor him in the ways of the elite. *O.K. Crackerby* (ABC, 1965–66) becomes a buddy show as "the two men split their time fighting with each other on an intellectual level and banding together to battle the social snobs on a personal level" (Brooks and Marsh). Hank Dearborn (Dick Kallman) is a young man raising his younger sister, Tina (Katie Sweet) after their parents are killed in a car accident in *Hank* (NBC, 1965–66). Determined to get an education, he attends classes at a local college without enrolling (or paying). Everyone is in on the plan, except the registrar, Dr. Lewis Royal (Howard St. John), who keeps trying to find the elusive pseudo-student. In spite of his status, Prof. McKillup (Lloyd Corrigan) is tolerant, and track coach Ossie Weiss (Dabbs Greer) wants him to join the team. Losing a grip on realism almost altogether is *Malibu U* (ABC, 1967), which aired over two months during the summer of 1967. It is primarily a music show with Rick Nelson playing the "Dean of the Drop-Ins" (the opposite of drop-outs) at a "mythical college." "Guest professors" are popular singers who lecture (sing) to the student body—primarily young women in bathing suits (Brooks and Marsh 727)!

Two series featuring African Americans in the lead roles as teachers are significant shows for the era. *The Bill Cosby Show* and *Room 222* feature Blacks and Whites living and working together in an integrated world remarkably free of racial strife. Significantly, both began in 1969, the year after Martin Luther King, Jr. and Robert Kennedy were assassinated, while the Vietnam War was escalating and protests against the war and for civil rights and women's rights were rampant. Although there was little or no racial friction in the world of *The Bill Cosby Show* and *Room 222*, both shows have been labeled "relevant" (Marc and Thompson 62) and fit into the category of social relevancy programming (Bindas and Heinman 31, Gitlin 203–211, MacDonald 166, Means Coleman and McIlwain 130–132). According to Phillip Brian Harper, shows of this type "would 'reflect' the social reality on which it was implicitly modeled" (70). *The Bill Cosby Show* and *Room 222* have also been called signs of social progress for race relations (Bogle 6), representing a new America in which African Americans and Whites work and go to school together harmoniously.

Race and Social Relevancy

In the sitcom *The Bill Cosby Show*, Cosby plays physical education teacher Chet Kincaid. This show was unconventional because it had no laugh track and used single-camera shoots on location. The show follows Cosby's historic co-starring role in *I Spy* (NBC, 1965–68) that marked the reintroduction of an African American character in a major role on primetime programming for the first time since "dialect comedies" such as *Amos 'n' Andy* in the mid-1950s.

Room 222 also is set in Los Angeles and features African Americans in the starring roles. A dramedy, *Room 222* complements the tone and overall style of *The Bill Cosby Show*. Many episodes of each series are structured around imparting a moral (as are most sitcoms), usually a general lesson of tolerance designed to have universal appeal. These programs contrast sharply in tone with the better-known social relevancy sitcoms on the horizon such as *All in the Family*, *Maude*, and *Good Times*, and may be regarded as precursors to these more topical series that follow.

Although both shows revolve around African Americans in starring roles, they were criticized for having little to do with the real world lives of African Americans. In a July 1970 issue of *TV Guide*, the author criticizes *Room 222*: "The black folk here are full of understanding and wisdom, sympathetic all the way. No basic problems between races. All men are brothers, right? An undramatic, middle-classish situation that hardly has anything to do with the Black experience" (qtd. in Harper 71). Although both programs show an integrated America, there is an ambiguity about race; integration is ubiquitous, with African Americans and Whites co-existing in a seemingly color blind world. Although *Room 222* addresses racial issues from time to time, for the most part the race of the characters is backgrounded. That there are African Americans on these shows makes little difference to the narratives. Phillip Brian Harper states that "*Room 222* is not primarily about racial integration at all; rather, it always represents an allegorical narrative about social differentiation among black subjects" (77). This social differentiation is manifested socioeconomically on *Room 222* by showcasing a disadvantaged student and on *The Bill Cosby Show* by foregrounding Chet Kincaid's brother and his job as a garbage collector.

Donald Bogle writes that *The Bill Cosby Show* was "insistent upon *not* rattling its mainstream viewers" (emphasis in the original, 167), and the same could be said for *Room 222*. J. Fred MacDonald writes that "although [*The Bill Cosby Show*] projected life in racial harmony, this program was extracted from the black experience, and possessed an esoteric quality African Americans alone could understand" (126). He goes on to write that the show had a "black ambiance" that can be seen in the Afro hairstyles and dashiki shirts (127) and that "the series was a statement about black life, an endorsement of the middle-class, educated black man who has not deserted the ghetto, but moves gracefully between both worlds" (127). This is only partially true of *Room 222* where Pete Dixon and Liz McIntyre are both middle-class and educated, but they are fully acclimated to the perfectly integrated world of Walt Whitman High. "Better than any other program focusing on blacks in the Golden Age [of Blacks in television], *Room 222* mirrored the ambiance of social change that was a part of the late 1960s, while operating within the boundaries of cultural possibility" (MacDonald 136). The characters of *Room 222* are safe characters. "There was no rage here.... The black heroes were allowed vestiges of African-American culture—Afros, colorful clothing, and a sensitivity toward younger 'brothers' and 'sisters' seeking equal opportunity. But the same central characters were well adjusted to the suit-and-tie regimentation of their careers and identities within the mainstream" (MacDonald 137). And although there were riots in the streets of America about civil rights (and other social movements including anti-war protests), little of it was reflected on either of these shows.

The Bill Cosby Show

The Bill Cosby Show (NBC, 1969–71) features Bill Cosby as high school coach and physical education teacher Chet Kincaid. And, as the name of the show suggests, it is Cosby's show; he is the star and one of the producers. Although the main character is a teacher, not many of the episodes involve teaching (or coaching for that matter). The show is primarily about a young African American man who happens to be a high school coach; only half of the episodes are set at the school, and even within those shows Kincaid is rarely shown teaching. The program tries hard to show that African Americans and Whites (and Hispanics and Asians) aren't very different from one another. As Robin Means Coleman and Charlton D. McIlwain state: "*The Bill Cosby Show* likewise depicted a world that was wholly integrated and without conflict.... offer[ing] a racist ideology that Black culture was most prized when it approached the norms and values of Whiteness" (130). They go on to write that this show (as well as *I Spy* and *Julia*) "sent a placating message, presenting Blacks as accommodating, docile, and nonthreatening" (130). (Interestingly, they don't mention *Room 222* at all.) As noted in the documentary *Color Adjustment*, it was a difficult time for producers who wanted to bring African Americans to the small screen but also wanted to keep their sponsors and their viewers.

Although he is a high school teacher and coach on the show, almost half the shows feature Kincaid outside the school environment. Many involve him helping family members (delivering papers for his sick nephew, refereeing a bickering aunt and uncle or brother and sister-in-law, babysitting his niece and nephews), volunteering (helping at the local community center, coaching a Little League team), dating, and miscellaneous escapades (coping all night with a barking dog, taping a television commercial, being trapped in an elevator). In plots that increase the social relevancy of the show, two episodes involve Kincaid being questioned or arrested by the police although he is exonerated in both cases. In both instances there are White and Black police officers involved, thereby maintaining the colorblindness of the show. No matter what, Kincaid is always portrayed as smart (albeit a little smart-alecky), competent, and easy-going.

Figure 3.3. Bill Cosby as Chet Kincaid in *The Bill Cosby Show* (NBC, 1969–71). Photo courtesy of Photofest. Used by permission.

Several episodes occur at school but do not involve teaching. In one, a female student is trying to fix him up with her mother ("To Kincaid, with Love"), and in a different episode he is fixed up with another teacher to chaperone a high school dance ("Growing Growing Grown"). This follows the Hollywood Model: Kincaid is allowed to have a social life whereas female teachers are not. In "How You Play the Game," Kincaid is asked to drop a talented halfback from the football team because the student is so depressed about losing a game that he is failing algebra. Kincaid tells the student that it's not whether you win or lose, it's how you play the game. The moral doesn't sink in with the student until he sees Kincaid blow his cool while losing a championship handball game. Only when Kincaid learns his own lesson does the student come to understand good sportsmanship. In the second season, Kincaid wins an award for teacher of the year but has a hard time getting the other teachers to attend the awards banquet ("Teacher of the Year"). In "Tobacco Road," Kincaid helps a teacher quit smoking.

There is a modicum of teaching involved in the show, however. In an early episode, Mr. Kincaid—and he is called Mr. Kincaid by students and teachers—holds tryouts for the basketball team ("Best Hook Shot in the World"). He is shown coaching during the tryouts and also during the game. This is an interesting episode because prejudice plays a role but not prejudice based on skin color. In this episode, Kincaid pays scant attention to a particular player trying out and is accused by the student of being prejudiced—not because the student is Black, because he is short. The student challenges Kincaid to a game of one-on-one and wins, thereby proving that he is good enough for the team and demonstrating that prejudice can come in many guises. To make sure this is perfectly clear to the television audience, the White guidance counselor tells Kincaid: "It is not unusual to pre-judge people before you know who they are or what they can do. And when you pre-judge, that's prejudice." In other episodes Kincaid helps a student athlete clean up his language ("This Mouth Is Rated X"), films the football team so they can see how to play better ("Anytime You're Ready, C.K."), encourages a young artist ("The Artist"), discovers a young poet is plagiarizing ("The Poet"), and tutors a Mexican immigrant ("Viva Ortega").

In several episodes, Kincaid has to substitute for other teachers in other subjects. In one instance, he has to teach an algebra class for a few days ("Let X Equal a Lousy Weekend"). His plan to use the smart students and the answer guide to teach the class backfires when he discovers that a few pages are missing from the answer book and even the smartest student can't solve one of the problems. He sidesteps the issue of actually teaching by saying, "I don't think you can learn just by following the teacher's footsteps." Ultimately (and luckily for Kincaid), the smartest student *does* solve the problem. In another substitute situation, Kincaid must step in to teach Biology 9, Sex Education ("The Substitute"). The all female class tells him they are on Chapter 9, "Preparing for Marriage." He tries to skip this chapter, but the students respond by telling him that their regular teacher doesn't like to skip around. He acquiesces, answers their questions, and tells them a little about the time he almost got married. Personalizing the curriculum is one way that Hollywood denotes a Good Teacher. In this case, Kincaid personalizes the curriculum by telling his story and the students (and the viewers) get to learn a little more about him.

Because Kincaid is a physical education teacher and coach, several episodes are devoted to his coaching. In addition to "Best Hook Shot in the World," mentioned above, there is "The Killer Instinct," in which he must cut a young man because he's not good enough, even though the student's father has pressured Kincaid to put his son on the team. Kincaid is shown coaching the team and then additionally helping the student outside of practice. When the father is impressed by Kincaid's integrity (because he ultimately has to cut the student from the roster because he's really not good enough), the father offers him a job at two to three times his teacher's salary. Kincaid demurs saying, "I'm trying to learn to be a good school teacher." On television, Good Teachers sacrifice their own advancement for the good of their students.

In an interesting use of psychology in another episode ("Lover's Quarrel"), Kincaid motivates a student who has been slacking off in physical education class by goading him. The student hasn't been coming to class and always seems to have an excuse for why he can't attend. Kincaid tells him repeatedly that if he doesn't come to class and climb the rope (an activity guaranteed to elicit sympathy from the audience), Kincaid will have to give him an "F" for the semester. The student doesn't seem to care. The student's P.E teacher from the previous year says that the kid is a "zero." On the final day of the semester when the student walks through the gym, Kincaid tells him that he has a nasty attitude and that he doesn't like it. He continues goading the student, until the student gets mad and climbs the rope. Kincaid gives the student an "A" because he climbed the rope and touched the ceiling (the same criteria used for all the other students). Afterwards, Kincaid tells the other teacher, "Some people don't think you like them unless you're yelling at them." And although this ties into the parallel story in this episode (of Chet's bickering aunt and uncle), it seems odd from the vantage point of forty years later when goading and yelling at a student would be frowned upon, as would giving a student an A who hasn't been coming to class. Nevertheless, Kincaid personalizes the curriculum, engages the student, and ultimately motivates him to climb the rope.[2]

In another episode, Kincaid is being considered for a part-time driver's education position and agrees to teach the student who "drove" the former teacher to quit his job ("Driven to Distraction"). The student is so nervous and insecure that when she had her last driving class she wrecked the car. Kincaid tries many strategies to teach her and give her confidence, but it is only when he hurts his back and tells her to go get help, that she rises to the occasion and drives him back to the school. She learns to drive, and the Good Teacher once again motivates his student by getting personally involved, but he decides that teaching driver's education is not for him.

Many of the episodes have "lessons," typical of the sitcom genre: do the right thing, listen and help others, don't take advantage of people, respect your family, respect your elders, tell the truth. But there is one lesson that threads its way through much of *The Bill Cosby Show*: it is not important who wins, it's how you play the game. In "Let X Equal a Lousy Weekend," Kincaid tells his colleagues in the teacher's lounge who have been criticizing his coaching, "It's not important to me, the winning or the losing. What is important is the making of the man." Although viewers don't see Kincaid teaching very much, he puts students first. In another episode he says, "There's no labor or work that a man can do that is undignified, you know; it just depends on how well he does it, that's all" ("Going the Route"). This is an oblique reference to, and support of, his brother, the garbage collector. Chet Kincaid is an upstanding man, and we assume he is also a good teacher based on the evidence seen in the show. He says and does the right thing.

Although Chet Kincaid fits the model of a Good Teacher in many ways—he has a ready sense of humor, gets involved with the students on a personal level and learns from them, and he personalizes the curriculum when necessary—he does not fit the Hollywood Model in that he is not an outsider (his Blackness notwithstanding) nor is he disliked by his colleagues. Kincaid may try to cut through red tape and coach the way he thinks best, not the way his colleagues recommend, but for the most part he fits it. He may not fit the stereotype of a "good teacher" perfectly, but he is a Good Teacher nevertheless.

Room 222

Room 222 is a more realistic program than *The Bill Cosby Show* even if its world is also perfectly integrated. This is probably because the series is more dramedy than sitcom. (It's listed as a "school drama" in Brooks and Marsh, 1011.) *Room 222* revolves around Pete Dixon (Lloyd Haynes), a high school history teacher; guidance counselor Liz McIntyre (Denise Nicholas); rookie teacher Alice Johnson (Karen Valentine); and principal Seymour Kaufman (Michael Constantine). It shows in "different ways the social dynamics among teens and

Figure 3.4. (top row, left to right) Denise Nicholas as Liz McIntyre and Karen Valentine as Alice Johnson, (bottom row, left to right) Michael Constantine as Principal Seymour Kaufman and Lloyd Haynes as Pete Dixon in *Room 222* (ABC, 1969–74). Photo courtesy of Photofest. Used by permission.

between teens and adult authority figures such as teachers, administrators, and parents" (Forman 70), yet these portrayals are all overly idealistic. In a perfect world, this is how teachers, students and administrators would behave. In addition, *Room 222* shows us how schools could be if they were integrated, a fairly radical notion for 1969 when most schools were still segregated.

The action takes place predominantly at Walt Whitman High School and was shot at Los Angeles High School, enhancing the reality of the show (Brooks and Marsh 1011). While other teacher shows from the 1960s rarely show classrooms (even *Mr. Novak* and *The Bill Cosby Show* emphasize non-schoolroom spaces), *Room 222* shows teachers and students in the classroom teaching and learning. Action also occurs in the offices of the principal and guidance counselor, the nurse's room, the gym, hallways, and school grounds as in the other shows, but it is the classroom scenes that make *Room 222* stand out. Not only do the students learn, but the audience is drawn into the process.

Because Pete Dixon is a history teacher, the writers and producers were able to use historical events to highlight current events. Dixon uses the impeachment of President Andrew Johnson to talk about how government works ("Seventeen Going on Twenty-Eight"); the class discusses prohibition, and the students relate it to marijuana laws ("Goodbye, Mr. Hip"); discussion of Native American history is related to a new student who belongs to the Navaho tribe ("House Made of Dark Mist"). The classroom discussion of impeachment is prescient. The episode aired originally on December 12, 1969, several years before President Richard Nixon resigned under threat of impeachment. In each instance, the teacher personalizes the curriculum, supporting the Hollywood Model of a Good Teacher.

In other episodes, additional socially relevant issues are tackled, including service in the Peace Corps, freedom of speech, homosexuality, high school retention, and poetry in modern song lyrics. In "The Valedictorian," the students propose that a competition be held to determine who will be the valedictorian rather than using the highest grade point average. The authors of the top three speeches are chosen to deliver their speeches during graduation. A young Richard Dreyfus plays a mediocre student whose speech is nevertheless ranked among the top three. After he appears (with two other students) on a local television show saying disparaging things about the state of education, faculty and students are split on whether he should be allowed to give his speech because it is feared that he will use the opportunity to speak out. They ultimately allow him to make his speech, and he uses his platform to inform the graduating seniors, teachers and parents:

We have to get better grades than the next kid so that we go to college where we learn more useless junk that has nothing whatever to do with what we need. The world is burning. Races are at one another's throats. There are wars; millions of people starving. Why don't you teach us how to build a better world? We can't change the mess that you've given us by learning trigonometry.

Some parents in the audience protest; others are supportive; the principal supports the student's right to speak. Nothing is solved in this episode except to reinforce the idea that it is important to maintain dialogue.

Room 222 also incorporates lessons about teaching. Not only do we see Dixon, Johnson and others teaching, and McIntyre and Kaufman talking with and disciplining students, there are numerous scenes in which the characters talk about teaching. In "The Exchange Teacher," a enthusiastic but unorthodox British teacher connects with the students by making her classes lively and relevant but runs afoul of the administration when she fails to follow the rules by not taking attendance, having assigned seats, ignoring the period change bell, or having formal assignments. She ultimately chooses to return to England early rather than follow these rules. In another episode, Johnson is persuaded by her students to let them perform the last scene in their production of Shakespeare's *Twelfth Night* in the nude ("Naked Came We into the World"). In the end, the kids decide they really don't want to take off their clothes, but Miss Johnson wins their respect by allowing them to find their own way. In "Goodbye, Mr. Hip," a teacher trying to be cool by wearing hip clothes, long hair, and using slang, doesn't fool the students when he leads them to think that it's okay to smoke marijuana. He ultimately looks foolish when the students place a fake marijuana cigarette on his desk and he becomes upset. Dixon advises the teacher to be honest with the students. Although he is mad at the students for tricking him and at Dixon for telling him what he already knows, he returns to the classroom and admits he was scared when he found the marijuana cigarette. The students accept his confession; he vows to act more like a teacher, and they respect him for it. In both these instances, the teachers don't fit the Hollywood Model, they must either accommodate or leave. In the first instance, the visiting teacher chooses to leave early rather than compromise, and in the second instance, the "hip" teacher decides to behave more like a teacher, to fit in, and stay. Both end up gaining the respect of their colleagues and the students.

The downside of teaching is exposed in at least two episodes. In one, Principal Kaufman describes teaching as an "unexciting job" with a "pitiful salary and very limited prospects for the future" ("Seventeen Going on Twenty-Eight"). In another, a potential replacement for Kaufman (if he decides to take a sabbatical) is a strict authoritarian who says that you "have to sacrifice the bad apples to save the good ones." He reiterates his point when he says "schools have their function and jails have theirs." This may be the view of some but not among the teachers at Walt Whitman High. Upon hearing this man's philosophy, Mr. Kaufman decides to forego his sabbatical.

The world of Walt Whitman High is a rarefied world. *Room 222* tries to show the promise of social change of the era but within the realm of possibility. And although Dixon has been called an idealist, all the recurring characters share his outlook, striving for understanding and tolerance (Brooks and Marsh 1011). This need to unify is utopian and distances the main characters from the established Hollywood Model by eliminating the conflicts caused by positioning good teachers as outsiders at odds with the administrators and contentious colleagues. *Room 222* is a world in which everyone works together to create a wholly integrated school where all can learn.

Conclusion

The 1960s were a time of turmoil in American culture, but little of that turmoil was shown in primetime television programming. With the exception of a few socially relevant shows, what was seen on television news contrasted sharply with what was seen during primetime programming. Three of these socially relevant shows feature teachers: *Mr. Novak*, *The Bill Cosby Show*, and *Room 222*. Only *The Bill Cosby Show* and *Room 222* provide any ongoing references to race and neither addresses race directly, either on a societal or on a personal level (although *The Bill Cosby Show* makes a few indirect references). And while *Mr. Novak* backgrounds African Americans, *The Bill Cosby Show* and *Room 222* both present fully integrated environments in which the color of a person's skin is irrelevant. Even on those rare occasions when race is dealt with directly in either show, it is addressed obliquely. In both cases, hair styles and dress are used to signify African American culture; in *The Bill Cosby Show* the lead character sometimes wears a dashiki. Music, supporting characters, and asides are also used in this way. In *Room 222*, African American hairstyles and dress are seen only on students.

It could be said that the very fact that these shows tiptoe around race and race-related issues makes them representative of their era. In a time when the country was in turmoil, it was reassuring for audiences to be able to see a color-blind world where everyone was trying to do the right thing. And these shows *do* tackle other socially relevant topics and seek to demonstrate that the dream of integrated schools could be realized, even if only on primetime television.

The socially relevant portrayal of teachers on television in the 1960s gives way to the quest of ideological neutrality in the 1970s with *Welcome Back, Kotter* and *The Paper Chase*. The avoidance of reality continues.

FOUR

1970s Ideology and Social Class

Welcome Back, Kotter and *The Paper Chase*

The 1970s was a decade of upheaval and unrest. It began with continuing protests against the escalating Vietnam War and the killing of four students at Kent State University by the Ohio National Guard and ended with the election of a former Hollywood movie star as president of the United States in 1980. In between there was the Watergate scandal; the end of the war and reunification of Vietnam; resignations of U.S. Vice-President Spiro Agnew, amid a scandal, and President Richard Nixon, under threat of impeachment for lying to Congress. Margaret Thatcher became the first woman elected prime minister of England. The first test-tube baby was born, and abortion was legalized in the U.S. Elvis Presley died, and rumors of Elvis sightings ran rampant as his fans refused to admit he was gone. An African American tennis pro, Arthur Ashe, won at Wimbledon for the first time. Gay rights became a prominent feature of identity politics. The film *Star Wars* was released, creating an empire so popular that it spawned two sequels and three prequels. Pocket calculators and video cassette recorders were introduced. And, two oil embargos fueled a recession in the U.S., serving to increase a widespread sense of disillusionment with government and politics.

On television, ABC premiered *Monday Night Football* in 1970, and over eleven million viewers watched the Cleveland Browns defeat the New York Jets. Early in the decade, Norman Lear's controversial *All in the Family* (CBS, 1971–79) began, and PBS imported highbrow programming for its new Sunday night show, *Masterpiece Theatre* (1971–). *Saturday Night Live* premiered on NBC in 1975 and is still going strong, and ABC brought the first female news anchor to the airwaves in 1976 when Barbara Walters began hosting the *ABC Evening News* with Harry Reasoner. In 1977, the groundbreaking miniseries *Roots* aired for eight consecutive nights on ABC, creating a national dialog about race. The role of a lovable alien on *Mork and Mindy* catapulted Robin Williams to stardom in 1978. And, in 1979, ESPN became the first cable network to specialize in sports programming.

The 1970s saw the baby boomers transformed into consumers in what author Tom Wolfe called the "Me Decade." Although Thorstein Veblen coined the term conspicuous consumption in his 1902 book *Theory of the Leisure Class*, it seemed to reach its apotheosis in the 1970s. As people turned inward, social class, long denied as a barrier to success by the proponents of the American Dream, became even less visible as an issue.

The ideology of social class in the classroom remained implicit on television as producers, and writers tried to maintain impartiality in entertainment that often featured more meaningful cultural critiques. Social relevancy programs, such as *All in the Family* and *Maude*, sidestepped classroom settings, perhaps because students provided so much impetus to social movements in real life that it was a subject TV producers wished to avoid. As a consequence, mainstream television programs appeared bland in comparison to the stories on the evening news. Although there was a nominal increase in television shows featuring teachers during the 1970s compared to the 1960s, many of them either were on the air for a short period of time or the teacher characters were minor, or both. A few shows, most notably *The White Shadow*, tried to approach some of the troubling issues facing educators at the time, such as integration and race relations. For the most part, however, the retreat from reality was abject, as shows steered clear of controversial issues even while maintaining racially diverse casts.

Teachers on TV: The 1970s

Of the twenty-five shows with teacher characters in the 1970s, twelve are situation comedies, two are dramedies, nine are dramas, one is a drama anthology, and one is occult. In most of these shows, the teacher characters or their teaching is peripheral, or the shows aired for less than a season. One, *Struck By Lightning*, lasted for only three episodes!

Several shows featuring educators in starring or key roles are noteworthy for their portrayals of teachers actually teaching. One of these is *The Headmaster* (CBS, 1970–71), starring Andy Griffith as Andy Thompson, headmaster of a private high school, in his first role after his iconic turn as Sheriff Andy Taylor on *The Andy Griffith Show*. The main focus of this series is the teachers and students. Thompson's wife, Margaret (Claudette Nevins), is an English teacher, and his best friend, Jerry Brownell (Jerry Van Dyke, predating and foreshadowing his appearance on *Coach* by more than fifteen years) is the coach and physical education teacher. According to Brooks and Marsh, the public wasn't ready to accept Andy Griffith in a dramatic role, and the show lasted less than a year (596).

Another promising yet short-lived series focuses on a former baseball player[1] and sportswriter who becomes an English teacher in a suburban high school outside St. Louis. *Lucas Tanner* (NBC, 1974–75) features the title character with a "down-to-earth" teaching style that irritates his more traditional colleagues, but he manages to make his style work because his students care for him and he has the support of his principal. Tanner is portrayed by David Hartman, who became known as the host of the ABC morning show, *Good Morning, America*, from 1975 to 1987.

More rooted in reality in the surreal way that television has of distilling real-seeming events into palatable, just barely believable stories, *The White Shadow* (CBS, 1978–81) stars Ken Howard as former professional basketball player Ken Reeves. After being forced to retire from the Chicago Bulls because of knee injuries, Reeves becomes the basketball coach at the inner-city, racially-mixed Carver High School in Los Angeles. The show features African American principal Jim Willis (Jason Bernard, in the first episode, then Ed Bernard, no relation) and African American assistant principal Sybil Buchanan (Joan Pringle), who becomes the principal in the third season. *The White Shadow* is set primarily in and around the school. The prominently Black team includes Warren Coolidge (Byron Stewart), a student who reads at a third-grade level; James Hayward (Thomas Carter), who is arrested seventeen times over the course of the show (always escaping conviction); smart aleck Morris Thorpe (Kevin Hooks); pot smoker Curtis Jackson (Eric Kilpatrick); and Mario "Salami" Pettrino (Timothy Van Patten), the most prominent White player. Although the show deals with serious issues, including drugs, homosexuality, gambling, educational mainstreaming, physical and mental disabilities, sexually transmitted diseases, prostitution, and child abuse, it often undermines its own credibility by cutting to a silly reaction shot or inserting a laugh track. In keeping with the Hollywood Model of the Good Teacher, Reeves tells his team at the end of the big game in the first episode, "I'll be behind you every step of the way." A student player responds, "Yeah, like a white shadow."² Through it all, Ken Reeves is the father substitute (and Good Teacher) who never stops believing in his players.

Figure 4.1. Ken Howard as Ken Reeves and Jason Bernard as Jim Willis in *The White Shadow* (CBS, 1978–81). Photo courtesy of Photofest. Used by permission.

Three short-lived shows also feature characters who are used to the limelight and are new to the teaching profession. In *The Waverly Wonders* (NBC, 1978–78), former pro football quarterback Joe Namath takes on the role of retired pro basketball (yes, basketball!) player Joe Casey who becomes a high school history teacher and coach. He is inept as a teacher, and his team, the Waverly Wonders, can't play basketball. *Hanging In* (CBS, 1979–79) stars Bill Macy (previously of *Maude*) as Louis Harper, a former pro football (yes, football!) player who becomes the president of a university. In *Dorothy* (CBS,

1979–79), a different kind of professional, former showgirl Dorothy Banks (Dorothy Loudon), becomes a music and drama teacher at an exclusive school for girls. Although her students love her, the administration takes a dim view of her unorthodox teaching style. Each of these shows lasted less than a month on the air.

Although several situation comedies that debuted during the 1970s include teacher characters, few focus on teaching. In *Nanny and the Professor* (ABC, 1970–71), widowed mathematics professor Howard Everett (Richard Long) hires Phoebe Figalilly (Juliet Mills, who would later appear as Tabitha Lenox on *Passions* on USA, 1999–) as a nanny to care for his children. Sandy Stockton (Sandy Duncan) is a UCLA education major who works part time as an actress in *Funny Face* (CBS, 1971–71). Film star Jimmy Stewart adopts the persona of anthropology professor James K. Howard whose grown son, Peter (Jonathan Daly), moves in with him in *The Jimmy Stewart Show* (NBC, 1971–72). In *Anna and the King* (CBS, 1972–72), based on the film *The King and I*, Yul Brynner reprises his stage and film role as the King, and Anna, the impertinent teacher, is played by Samantha Egger. On *Bridget Loves Bernie* (CBS, 1972–73), a young Catholic newlywed, Bridget Fitzgerald Steinberg (Meredith Baxter, who would go on to star as the mother, Elyse Keaton on *Family Ties* on NBC, 1982–89 as Meredith Baxter-Birney) is an elementary teacher married to a Jewish writer, Bernie Steinberg (David Birney). Emily Hartley (Suzanne Pleshette), the wife of psychologist Bob Hartley (Bob Newhart), is an elementary school teacher on *The Bob Newhart Show* (CBS, 1972–78). *Delta House* (ABC, 1979–79) was based on the gross-out film *Animal House*, and takes place in a college fraternity house. And, in *Struck by Lightning* (CBS, 1979–79), a young science teacher, Ted Stein (Jeffrey Kramer), inherits an inn, learns he is Dr. Frankenstein's great-great-grandson, and caretakes a 231-year-old monster named Frank (Jack Elam). In all of these shows, the teachers are rarely, if ever, shown teaching.

Teaching was never the focus of *Happy Days* (ABC, 1974–84), but it is interesting that one of the ways the writers clean up a character's reputation is to have him become a teacher. The Cunninghams—parents Howard and Marion and teenagers Richie and Joanie (Ron Howard, a grown-up Opie from *The Andy Griffith Show*, and Erin Moran, also starring in *Joanie Loves Chachi*)—are the stereotypical 1950s family. Although both Cunningham kids and their friends matriculate, there are rarely scenes at school. Ultimately, the biggest star on the show is "The Fonz," a motorcycle tough whom all the kids look up to. Arthur "Fonzie" Fonzarelli (Henry Winkler) is a high school dropout, but as he gradually mellows into a more mainstream character, he attends night school and graduates at the same time as Richie and his friends. During the sixth season, Fonzie becomes almost respectable—he is co-owner of the local eatery, Arnold's, the operator of Bronco's Garage, and a shop teacher at the high school. In the last season, Fonzie becomes the Dean of Boys at a vocational high school where Joanie joins him as a trainee teacher. With so many teacher characters and so little teaching, it becomes clear that the occupation of teacher is convenient shorthand for intelligence and respectability.

Figure 4.2. Melissa Gilbert as Laura Ingalls in *Little House on the Prairie* (NBC, 1974–83). Photo courtesy of Photofest. Used by permission.

Figure 4.3. Richard Thomas as Jim Warner, Fay Hauser as Carrie Barden, and Henry Fonda as Col. Warner in *Roots: The Next Generations* (ABC, 1979–81). Photo courtesy of Photofest. Used by permission.

Two dramedies during the decade have teacher characters. Sandra Sue Abbott "Abby" Bradford (Betty Buckley, who is a singer and actor and portrayed Suzanne Fitzgerald for two seasons on the HBO series *Oz* 1997–2003); stepmother on *Eight Is Enough* (ABC, 1977–81), is a teacher who completes her Ph.D. in education over the course of the show. And, in *Shirley* (NBC, 1979–80), Shirley Miller (Shirley Jones, best known as the mom on *The Partridge Family)*, is a widowed New York teacher who can't get a full-time teaching position after she relocates her family to Lake Tahoe, California. Her children attend the local schools, but Shirley has to settle for non-teaching, part-time jobs for income.

Several dramas during the 1970s have teacher characters. The occult show *The Sixth Sense* (ABC, 1972–72) features college professor Dr. Michael Rhodes (Gary Collins), whose studies in parapsychology involve him in a story about various psychic phenomena every week. On *Little House on the Prairie* (NBC, 1974–83), two of the daughters grow up to be teachers. As an adult, Mary Ingalls (Melissa Sue Anderson) marries her teacher, Adam Kendall (Linwood

Boomer) and then becomes a teacher, and later her sister, Laura (Melissa Gilbert), also becomes a teacher. On *James at 15* (NBC, 1977–78), the father, Paul Hunter (Linden Chiles), is a college professor. The dramatic anthology *What Really Happened to the Class of 1965?* (NBC, 1977–78) features a different graduate's story each week. The only continuing role is that of one member of the class, Sam Ashley (Tony Bill), who has returned to teach at the school. Psychologist David McKay (Robert Reed, remembered for his portrayal of the father on *The Brady Bunch*) has a girlfriend, Karen Wingate (Karen Machon), who is a college dean on *The Runaways* (NBC, 1978–79). Although there are only a few recurring teacher characters on the long-running series *The Waltons* (CBS, 1972–81), Miss Hunter (Mariclare Costello) ultimately teaches all the Walton children at Walton's Mountain School and even upsets parents when she teaches evolution in "The Fire." In "The Scholar," John-Boy (Richard Thomas) is asked to tutor others, and in "The Sermon," mother Olivia Walton (Michael Learned) is asked to be a substitute teacher. A smart but inexperienced teacher causes problems at Walton's Mountain School in "The Substitute," and in "The Romance," Olivia's night school art teacher makes makes a pass at her. When John-Boy goes to Boatwright University, and later Jason goes to Klineberg Conservatory, they both encounter professors. Only two professors have recurring roles: Professor Parks (Paul Jenkins) and Professor Thaxton (Jay Robinson). In a socially relevant plot line on *Roots: The Next Generations* (ABC, 1979–81), wealthy, white patriarch Colonel Warner (film icon Henry Fonda), disowns his son, Jim (Richard Thomas previously of *The Waltons*), when Jim marries Black school teacher Carrie Barden (Fay Hauser). Another character, Simon Haley (Dorian Harewood,), teaches agriculture at a Black college.

Two teacher shows from this decade deserve a closer look for the ways in which they represent upper and lower class student populations but relegate social class to the background: *Welcome Back, Kotter* (ABC, 1975–79) and *The Paper Chase* (CBS, 1978–79 & Showtime, 1983–86). Although the shows can be seen as bookends—one deals with lower socioeconomic teens in an inner-city school and the other concerns the rarefied world of an elite law school—they both illustrate the dominant ideology that social class doesn't matter in America because people believe that America is the land of opportunity. Both shows focus on education and treat the students in an idealized fashion.

Ideology and Social Class

Social class has become a more difficult marker by which to categorize people since the 1970s because the indicators of socioeconomic status are not as readily visible as they once were. In their 2005 series on class for the *New York Times*, Janny Scott and David Leonhardt said, "There was a time when Americans thought they understood class. The upper crust vacationed in Europe and worshiped an Episcopal God. The middle class drove Ford Fairlanes, settled in the San Fernando Valley, and enlisted as company men. The working class belonged to the A.F.L.-C.I.O., voted Democratic, and did not take cruises to the Caribbean." Now, because of the magnitude of consumer wealth, it is harder to discern a person's social class. The consumer trappings of the upper class are more readily available to many more people who are able to take a European vacation or lease a fancy car.

According to the dominant ideology, class is less relevant to us because we believe that anyone can "make it" in America if they just work hard enough. Yet, there are certain markers that can place you in one class or another. These include how you speak, what you wear, where you live, what you buy, how much education you have, whom you socialize with, and your choice of entertainment (including what you watch on television). According to Scott and Leonhardt, class "means different things to different people. Class is rank; it is tribe; it is culture and taste. It is attitudes and assumptions, a source of identity, a system of exclusion. To some, it is just money. It is an accident of birth that can influence the outcome of a life. Some Americans barely notice it; others feel its weight in powerful ways." Although social class is seldom addressed directly in American society, it is a constant undercurrent in many people's lives.

Between 1950 and 1970, most people born into a particular social class stayed in that class or moved up. This began changing in the 1970s, as more people started moving down as well. By the end of the decade, there was a growing divergence between the rich and the poor, a disparity that continues into the present (Bradbury and Katz 3). The 2005 *New York Times* study showed that the economic status of Americans was shifting. The wealthiest people and the poorest people tended to stay wealthy or poor, but the rest of us had more social mobility (Scott and Leonhardt). This income mobility leads people to think that we live in a classless society, or that, if classes do exist, we can better ourselves and move into a higher class if we want to and just work hard enough. Yet, social mobility has actually slowed since 1975 due to the concentration of wealth among the elite (Beller and Hout 19).

One of the major ways we are told that we can better our lot in life is to get a good education. Statistically, however, it's who your parents are and how wealthy they are that has a greater impact than any other factors (McNamee and Miller 13). Nevertheless, education is seen as the key that can unlock the doors for many to move ahead. Access to better educational opportunities from pre-school to college can influence mobility positively or negatively, but it is not everything, and sometimes the very system that is set up to help us is class-based. Pedagogic literature has chronicled the ways in which the education system treats students differently based on their socioeconomic backgrounds.

In her seminal study in the late 1970s (the time frame for the shows discussed in this chapter), Jean Anyon notes that students in the schools she observed were rewarded for classroom behaviors that corresponded to various occupations for which they were deemed likely candidates. For example, working class students were rewarded for docility and obedience whereas in middle and upper class schools, students were rewarded for initiative and assertiveness. According to this "hidden curriculum," schools prepare students from different socioeconomic groups for jobs that correspond to those strata.[3] The curriculum at the working class schools focused on rote learning with little decision making. Students were graded on whether or not they followed the rules. On the other hand, students at upper middle class and upper class schools were graded on how well they worked creatively, analytically, and independently. This research is not reflected in *Welcome Back, Kotter* and *The Paper Chase*, which serve as examples of how the influence of social class is blunted on television. The shows' creators imply ideology in the classroom settings of a working class school and an Ivy League school, yet play down the explicitly political in favor of storylines that focus on the personal.

Although the students are from lower class families in *Welcome Back, Kotter*, the show does not focus overtly on social class. The inner-city location and vocational approach to education brought to film twenty years earlier in *Blackboard Jungle* is echoed on *Welcome Back, Kotter*. Former student Gabe Kotter returns to teach history at his alma mater, but the television series substantially removes both the threat and the promise of the students along with any compelling representation of their status in the underclass. Kotter has managed to ascend to the middle class as a teacher without any discernable improvement to his living situation, which makes his status analogous to that of his students and blurs the socioeconomic lines between them. Kotter treats them with respect, telling the students they are worthy and that they need to try harder. At the other end of the spectrum, the main student character on *The Paper Chase* hails from a middle-class upbringing in Iowa, yet his primary law professor is upper class, as is the school, and the elitism of the setting is assumed. Even though social class was being questioned in society during the 1970s, in both these shows class is rarely foregrounded. By ignoring the consequences and implications of social class, these series minimize the importance of class in America across the spectrum.

Welcome Back, Kotter

Welcome Back, Kotter takes place in James Buchanan High School in the Bensonhurst neighborhood of Brooklyn, New York. Although there are other characters and settings within the school, the show focuses on a history class, as in *Room 222* and *Head of the Class*, except these are remedial students. The core of the class is comprised of a group of students who call themselves the Sweathogs. The teacher is Gabe Kotter (standup comedian Gabriel Kaplan), a former Sweathog, who has returned to teach in his former high school. A multicultural underclass composes The Sweathogs. The main characters are: the cool Italian heartthrob Vinnie Barbarino (John Travolta in his first major role),[4] who is the ringleader; tough Jewish-Puerto Rican Juan Luis Pedro "Epstein" Phillipo de Heuvos Epstein (Robert Hegyes); hip African American Freddie "Boom Boom" Washington (Lawrence-Hilton Jacobs); and shy class clown Arnold Horshack (Ron Palillo). A recurring classmate is Verna Jean (Vernee Watson), another African American who has a small speaking role in a number of episodes. Two other Sweathogs appear later in the series: Polish Angie Globagoski (Melonie Haller) and Southern smooth-talker Beau De Labarre (Stephen Shortridge). Although there are always other students in the room, most are extras and speak only occasionally in response to main characters. In addition to the featured students and their teacher, Michael Woodman (John Sylvester White) is the assistant principal and Kotter's sometimes nemesis. Kotter's wife, Julie (Marcia Strassman), appears at the beginning and end of most episodes in bookend sequences in which she plays straight person for Kotter's opening and closing jokes.[5] She is featured in a quite a few episodes, especially in the last two seasons when Gabe Kaplan's appearances were intermittent.

When the show first began airing on ABC in 1975, it was not carried by the Boston affiliate because the station executives felt that the show was in poor taste for their viewers in light of all the consternation at the time about school integration. Even though the landmark Supreme Court case of *Brown v. Board of Education* found segregated schools unconstitutional in 1954, school integration was very slow to occur in many locales. In some areas, such as Boston, court-ordered school busing and integration were met with riots in the 1970s. The local affiliate thought that showing "rebellious" students in an integrated school, even in a fictional setting, might not be welcomed by their viewers. The show began airing in Boston with the fifth episode (O'Connor). The Sweathogs cannot be called rebellious, for the most part everyone gets along, but Buchanan High School is a decidedly integrated setting.

Across the ninety-four episodes that were produced, twenty-nine deal di-

Figure 4.4. (top row) Gabe Kaplan as Gabe Kotter, (bottom row, left to right) Robert Hegyes as Juan Luis Pedro Phillipo de Huevos Epstein, Lawrence-Hilton Jacobs as Freddie "Boom Boom" Washington, John Travolta as Vinnie Barbarino, and Ron Palillo as Arnold Horshack in *Welcome Back, Kotter* (ABC, 1975–79). Photo courtesy of Photofest. Used by permission.

rectly with education issues, including teaching, learning, the state of education, sports versus education, sex education, cheating, and dissection. Other issues of note include the Constitution, non-violence, investigative journalism, the Equal Rights Amendment, elections and the electoral process, the legal system, death and suicide, addiction and alcoholism, marriage, unwanted pregnancy, gangs, wealth, lottery, bribery, and sexual molestation. These are serious issues but rarely get serious treatment on the show. Most topics are ameliorated by jokes. In true sitcom form, the jokes take precedence, but it was uncommon at the time for such weighty topics to be broached, even superficially.

Between the jokes and wisecracks, Gabe Kotter is a dedicated teacher. He and his wife live in a one-room apartment in Brooklyn and barely get by financially. They live in a poor, dangerous neighborhood, but the setting is rarely noted as such. Kotter is generally unflappable, whether at school or at home, and because he remembers his time as a Sweathog, he is dedicated to helping his students. Although Kotter sometimes seems smug, he nevertheless believes in himself and his students and their abilities. He is portrayed as a model of the upward mobility available to his students if they work hard.

Although social class is not addressed directly on the show, implicit in Kotter's classroom approach is a belief that education is the key to getting ahead. The working class students at Buchanan High School are not focused on rote learning, however, nor are they graded by whether they follow the rules or not, as Anyon found in her study mentioned above. The Sweathogs are encouraged to think and to think outside the box. Their socioeconomic status doesn't influence how Kotter teaches them; in fact, according to Anyon's research, these students are treated more like upper middle to upper class students. They are encouraged to be creative, independent, and think for themselves. In Anyon's studies, she found that lower class students were given rote work and rewarded for their docility. This is a far cry from how Kotter treats the Sweathogs.

In "The Debate," Kotter encourages his students to compete against Buchanan's debate team.[6] They do, and they win, but not because they prepare in a traditional way by researching the issue, "Are human beings naturally aggressive?" Instead they win by using showmanship, real life experiences, and ultimately cause the other team to lose its cool, with one opposing team member even becoming aggressive. Kotter tells his students he is proud of them for having a plan, even though they have a long way to go. They are encouraged to think creatively and independently.

In "Mr. Kotter, Teacher," Kotter's teaching style is criticized, and he is suspended. The charges against him are that he refuses to use the outdated textbooks and the prescribed curriculum (personalizing the curriculum is one of the characteristics of a Good Teacher). Kotter's students crash the hearing to defend him. When asked where and how they got the information they use in his defense, they respond that they went to the library. Kotter tells the review board: "Unfortunately, normal teaching didn't seem to work for these kids. I mean, if it did, well, they wouldn't be Sweathogs. Don't you see, they're gonna have to survive in the world of the future. If they learn how to learn . . . they'll be able to survive anywhere." Kotter is reinstated.

In "The Telethon," Kotter and his class are told there isn't enough money to continue their remedial class for the rest of the year and that the Sweathogs will be put in regular classrooms. Horshack comes up with the idea to hold a telethon on the local Brooklyn public access television station. Everyone performs—Kotter, each student (with John Travolta's character, Barbarino, in a gold lame jump suit imitating Elvis, a foreshadowing of his performance in *Saturday Night Fever* in 1977), Mr. Woodman, and even Kotter's wife, Julie. At the end of the telecast, they issue a special appeal to all the teachers of "normal" students to donate to keep the Sweathogs out of their "normal" classrooms. The students' status as Sweathogs is discussed, but their social class is not. Of course, this may be because almost all the students at the school are from working class families.

In "One Flu over the Cuckoo's Nest," the students chafe at having the normal kids added to their class during a flu outbreak. The normal kids always do their homework and always know the answers to Kotter's questions. Frustrated, the Sweathogs say that all they have are a lot of questions. Kotter assures them that asking questions is how they learn. In "The Sit-In," the students learn about non-violent demonstrations and hold a sit-in to protest the serving of liver in the cafeteria. In "The Election," Kotter teaches the electoral system using jokes, and when Mr. Woodman substitutes for Kotter in "No More Mister Nice Guy," he teaches the American Revolution using many costume changes. Although Kotter's use of jokes is in character for him, Mr. Woodman's use of non-conventional methods is totally out of character for him and is played for laughs. The use of these upper middle and upper class tactics serves to minimize the effect of social class by relegating it to the background. By avoiding the effect of social class, this series also minimizes the apparent importance of class in America and suggests fluidity among the social classes.

Social class is rarely highlighted on *Welcome Back, Kotter*, but in several instances references are made to the lower class setting or social position of the teacher or students. In "Hello, Ms. Chips," a student teacher comes to observe and teach in Kotter's class. She tells Kotter that her college program is called Educational Development and Guidance. He responds by saying that he majored in the same thing: Slum Training 101. In "Career Day," Kotter is offered a job with a company in Chicago making three times his teaching salary. He ultimately decides to remain in teaching and tells his students, "You know how good I feel every time I teach you people something? You know, I feel good, really good. When I help you discover that you're smart, not dumb. . . . You know, I don't do it for the money. I learn things from you people, too." Teaching is his vocation. At the end of the episode, he encourages the Sweathogs to become teachers, ostensibly to better their social class but also for self-fulfillment. Arnold is promoted to a regular class in "Arrividerci, Arnold." After a few days, he tells the Sweathogs and Kotter, "You don't know what a regular class is like: no jokes, no costumes, no impressions." Ultimately, Kotter realizes the reason Horshack was doing well in his class, and he tells Assistant Principal Woodman, "If Arnold learned anything, he learned it in this classroom. . . . because for someone to learn, they have to feel secure. They have to feel like they belong." Horshack is allowed to return to the Sweathogs. In "The Museum," Principal Woodman doesn't think the class should go on a field trip to a museum. He doesn't think they are responsible enough; yet, in the end, it is the students who are the most responsible and figure out a way for everyone to escape after they are trapped in a special exhibits room. The students are treated like middle class students, not like lower class students. In all these examples, the storylines focus on the personal to avoid the politics of social class.

Buchanan High School is shown as a working class school but not emphasized as such. In fact, the school has certain activities that might not be expected in a lower class school, such as sports teams, a school newspaper, a debate team, and a radio station. These extracurricular activities neutralize the effect of references to the socioeconomic status of the school, thereby rendering social class invisible. The Sweathogs are told repeatedly that what they need to do is believe, to work hard, and they can get ahead. This is a message that appears in almost *all* television teacher shows, but on *Welcome Back, Kotter*, the exhortation to think creatively, work hard, and believe in themselves is a constant refrain that buoys the students. The tacit understanding is that the Sweathogs' prospects are dim if they do not heed Kotter's advice. In *The Paper Chase*, this message is less urgent; because the students are all middle to upper class, they are already "ahead." As in *Welcome Back, Kotter*, social class is relegated to the background, and stories focus on the study of law and personal relationships.

The Paper Chase

The Paper Chase (CBS, 1978–79; Showtime, 1983–86) is the story of a law student's experiences at an unnamed Ivy League school and his relationship with a brilliant, yet cantankerous, professor. The show was based on the 1973 movie, which was based on a 1970 novel, both of the same title. Even though CBS aggressively promoted the show and it was said at the time to be "one of the best programs on the air" (Harmetz "CBS"), *The Paper Chase* never found the audience that CBS hoped for.[7] Low ratings could have been expected since it was competing with two of the top-rated shows that year, *Happy Days* and *Laverne and Shirley*, in what was sometimes called "the death slot" or "murderer's row" (Houseman 82). While only eight and a half million households were watching *The Paper Chase*, fifteen million households were laughing along with its competition on ABC (Houseman 84). Even after CBS moved the show to a different time slot (and then back), it never garnered the ratings the network wanted or needed. When CBS cancelled the show after its first season, the network received tens of thousands of letters in protest but refused to reconsider the cancellation (O'Connor "Old Friends," Schneider, Harmetz *"Paper Chase"*). In a remarkable move for the time, PBS rebroadcast thirteen of the original episodes in 1981. This was the first time a show had made a move from commercial to public television (Schneider). Then, in another extraordinary turn of events, pay cable network Showtime optioned new episodes. *The Paper Chase* became the first show to be produced especially for pay cable television and remained on Showtime for three seasons (Harmetz *"Paper Chase"*).

Although the show deals with many legal issues, such as privacy, search and seizure, contracts, constitutional law, and defamation, to name a few, it also tackles issues related to education like cheating, plagiarism, affirmative action, study skills, and tenure. *The Paper Chase* touches on other subjects, such as love and friendship, gambling, death, sexual harassment, racism, community action, aging, suicide, and anti-Semitism, but the focus is the law, law school, and the relationships of the characters.

James T. Hart (James Stephens) comes from a farm in Iowa and has worked hard to get where he is, but he is challenged by the level of work and the ruthlessness of law school. His nemesis is Professor Charles W. Kingsfield, Jr. (John Houseman reprising the role for which he won a best supporting Oscar in the 1973 film). Kingsfield has been variously described as authoritarian, tyrannical, ferocious, intellectual, wise, crusty, stern, brilliant, headstrong, demanding, awesome, imperious, challenging, and daunting.[8] Houseman called his character "old stoneface" (Schneider). Law school is a tense and stressful place, and Kingsfield strikes fear in the hearts of all his students. *The Paper Chase* shows students and professors studying the law, writing papers and briefs, and debating issues, and the massive law books in every school scene nearly become another character within the show. To cope with the workload, Hart joins a study group comprised of Tom Anderson (Robert Ginty), Willis Bell (James Keane), Jonathan Brooks (Jonathan Segal), and Franklin Ford III (Tom Fitzsimmons).

Figure 4.5. John Houseman as Charles W. Kingsfield, Jr., James Stephens as James T. Hart in *The Paper Chase* (CBS 1978, Showtime 1983–86). Photo courtesy of Photofest. Used by permission.

In the first year, Hart works at a pizza parlor to make ends meet. He is the only one with a job, and his work ethic extends to his studies. His job and his diligence to his studies suggest that he has to work harder because he has farther to climb. During the second year, he is appointed to the school's *Law Review*, and during the third year he is made editor, a plum position that is evidence that his work is paying off. Female characters are added during the second and third years. Especially noteworthy is Connie Lehman (Jane Kaczmarek, the wacky mother in *Malcolm in the Middle* from 2000 to 2006), a dedicated student who becomes a love interest for Hart, and a new instructor, Professor Tyler (Diana Douglas, film actor Michael Douglas' mother, has acted in films and television for over fifty years). Interestingly, an older former housewife, Rose Samuels (Lainie Kazan), is added to the student cast during the third year, broadening the range of female characters on the show.

Although the setting for *The Paper Chase* is an Ivy League school,[9] a seemingly upper class environment, social class is treated only indirectly. Professor Kingsfield shows all the characteristics of someone from the upper class: clothes, accent, language, and decorum. He has a regal bearing and a way of looking at people that lets them know that he is smarter than they are, and he knows it. We know little about the man, except that he is a widower, is in his late seventies (he turns eighty during season two), and was married to his wife for over fifty years. He has been a professor for over fifty years and has been considered twice for nomination to the United States Supreme Court. His huge corner office is large enough for his desk, a separate sitting area around the working fireplace, and a seminar table and chairs, and he has his own private secretary. It is unclear whether every professor at this school has her/his own secretary or if an exception is made for Kingsfield. The office and the secretary are both unremarked-upon symbols of Kingsfield's status. He seems to have been born into this elite arena. Yet, in spite of his bearing and the setting, his social class is never addressed explicitly. He seems above categorization.

Hart and most of the students seem middle to upper middle class except for the upper class Ford, a wealthy, "would-be third generation lawyer from a socially prominent family" (Brooks and Marsh 1048), and Bell, who seems to be lower to lower middle class because of his clothes and mannerisms. In their first year, students are encouraged to live in the dorm, and most do. This, in and of itself, is a leveling tactic. They all have the same rooms, take the same classes, and study in the same library, creating an egalitarian atmosphere.

Kingsfield treats all the students the same, for the most part, but he does seem to be harder on Hart than the others. This is Hart's story, so it is understandable that the focus would be on him, but the fact that he is from a Midwest farm also sets him apart. As the show progresses, his intellect is played up in the stories; he is very smart, and he is the only one to make an A in Kingsfield's contracts class. Hart's personal background is noted by other characters but is never dwelled on, just as Ford's background is mentioned but is not the focus. Hart's intellect *is* noted, however. In "Outline Fever," the first episode of the second season, Hart and his study group are now second year students. The new first year students all want to buy Hart's outline (as big as a book!) for Kingsfield's class. Hart doesn't want to sell it because he feels that the other students will learn more if they do the work themselves. Ultimately, the members of the study group coax him into letting them sell the outline. They auction it to the highest bidder, who discovers that the law is constantly changing and that even the best outline is already dated. As Kingsfield tells the student in class, "There are no shortcuts. You are responsible for not only last year's law but present law as well." In "My Dinner with Kingsfield," a snowstorm leads Kingsfield to have dinner with Hart at the student's apartment instead of Hart's expected guest, his girlfriend, who is trapped by the snow in New York. During the course of the evening, Hart complains that he worked harder than he has ever worked on his latest paper for Kingsfield and that the professor didn't seem to appreciate how good it is. Kingsfield tells him: "I am a professor. My job is to get the best work out of you, not to wet nurse you with lavish praise. . . . You're one of the better students in this institution. You should not need to be told that. You know your work is good. That's all that matters. Doing your best is its own reward, and you shouldn't need me to tell you about it." In both these instances, doing well is an individual task. To succeed, you must do your best, a sentiment that reinforces the idea of social mobility.

In "Plague of Locusts," law firm recruiters come to class to recruit second year students for summer internships. Many students are only looking for the highest paying positions, but Hart has a hard time deciding whether or not he wants to go for the money or choose a firm that does work he believes in. Recruiters are not allowed by school regulations to get grade point average (GPA) information about the students prior to the interview, but Ford's father's firm uses underhanded methods to get a list of all the GPAs for the entire second year student body and only interviews those at the top. (Although it's not noted, Mr. Ford seems to think that he deserves to know the GPA scores, an attitude indicative of his privileged social status.) Because Hart has the highest GPA, Mr. Ford gives him the royal treatment during his interview. Mr. Ford is unrepentant when confronted by his son, but the younger Ford will not turn him in to the school. He lets his father know that not only is he disappointed, he will not be coming to work in his father's firm. His father believes that their relationship is irreparably damaged, but Ford reaches out to him and tells him that although he's disappointed, he still loves him. Hart also decides not to go for the money, despite the wooing by the elite firm, after the editor of the *Law Review* tells him that he should go with a firm to "learn, not earn."

Although social class is rarely mentioned on the series, in "Birthday Party," Ford comes up with a system for him and Hart to signal one another when either has a girl in the apartment (tying a necktie on the doorknob). Hart is doubtful this is a good plan. Ford responds, "Trust me James. You went to public schools; this is an old prep school ploy." Later, when Hart's girlfriend spends the night, Ford is a little miffed and tells her that "owners shower first." In both these instances, Ford's upper class standing is noted in some way but is not dwelled on. In a parallel storyline in the same episode, a former student of Kingsfield's, now the U.S. attorney general, tells Hart he should "trust his gut" when deciding whether or not to honor Kingsfield on his eightieth birthday. Hart may not have the social training, but he can reliably "trust his gut."

Even though *The Paper Chase* is about law school and legal issues, and in spite of the fact that the setting is an Ivy League school, the show highlights learning and the general educational process. The series is more representative of the progressive tradition of John Dewey than the cultural elitism of Harold Bloom, providing further evidence that the rarefied Ivy League environment is moderated on television to minimize class divisions. In "The Burden of Proof," Hart has an internship in the public defender's office in addition to his position at the *Law Review*. Kingsfield asks Hart if he is aware that his performance in class has been below the usual standards. Although Kingsfield knows about the internship, he tells Hart, "Your academic work remains of paramount importance." Hart is chagrined but assures Kingsfield that he can do the work. Later, when Kingsfield is mugged, Hart is assigned to work on the case defending the mugger. At first Hart is enthusiastic about the case because he believes that his client is innocent. When he learns that his client is guilty, he is torn about whether or not he should defend him. His classmates think he is betraying Kingsfield. When Hart confides in Kingsfield, he is chastised for even talking to him because that's not the behavior of a lawyer. Hart decides to defend the accused, and Kingsfield attends the trial. Even though Hart is divided between his loyalty to Kingsfield and his loyalty to the law, he determines that the evidence was obtained through an illegal search, and his work results in the mugger being released. Kingsfield reminds Hart that this experience is part of his education and that sometimes the law can be used to impede justice. The overall tone of the show tends to blur distinctions between upper and lower class. The characterization of muggers as lower class people and of elites using their power to influence the system, as in the next example, could serve to reinforce the stereotypes about both classes. In both instances, however, their socioeconomic status is truncated to minimize class identification.

In "Security," Hart and Kingsfield unite to help Kingsfield's old friend and former editor of the *Law Review*, Jeremy Brooks (John Randolph), get his social security benefits after he is debilitated by a stroke. After much research and study, and additional help from Brooks, they sue the U.S. Social Security Administration and win. At the end of the episode, Brooks gives a speech about "our obligations to others" at the annual *Law Review* dinner. He says "the strong have nothing to worry about, but the weak and old fall by the wayside. We must choose between greed and compassion, between words and deeds." Once again, members of the educated, upper class have the knowledge and money to fight, but they find that many people are denied benefits who don't have the ability to fight the system. But the emphasis is placed on personal virtue rather than on any broader class consciousness. To a viewer, who may not be seeking such distinctions, evidence of class privilege is downplayed.

The Paper Chase could have veered into elitism in almost every episode, but it puts social class in the background, confined to the setting of the show, while the narrative focus remains on learning, legal issues, and relationships. One could say that the stories are life lessons. The rarefied atmosphere of the Ivy League law school is downplayed, in spite of Kingsfield's demeanor and the setting, in order to highlight teaching, learning, and the educational process.

Conclusion

In these two television shows, both lower and upper ends of the class spectrum are pulled toward a middle ground where predictable storylines about relationships are developed instead of overtly socioeconomic narratives. *Welcome Back Kotter* reproduces the inner-city location of the *Blackboard Jungle* and removes compelling representations of the students' status in the underclass. At the other end of the spectrum, *The Paper Chase* follows an Ivy League law school student and his relationship with an elitist professor, who is both aloof and certain of his place at the top, yet the show plays down the upper class environment. The downplaying of the implicit ideology of the settings minimizes the consequences and implications of social class at both ends of the spectrum. By focusing on personal stories, these series also minimize the apparent importance of class in America. The curtailing continues during the next decade in *The Facts of Life* and *Head of the Class*, both shows where social class is backgrounded and educational privileges for elite students are validated.

FIVE

1980s Normalizing Meritocracy

The Facts of Life and *Head of the Class*

The decade began with a certain amount of drama. There was the failed attempt to rescue the hostages being held in Tehran, Iran, and Mount St. Helens in Washington State erupted for the first time in over a hundred years. Ronald Reagan was elected president of the United States in November, and John Lennon was assassinated in December. When launching his presidential campaign in 1991, candidate Bill Clinton referred to the decade in this way: "The Reagan-Bush years exalted private gain over public obligation, special interests over the common good, wealth and fame over work and family. The 1980s ushered in a Gilded Age of greed and selfishness, of irresponsibility and excess, and of neglect" (Troy 16). This is an apt description for an era in which unemployment reached nine and a half percent, and there was a fifteen percent overall poverty rate. The term "yuppie" was coined to describe "young, urban professionals," the well-educated, new middle class with the purchasing power to consume conspicuously. Another term that came into widespread use to refer to President Reagan's economic program was Reaganomics. This program stressed low taxes and reduced government spending—except for the military—and was said to have contributed to the large budget deficits that plagued the country at the end of the decade. And, in an era when over-the-top fashion and big hair prevailed, and personal computers, video games, and mobile phones made their debuts, the 1980s lived up to Clinton's description.

Of course, there were also several notable signs of progress. During the 1980s, the first woman, Sandra Day O'Connor, was appointed to the Supreme Court; Sally Ride became the first American woman astronaut; the environmental movement became mainstream; and, the Cold War with the Soviet Union ended with the fall of the Berlin Wall in 1989. In the popular culture realm, MTV was launched; Oprah Winfrey began her talk show career; Ted Turner started CNN, a twenty-four hour news channel (albeit to much skepticism); and Rush Limbaugh catalyzed the conservative talk show movement with his AM radio show. On television, the animated sitcom *The Simpsons* debuted; and *The Cosby Show*, a sitcom about an upper middle class African American family, was rated the number one show in America for five years running.

Overall, the decade was one of unease demonstrated by a number of incidents, including a student massacre in Tiananmen Square in Beijing, China, and a catastrophic nuclear accident at the Chernobyl reactor in Ukraine. President Reagan's Strategic Defense Initiative (nicknamed Star Wars) was begun in the hopes of providing a shield against a nuclear weapons attack. In 1986, the *Challenger* space shuttle exploded killing all aboard, including school teacher Christa McAuliffe, the first civilian and the first teacher in space. The AIDS epidemic was discovered early in the decade and declared a pandemic in 1986. A significant increase in violent crime was predicated on a crack cocaine epidemic in urban areas. Through it all, the divide between the rich and the poor was increasing, causing widespread anxiety as the middle class saw its share of the pie decreasing. According to the U.S. Bureau of the Census, the average SAT (Scholastic Aptitude Test) score was 977 in 1985, down from 992 in 1980 (175). The starting salary in 1985 for a typical public school teacher was $15,460, and the average salary was $23,600 (165). At these levels of compensation, the profession was having a hard time attracting the best and the brightest. Classroom teachers were feeling the squeeze, a situation that was generally ignored on television.

Teachers on TV: The 1980s

The depiction of teachers on television proliferated with thirty-four shows airing during the 1980s that either featured teacher characters in non-classroom roles or in active teaching roles. Yet, most of the shows were not on the air for very long. Twenty-three of the thirty-four shows were situation comedies, eight were dramas, and three were either adventure or science fiction. Of the situation comedies, all but two lasted fourteen months or less on the air, and eleven featured teacher characters teaching. Of these, the two sitcoms on the air the longest were *The Facts of Life* and *Head of the Class*. These two shows deserve a closer look for how they portray teaching, education, and meritocracy and will be examined in more detail later in this chapter.

Nine other sitcoms feature active teacher characters. Four lasted three months or less. One is *Making the Grade* (CBS, 1982–82), which was on the air for five weeks and includes characters straight out of central casting: dedicated dean of boys Harry Barnes (James Naughton); pretentious, dreary assistant principal Jack Felspar (Graham Jarvis); young, attractive drama teacher Sara Conover (Alley Mills); playboy English teacher David Wasserman (Philip Charles MacKenzie); cash-poor Latin teacher Anton Zemeckis (Zane Lasky); and hyper-athletic physical education teacher Gus Bertoia (George Wendt, just before he began his stint on *Cheers*). Another short-lived teacher sitcom is *Fast Times* (CBS, 1986–86). Based on the film *Fast Times at Ridgemont High* (1982), the show features two of the film's actors reprising their roles: Ray Walston (of *My Favorite Martian* and *Picket Fences* and others on television and multiple feature films) as Arnold Hand, an authoritarian history teacher, and Vincent Schiavelli as Hector Vargas, an unconventional science teacher. Another featured faculty member is life studies teacher Leslie Melon (Kit McDonough), who likes to get personally involved in her students' lives. Although the movie was fairly successful, the television show lasted only seven weeks. What some might say is an aptly titled show about college teaching, *Pursuit of Happiness* (ABC, 1987–88), features an idealistic young man who decides to try teaching history at a small college after years of wandering the country searching for meaning in his life. Assistant Professor David Hanley (Paul Provenza) becomes the protégé of his idol, Professor Roland C. Duncan (Brian Keith of *Family Affair* and *Hardcastle and McCormick*, among others, on television and multiple feature films), a brusque, matter-of-fact man. Other eccentrics inhabit this collegial world, but perhaps the most fascinating aspect of the show is that David "consults" President Thomas Jefferson (Kevin Scannell) and Los Angeles Laker Magic Johnson (Himself) for advice about his life! This show lasted two and a half months. *Homeroom* (ABC, 1989–89), lasted a little longer, three months, and features Darryl Harper (Darryle Sivad) as an advertising jingles writer who gives up his career to become a fourth grade teacher.

Four other shows with active teachers were on the air for more than half a year. *Mr. Sunshine* (ABC, 1986–86) stars Jeffrey Tambor as Professor Paul Stark, an embittered, domineering English professor who loses his eyesight in an accident and is divorced by his wife. He has a sarcastic secretary, Grace D'Angelo (Nan Martin), and a drama professor, Leon Walters (Leonard Frey), for a colleague. This is an interesting premise but may have been too depressing for audiences to embrace. In *Spencer*, the star of the show is teenager Spencer Winger (Chad Lowe), but his interactions with his teachers are central to the narrative. Teacher figures are the school guidance counselor, Benjamin Beanley (Richard Sanders), and Miss Spier (Beverly Archer), the English teacher. After the actor portraying the teenager quit the show, the network repackaged the show and changed its name to *Under One Roof*. Mr. Beanley became the principal and Miss Spier became a Spanish teacher. The confusion about the show was exacerbated when the network aired reruns of *Spencer* while simultaneously airing its newer incarnation, *Under One Roof*. Most of the action in *Teachers Only* (NBC, 1982–83) takes place in the teacher's lounge and the faculty lunchroom. Teachers include Diana Swanson (Lynn Redgrave[1]), a dedicated, rigorous, and popular English teacher; Ben Cooper (Norman Fell, who plays Mr. Roper on *Three's Company*), the warm-hearted but gruff principal; Mr. Brody (Norman Bartold), the assistant principal; teachers Michael Horne (Tim Reid) and Gwen Edwards (Van Nessa Clarke). In a mid-season shake-up because of low ratings, the producers brought in a new cast except for Diana Swanson and Ben Cooper. New additions included gym teacher and coach Spud Le Boone (Joel Brooks) and teacher Sam Keating (Teresa Ganzel). The changes didn't help the ratings, and the show was cancelled after being on the air for seven months. Finally, one of several syndicated teacher shows listed in Brooks and Marsh's *Complete Directory of Prime-Time Network and Cable TV Shows* stars standup comedian, actor, and author Yakov Smirnoff as Nikolai Rostapovich, a Russian immigrant who is a student in an English-as-a-second-language class. In addition to Smirnoff as a student, *What a Country* (Syndicated, 1986–87) features young, idealistic teacher Taylor Brown (Garrett M. Brown) and assertive principal Joan Courtney (Gail Strickland). Courtney was replaced by F. Jerry "Bud" McPherson (Don Knotts, best known for his role as Deputy Barney Fife on *The Andy Griffith Show* in the 1960s) halfway through the series' twenty-six episode run.

Of the remaining sitcoms, eleven feature teacher characters but little teaching, and one focuses on a board of education and rarely shows teachers at all. *Nearly Departed* (NBC, April-May 1989) stars Eric Idle (of Monty Python fame) as Grant Pritchard, a college professor who is killed along with his wife, Claire (Caroline McWilliams) in a car accident, yet decides to stay and haunt the family who moves into the ghosts' house. In *Better Days* (CBS, October 1–29, 1986), California teenager Brian McGuire (Raphael Sbarge) is sent to Brooklyn to live with his grandfather (Dick O'Neill) and attend the local high school. Harriet Winners (Randee Heller) is his contemptuous English teacher. R&B singer Gladys Knight and comedian Flip Wilson co-star as wife and husband in *Charlie & Co.* (CBS, 1985–86). Knight is elementary school teacher Dianna Richmond, and Wilson is her husband, Charlie. According to Brooks and Marsh, many critics called this show a poor-man's version of *The Cosby Show* (237). *Square Pegs* (CBS, 1982–83) follows two friends, Patty Greene (Sarah Jessica Parker, who would go on to portray Carrie Bradshaw on the HBO television sitcom *Sex and the City*, which aired on HBO from 1998–2004, and in the feature film of the same name in 2008) and Lauren Hutchinson (Amy Linker), and their trials and tribulations as new high school freshmen. Principal Dingleman (Basil Hoffman) and teachers Mr. Donovan (Steven Peterman) and Ms. Loomis (Catlin Adams) are peripheral characters. The syndicated show *Learning the Ropes* (1988–89, 26 episodes) features a private high school history teacher and assistant principal, Robert Randall (Lyle Alzado), who moonlights as "The Masked Maniac," a professional wrestler. Although *Doctor, Doctor* (CBS, 1989–91) is a sitcom about a group of physicians, one of the main characters, Dr. Mike Stratford's (Matt Frewer who got his break portraying Max Headroom) brother, Richard (Tony Carreiro), is a college English professor. In a spin-off of the popular *Growing Pains* (ABC, 1985–92), Coach Lubbock (Bill Kirchenbauer) moves his family to California to accept a position at a Catholic boys school in *Just the Ten of Us* (ABC, 1988–90). Other school staff include Father Hargis (Frank Bonner) as the forgetful headmaster, Sister Ethel (Maxine Elliott) as the absentminded nun, and Coach Duane Johnson (Dennis Haysbert, who plays U.S. President David Palmer on *24*, FOX, 2001–, and then Sgt. Major Jonas Blane on *The Unit*, CBS, 2006– .). In one of only two instances where a television series was based on a phonograph record,[2] *Harper Valley P.T.A.* (NBC, 1981–82) revolves around a mother of a 13-year-old who challenges the P.T.A. board and is eventually elected a board member. Barbara Eden (best known for her role as Jeannie in *I Dream of Jeannie* in the 1960s) stars as Stella Johnson, a woman with liberal attitudes and sexy attire who takes the conservative members of the board and the community by storm. During the last half of the series, the P.T.A. board was dropped, the series name changed to *Harper Valley*, and teachers became tangential to the storylines.

Three sitcoms had substantial runs; these include *Dear John*, *A Different World*, and *Out of This World*. In *Dear John* (NBC, 1988–92), high school English teacher John Lacey (Judd Hirsch) joins a singles support group after his wife leaves him and takes everything, including their son. The show revolves around the relationship between the group's members. *A Different World* (NBC, 1987–93) is a spin-off of *The Cosby Show* (NBC, 1984–92) and takes place at primarily African American Hillman College. The only recurring teacher character is Col. Clayton Taylor (Glynn Turman), a tough calculus professor nicknamed "Dr. War," who appears in almost a third of the 144 episodes. In "To Whit, with Love," socialite and former student Whitley Gilbert (Jasmine Guy) substitutes in a remedial class in a marginal junior high school, and in "We've Only Just Begun," graduate student Dwayne Wayne (Kadeem Hardison) begins teaching classes at Hillman. A few other teachers are shown, including Professor Lawrence (Keenen Ivory Wayans, who created and starred on *In Living Color*, a comedy/variety show that aired on FOX from 1990–94, Professor Byron Walcott (David Alan Grier, also of *In Living Color* fame and a regular on *Life with Bonnie*, an ABC sitcom from 2002–04), and Professor Barnabus Foster (Roscoe Lee Browne). For the most part, however, teachers are rarely seen on the show. Another show about a private school, *Out of This World* (Syndicated, 1987–91, 96 episodes), features high school student Evie Garland (Maureen Flannigan), whose mother, Donna Garland (Donna Pescow), is a human, and whose father, Troy (Burt Reynolds in voice only), is an extraterrestrial. Evie has strange powers and is able to stop time and make things appear just by thinking about them. Teachers are peripheral on this show (none are listed in the cast list in Brooks and Marsh, 1037.)

Eight drama series from this decade feature teachers. Three of these were on air from one to four months. *The Contender* (CBS, April 1980–May 1980) features Johnny Captor (Marc Singer) as a young man who drops out of college to become a boxer. His girlfriend, Jill Sindon (Katherine Cannon), a teacher at the college, doesn't approve. In the primetime soap opera *King's Crossing* (ABC, January 1982–February 1982), family patriarch Paul Hollister (Bradford Dillman) is an alcoholic teacher trying to get his life in order. In *TV 101* (CBS, 1988–89), Kevin Keegan (Sam Robards), a former disruptive student, now TV news photographer, comes back to his old high school to teach broadcast journalism. His former journalism teacher, Emilie Walker (Brynn Thayer), is his ally, and his nemesis is Principal Edward Steadman (Leon Russom). One of the students is played by Matt LeBlanc, in his first television role. LeBlanc would go on to play Joey Tripiani on *Friends* (NBC, 1994–2004).

Other shows had more extended runs and more substantial characters. In *The Bronx Zoo* (NBC, 1987–88), Ed Asner plays Principal Joe Danzig who tries to bring order and hope to a violent, inner city high school. (Asner played journalist Lou Grant on *The Mary Tyler Moore Show* on CBS, 1970–77, and *Lou Grant* on CBS, 1977–82. He is helped by vice principal Jack Felspar (Nicholas Pryor), naïve English teacher Sara Newhouse (Kathryn Harrold), and streetwise history teacher Harry Barnes (David Wilson). Other teachers include independent art and drama teacher Mary Caitlin Callahan (Kathleen Beller),

Figure 5.1. (top row, left to right) Morgan Stevens as David Reardon, Lori Singer as Julie Miller, and Lee Curreri as Bruno Martelli, (middle row, left to right) Gene Anthony Ray as Leroy Johnson, Carol Mayo Jenkins as Elizabeth Sherwood, Albert Hague as Mr. Benjamin Shorofsky, and Erica Gimpel as Coco Hernandez (bottom row, left to right) Valerie Landsburg as Doris Rene Schwartz, Debbie Allen as Lydia Grant, and Carlo Imperato as Danny Amatullo in *Fame* NBC, 1982–83. Photo courtesy of Photofest. Used by permission.

former lawyer/current math teacher Matthew Littman (Jerry Levine), and African American basketball coach and science teacher Gus Butterfield (Mykel T. Williamson). A standout feature of the show is the juxtaposition of Danzig's (and others') idealism and the violence occurring at the school.

Based on the 1980 film of the same name, *Fame* (NBC, 1982–83; Syndicated 1983–87) is set in New York City's High School for the Performing Arts. Several of the film's stars reprise their roles: Debbie Allen as beautiful and driven dance teacher Lydia Grant, Albert Hague as music teacher Benjamin Shorofsky, Lee Curreri as student Bruno Martelli, and Gene Anthony Ray as student Leroy Johnson. The school's curriculum prepares its graduates for careers in show business and is very competitive. The show is notable for its realistic portrayal of the students' commitment to their arts coupled with the angst of high school, and the teachers who are even more dedicated than the students, especially Lydia Grant.

In a spin-off from *Little House on the Prairie* (NBC, 1974–83), Merlin Olsen recreates his role as John Michael Murphy in *Father Murphy* (NBC, 1981–84). John Murphy is a drifter who poses as a priest in the Dakota Territory in the 1870s. With the help of a young teacher, Mae Woodward (Katharine Cannon), he cares for two dozen orphans after their parents are murdered in a labor dispute in a mining camp. Murphy and Woodward teach their charges, but have to deal with officials who want to put the children in an orphanage. Eventually they marry and adopt all the children.

In an interesting synthesis of teaching and crime, *Snoops* (CBS, 1989–90) features a criminology professor solving crimes with his wife. Chance Dennis (Tim Reid) is the professor, and his wife, Micki Dennis (Daphne Maxwell Reid), is deputy chief of protocol for the State Department.[3] This show is reminiscent of 1940s *Thin Man* film series featuring Dick Powell and Myrna Loy. One other drama from the 1980s features a teacher character. *thirtysomething* (ABC, 1987–91) is about a group of people (two couples and three singles) accepting and/or avoiding the responsibilities of adulthood. Classics Professor Gary Shepherd (Peter Horton) is a nonconformist who is ultimately fired from his job and suddenly dies in the last half of the last season.

Three other shows feature teachers during this decade. In the science fiction show *The Powers of Matthew Star* (NBC, 1982–83), high school student Matthew Star (Peter Barton) is a crown prince from another planet. His guardian, Walt Shephard (Louis Gossett, Jr., who won an Oscar for Best Actor in a Supporting Role for *An Officer and a Gentleman*, 1982), is a high school science teacher and football coach. As Matthew's powers increase, the stories shift from school to fighting crime for the government. *The New Adventures of Beans Baxter* (FOX, 1987–88) is a farcical adventure/espionage show in which high school student Beans (Jonathan Ward) takes over as a courier-spy at an intelligence agency after his father is kidnapped by agents for the Underground Government Liberation Intergroup (U.G.L.I.). Beans, who doesn't have a car, rides his bicycle to secret hideouts. The adventure series *Gideon Oliver* (ABC, February–September 1989) stars Louis Gossett, Jr. in the title role, a Columbia University anthropology professor who is also an amateur sleuth. When he is not helping the police get to the bottom of cases, he is solving crimes in exotic locations. The focus is more on the sleuthing than the teaching.

One show deserves special mention because of its popularity and its reflection of the rising conservatism in American politics during the 1980s. *Family Ties* (NBC, 1982–89) showcases the Keaton family where teenager Alex (Michael J. Fox in his breakout role[4]) is a young conservative and his parents, Elyse and Steve (Meredith Baxter-Birney and Michael Gross) are laid-back liberals. Most of the scenes take place in the Keaton home, but with three children (four, after baby Andrew was born) in the house, school and teachers are featured in a few episodes. Alex's favorite college professor is Professor Ephraim Bronski (Michale McGuire), yet he only appears in one episode. In "My Tutor," Alex, who is very smart, hires a tutor to help him with math and is chagrined when he learns that the tutor is thirteen-year-old genius Eugene Forbes (River Phoenix, who went on to a promising film career before his untimely death in 1993 at age 23). *Family Ties* may not adequately portray teachers on television, but it brought the 1980s conservative/liberal debate into American living rooms.

Two other popular television sitcoms also reflect conservative themes by validating educational privileges for elite students; *The Facts of Life* and *Head of the Class* take two groups of students and accord them special status at school. *The Facts of Life* is set at an elite boarding school for girls, and *Head of the Class* is situated in a special program for academically gifted students at an urban public high school. In both cases, the shows suggest that the students have earned their rightful places of privilege, and their teachers (and housemothers) are complicit in perpetuating the myth of meritocracy.

Meritocracy

The Facts of Life (NBC, 1979–88) and *Head of the Class* (ABC, 1986–91) exemplify the dominant ideology of meritocracy as described by McNamee and Miller in the opening of their book, *The Meritocracy Myth*: "In the image of the American Dream, America is the land of opportunity. If you work hard enough and are talented enough, you can overcome any obstacle and achieve success. No matter where you start out in life, the sky is the limit. You can go as far as your talents and abilities can take you" (1). This "lift yourself up by your bootstraps" story has fueled the dreams and dominated the biographies of Americans from Benjamin Franklin to Abe Lincoln to Bill Clinton. We are told that anyone can make it if they have a good work ethic, good character, and the right attitude. And, according to a number of researchers, not only do most Americans believe that this is how the system should work; they think that this is how it *does* work (e.g., Huber and Form, Kluegel and Smith, Ladd, Lubrano, and McNamee and Miller).

Of course, in actuality, there is a gap in how people think the system works and how it *really* works. McNamee and Miller quote George Carlin as saying "The reason they call it the American Dream is because you have to be asleep to believe it" (1). The meritocracy myth says that the system distributes resources based on the merit of individuals. The truth is that there are many factors unrelated to merit that influence upward and downward mobility. These factors include inheritance, luck, number and types of jobs, education, self-employment (or entrepreneurship), and discrimination. Inheritance refers not just to the receipt of family money but to the inheritance of high living standards, access to social contacts, educational expectations and opportunities, and the prevention of downward mobility. Luck refers to any number of happenstances and eventualities that might help someone get ahead. Number and types of jobs refer to being laid off from a job, preparing for a job that doesn't exist because of a decline in demand, availability of training, and other employment mobility variables (McNamee and Miller).

Access to better educational opportunities from pre-school to college can also influence socioeconomic mobility, whether positively or negatively. Pedagogic literature has chronicled the ways in which the educational system treats students differently based on the students' socioeconomic backgrounds. As mentioned in the previous chapter, Jean Anyon discovered a hidden curriculum in schools serving children from different socioeconomic backgrounds. For example, students in working class schools were evaluated on how well they followed the rules and how obedient they were. On the other hand, students in upper middle class and upper class schools were encouraged to think critically and creatively and were rewarded for their independence. In her recent research, Anyon concludes that not only do the schools "reproduce social inequality . . . [they] exacerbate it by supporting a bifurcation of incomes and class structure" (Anyon "Social Class, School Knowledge" 38).

The myth of meritocracy states that anyone can make it if they work hard enough and maintain a good attitude, yet there are barriers to upward mobility. In the past, self-employment provided a clear path to move up in the world, yet there are fewer and fewer opportunities in this arena. The corporatized world of bigger and bigger businesses coupled with government regulations make the cost of doing business too high for many small business owners. In 2002, only seven percent of Americans were self-employed. Because self-employment offers fewer and fewer opportunities for upward mobility, there is less chance for upward mobility by this path now than in the past.

Discrimination is another recognized barrier to upward mobility. The most prevalent forms of discrimination are racism and sexism, but discrimination comes in any number of forms including age, sexual orientation, religion, mental or physical disability, and socioeconomic status. Lookism refers to the privileged treatment that a person receives because of his or her attractive appearance. De-emphasis of the barriers to upward mobility is one way that the myth of meritocracy is perpetuated, and, although all of these barriers are not explicitly shown on *The Facts of Life* or *Head of the Class*, many *are* shown, and are worth examining.

The Facts of Life

A spin-off of *Diff'rent Strokes*, *The Facts of Life* is the story of former housekeeper Edna Garrett (Charlotte Rae) becoming a housemother (and later a dietician) at Eastland School, a prestigious girls school in Peekskill, New York. For seven of the show's nine seasons, her charges include four young women, three of whom are White. The oldest is Joanna Marie "Jo" Polniaczek (Nancy McKeon), a tomboy from The Bronx attending Eastland on a scholarship. Blair Warner (Lisa Whelchel) is the spoiled, rich girl who dwells on her appearance. Natalie Green (Mindy Cohn) is fun-loving, impressionable, and loves to eat. The youngest, Dorothy "Tootie" Ramsey (Kim Fields), is an inquisitive African American, who is an aspiring actress.[5]

The things that give the girls their advantages—inheritance, luck, and education—are implied, but it is taken for granted that they belong at the school. Although Eastland is an elite school, only Blair is portrayed as rich. The other three main student characters come from various upper middle to upper class backgrounds: Tootie is the daughter of two attorneys; Natalie is the adopted daughter of seemingly financially secure parents; and Jo attends Eastland on a scholarship. For the most part, their backgrounds are downplayed, and the setting helps. Although Eastland is supposed to be a prestigious boarding school, the sets are very unpretentious.

Edna Garrett, the former housekeeper for the Drummond family on *Diff'rent Strokes* (NBC, 1978–86), becomes a housemother at Eastland School on *The Facts of Life* in the summer of 1979, but in the retooled version of the

Figure 5.2. (back row) Julie Anne Haddock as Cindy Webster, Lisa Whelchel as Blair Warner, Charlotte Rae as Edna Garrett, John Lawlor as Headmaster Stephen Bradley, and Felice Schachter as Nancy Olson, (front row) Mindy Cohn as Natalie Green, Molly Ringwald as Molly Parker, Julie Piekarski as Sue Ann Weaver, and Kim Fields as Dorothy "Tootie" Ramsey in *Facts of Life* (NBC, 1979–88). Photo courtesy of Photofest. Used by permission.

show in spring of 1980, she becomes the school dietician. Originally, she is a major focus, but in a very short period of time, the narratives revolve primarily around her four charges. And, although the focus is not on her, Mrs. Garrett is the "real" teacher on the show. It is she who counsels the girls, providing the obligatory lessons and "facts of life" in each episode. True to the Hollywood Model, when she is allowed to have a personal life and gets married in the sixth season, she moves away and leaves the show. At that point, "care" of the girls, who are almost adults, falls to her sister, Beverly Ann Stickle (Cloris Leachman[6]). The portrayal of the headmaster is also in keeping with the Hollywood Model. In season one, Steven Bradley (John Lawlor) is sometimes clueless, saying and doing the wrong thing, but seems like a decent man. For two seasons beginning in 1981, Charles Parker (Roger Perry) is a more bureaucratic headmaster.

The show tackles major, sometimes controversial, issues, and in almost every episode a lesson is learned. Topics include honesty, suicide, lesbianism, book banning, rape, date rape, alcoholism, drug abuse, breast cancer, abortion, racial divisions, and shoplifting. Regardless of the topic, there is always a resolution by the final minutes of the episode in which ethical and practical "truths" are embraced.

Facts of Life suggests that the students have earned their rightful place of privilege at Eastland School. Although the myth of meritocracy says that people who work hard can achieve success and privilege, the four girls on *Facts of Life* have attained their status not through hard work but though inheritance, luck, education, lack of discrimination, or any combination of these. Jo and Mrs. Garrett change their lives the most over the course of the show, but the ways in which they overcome impediments to achievement are seldom mentioned; to do so would make clear the fact that there is no level playing field, a central tenet of the meritocracy myth. Garrett goes from housekeeper (for the Drummonds on *Diff'rent Strokes*) to housemother to dietician to gourmet food shop owner to updated malt shop co-owner over the course of the show, clearly improving her socioeconomic status in the process. Jo escapes her working class background, goes to prep school, and then to college, also improving her status. There are relatively few barriers to upward mobility for the characters, and these barriers are unobtrusive and easily overcome.

The characteristics Anyon notes as being indicative of upper class schools—independence, creativity and analytical thinking—are all encouraged at Eastland. Independence is shown in many storylines. Although we rarely see the girls in the classroom, they are encouraged by Garrett to be independent and think for themselves. In an early example, "The New Girl Parts 1 & 2"), this independent thinking gets the girls in a lot of trouble. Jo, who already has a fake ID (and is trying to prove how cool she is), creates one for Blair so they can go to a bar to meet men. They allow Tootie and Natalie to come along even though the younger girls can't get into the bar. Jo hotwires the school van, because the girls don't have a car, and it is damaged while parked at the bar. Ultimately, all the girls are arrested (for driving without a license, having fake IDs, and soliciting) and expelled from Eastland, but they are put on probation and allowed to stay in school if they agree to live with Garrett over the cafeteria and work there to pay off the repair bill for the van. Although it may seem that meritocracy is at work here because they have to earn their way back into favor, they are only given a second chance because of who they are and who they know, not because they have worked hard and paid their dues.

In "Flash Flood," Blair and Tootie show their independence when they decide to save their pets, a horse and two rabbits, during a flood. After they are rescued by Mr. Bradley, and despite the fact they courted disaster by risking their lives, they, Mrs. Garrett, and the other girls show their independence again and stay to battle the rising waters instead of being evacuated with Mr. Bradley, who requires minor medical attention. Other episodes reinforce the value of independence. In "A Friend in Deed," Jo gets a part time job in a motorcycle shop; in "From Russia with Love," Blair and Tootie plan and execute a ski trip; and in multiple episodes, the girls—singly, in pairs, or all together—go to New York for dinner and/or a play, to visit family, or to see friends ("Pretty Babies," "Starstruck," "The Affair," "Runaway," "New York, New York," and "Big Apple Blues"). In "A Woman's Place," Jo is promoted over her boyfriend to weekend service manager, and in "All or Nothing," she takes on the administration of Langley College (where she and Blair are now students) when the school cuts scholarships in favor of a new athletic scoreboard. In all these episodes the girls exhibit the kind of independence expected of those who have been groomed to succeed.

The girls' creativity is nurtured as well. A student commits suicide in "Breaking Point," and Garrett tells the girls, "The best way you can let people know what is going on inside of you is to tell them. Now you girls are under a lot of pressure—to achieve, to succeed, to fit in, to grow up. And I want to tell you, it's okay to feel confused, and frightened, and insecure. We all do. And when you feel that way, . . . please talk about it." The girls decide they need a way to let students talk about issues before they get to the "breaking point." With Blair leading the charge, the girls establish a hotline at the school. As Anyon noted, showing this type of initiative is typical of upper-middle and upper class educational settings where students are not used to limits and boundaries but are encouraged to think creatively and to assume authority.

In "Read No Evil," the girls show their creativity and independence. Natalie loses her job as editor of the school newspaper after writing an editorial about the banning by the school board of a magazine (*Ms.*) and a few books (*Catch-22* and *Slaughterhouse Five*, among others) from the school library. Natalie, Jo, and Tootie reprint Natalie's editorial and mail it to all the parents with a notice on the outside of the envelope that reads "Expulsion Notice." This action results in many parents attending the board meeting to protest the book banning. Mrs. Garrett tells the girls that they did the right thing. In this and almost every other instance, the girls' creativity is championed, even when they are punished for going too far. Students who are not in this privileged setting would likely have been discouraged from taking such liberties and more seriously reprimanded for their actions. Instead the girls are praised even though they sent out a deceptive and inflammatory mailing to parents and called a special meeting of the board of trustees. Tootie's creativity as an actor and comedienne is mentioned throughout the series and is part of the storyline in "Me and Eleanor," "The Interview Show," "Born Too Late," "The Agent," "The Graduate," "Off-Broadway Baby," and "Rites of Passage." In "Dear Me," she writes fake love letters to herself to cover for the fact that she doesn't want to go on a camping trip with the other girls and their boyfriends. Her conceit is discovered, but her friends, rather than chastise her, are understanding and even a little in awe that she can write so well. Once again, the focus is on her creativity. There are no repercussions for her deception. By consistently highlighting the girls' creativity and ingenuity, the show reinforces the idea that the girls belong at Eastland, that they have earned their places of privilege.

Eastland School is a girls' preparatory school that caters to an upper and upper middle class clientele. It is implied that the school only accepts the best and the brightest students. In two episodes, "Overachieving" and "The Americanization of Miko," students' fathers want to withdraw their daughters because they think Eastland is not rigorous enough. In the first, Headmaster Bradley defends the school by saying, "This is not a school for rich, spoiled girls . . . Our teachers are rated highest in the state. We've got a ninety percent college placement. Our graduates represent a wide variety of professionals [sic] through the entire country." In the second episode listed above, Mrs. Garrett defends Eastland by saying, "It just so happens that this school turns out women of great accomplishment: doctors, lawyers, homemakers, businesswomen." While the school is for well-to-do girls, it prides itself on its educational rigor. The girls and Garrett take it for granted that they deserve to be there.

It is also taken for granted that the students at Eastland are intelligent. Natalie is shown to be exceptionally smart and in the episode "Advance Placement," she is allowed to take college level courses during her junior year at Eastland. She then learns that if she keeps her grade point average up, she'll be allowed to graduate early from Eastland and go to college. Part of this is a construct of the television milieu (the older Jo and Blair are attending college already, so the writers and producers want to keep the girls together even though there are seldom scenes at school), but this storyline also underscores that she deserves to attend college early. Although her achievement in the classroom is a direct result of her having access to the privileges of the elite mentioned above (inheritance, luck, education, and lack of discrimination), it is never a part of the show. Rather, it is implied that she deserves to be there because of her intrinsic ability and hard work.

In "Four Musketeers," after having caused the van to be wrecked in an earlier episode, the girls finally repay the cost of the repairs and are given the chance to move back into the dorm. After examining all the pros and cons, they decide to continue living above the cafeteria with Mrs. Garrett. They all realize that they love, support, and need one another. This reflects the critical thinking prized by the elite. The girls take what they have learned in the classroom and apply it in their lives, but they are able to do this because they have had the educational opportunities afforded to the elite.

The ability to be critically analytical is also held in high esteem on *Facts of Life*, just as it is in the larger culture. When Jo decides to get married (at 16!) in "Teenage Marriage 1 & 2," Mrs. Garrett and the girls try to talk her out of it by using rational arguments about money, high school and college education, children, etc. Getting married at such an early age would be unthinkable for the other girls, yet Jo digs in her heels and decides to elope with her Navy recruit boyfriend, Eddie Brennan, (Clark Brandon). It isn't until Jo thinks about what her friends have said and then talks to her fiancé that she realizes that she and Eddie want very different things from life. She decides she's too young to get married. There are competing messages provided by Jo's presence on the show. She is situated as an outsider, a working class girl from The Bronx, who has overcome obstacles to get to this elite school. In a few episodes ("Teenage Marriage 1 & 2" and "The Secret"), her background is treated explicitly in the story, but for the most part the show declines to seize the opportunity to look at the ways in which she and her family have had to sacrifice for her to get where she is. The characters on *Facts of Life*, including Jo, are blind to the privileges that allow them to be at Eastland.

Jo is different from the other girls in her tomboy demeanor, socioeconomic status, and attitude (with a capital A). She arrives for her first day at Eastland on a motorcycle with a smudge across her face and is mistaken for a delivery boy. She is set up to be the opposite of Blair, the debutante. And although Blair scored a ninety-six on her Eastland entrance exam, Jo scored a ninety-eight. These elements make for a convenient ongoing conflict between the two girls as well as a fish-out-of-water storyline for Jo.

In "Adoption," Blair uses her mother's connections to help Natalie find her birth mother. She calls a judge whom her mother once dated, and he is able to get the information about Natalie's adoption in less than a day. The connections that wealthy people have make it easy to accomplish many tasks, and no one is surprised that Blair is able to get the information and get it so quickly. Her privilege is not remarked upon by the others. On rare occasions, Blair acknowledges her favored status. As mentioned earlier, she prides herself on her good looks and isn't afraid of using them. For example, in "Rough Housing," she accepts the fact that she will win the Harvest Queen contest and is shocked when Cindy wins, and in "Double Standard," she is surprised when a boy asks Jo instead of her to the country club cotillion because she believes she deserves it. In "Breaking Point," Blair campaigns for class president telling her friends, "Being born with certain advantages gives me an obligation to serve." When she loses the election, she is taken aback. In each case, Blair assumes that she is worthy and is shocked when her privileged background or physical assets don't automatically translate into success. Her sense of entitlement is never actually challenged on the show despite these storylines. She's still the character whom lots of viewers want to be—beautiful, rich, attending an elite school, with her future secure—and because of this connection with the viewers, these storylines do not undermine the central validation of the meritocracy myth.

Discrimination comes up occasionally, but is talked about, worked through, and resolved so that the prejudicial words or actions are ameliorated. The show makes it easy for the characters to work through these barriers, so that the girls think they've achieved a certain status on their own when, in actuality, they were born into this privileged milieu. One episode stands out for its handling of racism. In "Who Am I?" Tootie, who is African American, meets a young Black man, Fred (Erik Moses), and begins to think about her race and how she fits in at Eastland School. She pulls away from her roommates and refuses to participate in the dance contest because her partner is White, even though the two of them won the dance contest the previous year. She tells Garrett and the other girls: "You think it's a terrific thing giving a Black girl a White education and White friends. Nobody cares that I'm going to wake up one morning and not know who I am. Well, I care. And I won't let that happen to me. I just won't." She ends up getting together with other Black girls on campus, but she finds that she has more in common with her roommates, who are all White. Because of her class privilege and her status as a student at an elite boarding school, Tootie is able to make a choice about where to fit in. Fred has told her that her close friends should be Black, but she finds that she can erase race if she wants. This minimizes the effects that race has on people's ability to succeed.

In the episodes "Teenage Marriage 1 & 2," part of the reason Jo decides not to get married is her fiancé's sexist attitude about marriage. He tells her that he wants a conventional construction of marriage where she will stay home and take care of the house and their children, Jo has bigger plans for herself because of the doors that have opened for her at Eastland School. She chooses to walk away from the romantic relationship while failing to recognize that most women don't have a range of choices, and this lack often binds them to a kind of oppression. She has been given this privilege, a choice not open to most people, because she is smart and she attends an elite school. Sexism comes up again in "A Friend in Deed" when Jo gets a job repairing motorcycles, not your usual job for a prep school girl, and in "A Woman's Place," when her co-worker boyfriend is upset after she gets a promotion to weekend manager. Sexism is one of the ways the myth of meritocracy is subverted. We all believe that a person can get ahead if they work hard enough, but in actuality, sexism, along with racism and ageism, serves to thwart people's quest for better lives.

Classism is dealt with in "The Secret" when Jo is embarrassed to tell anyone her father has been in prison and tries to keep him from attending her awards ceremony. When he does visit the school for the ceremony, everyone learns that he is an ex-con. He tells his daughter that he finished high school in prison. He has a knack for analyzing stocks, and although he knows that he can't be a broker, he wants to become a stock analyst. True to sitcom form, everyone is very accepting of him. This storyline helps support the myth of meritocracy: Jo can go to an elite prep school and her father can become a stock analyst because they are smart and work hard. In "Help from Home," Jo and Blair are accepted to Langley College, but Jo is anxious because she doesn't know how she's going to pay for it. In the end, she learns that her family can help her financially. Most people coming from Jo's background would have a much more difficult time dealing with these barriers to success, and Jo admits as much when she tells her father in "The Secret" that it's hard for her to attend a prep school, but Jo's problems are easily worked through. In this case she *has* worked hard to get where she is, but her effort is not shown. For most people, the socioeconomic status of their birth family determines their socioeconomic status later in life, even though the myth of meritocracy would have us believe that anyone can make it if they work hard enough. Jo is the exception to the deterministic rule, but as far as the viewer is concerned, she is an exception simply by virtue of being at Eastland. She assumes the privileges of her new set of peers.

Ageism refers to the discrimination that occurs because of a person's age. Usually this occurs because someone is seen as being too old or too young. Garrett doesn't have to face ageism when she returns to school. In both "E.G.O.C. (Edna Garrett on Campus)" and "The Rich Aren't Different," she is allowed to make her way with little resistance. In another episode, Garrett defies ageism by going sky diving ("I.Q."). Tootie experiences ageism in a few early episodes because she is the youngest of the girls. Although small comments are made on many episodes, on "Growing Pains," Tootie's status as the youngest is used for the main storyline. She expresses her feelings of alienation from the other girls by drinking a whole bottle of wine. In "Runaway," Tootie is not allowed to go with the other girls to see a play in New York because she is too young. She sneaks out with plans to meet the other girls. In both instances, there are little repercussions for her actions. Tootie feels abandoned in "Who's on First?" when Natalie starts dating before Tootie, but once Tootie begins dating in season five, issues about Tootie's age don't come up. Like racism, sexism, and classism, ageism is a barrier to social mobility, but all are downplayed on *The Facts of Life*.

In "Rough Housing," a student's sexual orientation is explored after Blair makes snide comments about her housemate, Cindy (known as the best athlete in school), and then suggests that she's "strange" when Cindy hugs another girl. Garrett has a long talk with Cindy about rates of development among girls and assures her that she'll develop when her "time clock" says it's time. Although not overtly spoken, the covert meaning comes through: it's okay to be who you are. The show deals with Blair's homophobia and discrimination, though, by implying that Cindy is just a late bloomer and not a lesbian. This convenient resolution allows the characters and the viewers to turn a blind eye to the discrimination most gays and lesbians feel on a daily basis, a discrimination that often forestalls self-improvement.

Discrimination based on mental and physical disability is shown in at least two episodes. In "Different Drummer," Blair has a hard time accepting her new friend's mental retardation, and in "Cousin Geri," Mrs. Garrett thinks Blair is embarrassed because Blair's cousin, Geri, has cerebral palsy and is in a wheelchair. But Blair really distances herself from Geri because her cousin is a successful comedienne, and Blair can't stand not being the center of attention. Physical and mental disabilities are shown not to be impediments; anyone can overcome barriers to achieving success. Once again, the meritocracy myth is perpetuated.

Lookism, the idea that people receive privileged treatment because of their good looks, plays a part in how the girls are treated, but it is almost always backgrounded. Two recurring instances of lookism occur. For most of the first two seasons, Tootie's character wears roller skates because the producers felt she was too short; and Blair, whose appearance is remarked on by her and the other characters frequently throughout the show's run, receives preferential treatment because of her looks, although not in the classroom. Further de-emphasizing appearance, the students wear uniforms, which levels the playing field somewhat. In three early episodes, lookism is foregrounded. In "Dieting," Sue Ann and Blair tease each other about their weight, but Sue Ann takes it too far by going on a starvation diet until she collapses. In "Bought and Sold," Blair gets a job selling cosmetics and turns Natalie into a walking billboard for her products. And, in "Pretty Babies," a talent scout comes to Eastland looking for "The Face of the '80s" and picks Tootie instead of Blair, surprising everyone. All the characters are fairly good looking—as are most television characters—so lookism isn't an overt issue on the show. Good looks become an obvious—though unstated—component of a certain level of success and acceptance, however. Many times when the overt storyline in these shows tells us one thing—looks don't matter, the larger context tells us something else—looks do matter.

For the most part, the characters of *Facts of Life* take it for granted that they belong at Eastland. They work creatively, independently, and analytically and are rewarded for it. Although barriers to mobility, such as discrimination in the areas of race, sex, age, sexual orientation, mental or physical disability, socioeconomic status, and appearance (lookism) are discussed and lessons are learned, the characters are not hampered in their educational goals. Their privileged status is uncontested. There is little classroom teaching on *Facts of Life*, but the students learn a great deal from Mrs. Garrett, who helps them confront life lessons every episode. This contrasts with *Head of the Class*, in which most of the interactions occur at school and in the classroom, but the myth of meritocracy continues to be upheld.

Head of the Class

Head of the Class (ABC, 1986–91) features a class of very intelligent, over-achieving students who have lots of "book smarts" but little "street smarts." Their substitute honors history teacher, aspiring actor Charlie Moore (Howard Hesseman), may not have as high an IQ as his gifted students, but he still has a lot to teach them about living. His substitute job at Millard Fillmore High School in Manhattan turns into a full time job after his first week on the job when the students' regular teacher quits. The honors students include Dennis Blunden (Daniel J. Schneider), the oversized computer geek; Maria Borges (Leslie Bega), a young woman who takes her studies very seriously (so seriously that she grounds herself when she gets a B); Jawaharlal Choudhury (Joher Coleman), the exchange student full of malapropisms; Arvid Engen (Dan

Frischman), the gawky nerd in big glasses with a pocket protector; Simone Foster (Khrystyne Haje), a shy, red-headed poet; Janice Lazarotto (Tannis Valleyly), a 12-year-old whiz kid; Eric Mardian (Brian Robbins), the cool student who's surprised and a little embarrassed to find himself in an honors class; Darlene Merriman (Robin Givens), a savvy, rich girl; optimistic Sarah Nevins (Kimberly Russell); and Alan Pinkard (Tony O'Dell), the straight-laced, yuppie Republican. A few of these students left the series over the years and were replaced by T.J. Jones (Rain Pryor), a problem student who works hard to get into the honors class; and less memorable Artistole McKenzie (De Voreaux White), Alex Torres (Michale DeLorenzo), Viki Amory (Lara Piper), and Jasper Kwong (Jonathon Ke Quan).

Figure 5.3. (back row) Dan Frischman as Arvid Engen, Brian Robbins as Eric Mardian, Tony O'Dell as Alan Pinkard, Joher Coleman as Jawaharlal Choudhury, Leslie Bega as Maria Borges, Howard Hesseman as Charlie Moore, William G. Schilling as Dr. Harold Samuels, and Jeanetta Arnette as Bernadette Meara (front row) Khrystyne Haje as Simone Foster, Tannis Valleyly as Janice Lazarotto, Daniel J. Schneider as Dennis Blunden, and Robin Givens as Darlene Merriman in *Head of the Class* (ABC, 1986–91). Photo courtesy of Photofest. Used by permission.

All of these students "deserve" to be in the IHP (Individualized Honors Program). They are smart and work hard. In fact, they work so hard that part of Moore's job as a teacher is to help them become more "well-rounded" by getting involved in other activities besides academics. The principal, Dr. Harold Samuels (William G. Schilling), considers the IHP class "his" pride and glory and prefers that Moore just let them study, rather that try to teach them anything. In the first episode, Samuels tells Moore, "Those kids represent culture, education, fine arts, the future of civilization. Don't mess with them. Just babysit, Mr. Moore, babysit." These are sharp kids—smarter than their teacher, for the most part—but there are still a few things Moore can teach them. In the first episode, he asks the students what baseball had to do with the Cuban Missile Crisis. He then tells them that Cuban President Fidel Castro had been a baseball player as a young adult, but that he wasn't good enough for the major leagues and went into politics instead. The students ponder not only what life would have been like with Castro as a baseball player, but what life would have been like if President Ronald Reagan had been a better actor and had not gone into politics.

According to the Hollywood Model, Moore is a good teacher. He cares about his students, and part of his job is to act as a buffer between the students and the administration. He helps the students make the transition from bookworms to more well-rounded teenagers. Moore is also an outsider—by vocation, he is an actor, not a trained teacher. (In the final season of the show, he leaves teaching for an acting job.[7]) The audience never sees Moore working in any other class, but we do see him teaching *this* class (even though he rarely gets very far in his lessons). Like Pete Dixon in *Room 222* and Gabe Kotter in *Welcome Back, Kotter*, Charlie Moore is a history teacher. His history lessons are filled with historical facts; his classroom is decorated with maps and pictures of Eleanor Roosevelt, Malcolm X, Bobby Kennedy, Golda Meir, and others. He has his emblematic battles with Dr. Samuels, and for the most part, he wins them. Samuels is portrayed as a buffoon, but with a good heart. The Vice Principal, Bernadette Meara (Jeanetta Arnette), is hardworking, level-headed, and has a sense of humor. As the show progresses, we learn that she is working on her Ph.D. in juvenile psychology.

All the students in *Head of the Class* are analytical. They are honors students who got where they are because they are gifted. Examples of their critical thinking skills occur in almost every episode because they are in school; there are scenes in almost every episode of the students paying attention, taking notes, and demonstrating their grasp of the subject matter. In one memorable story arc across two seasons (seasons one and three), the IHP competes against a visiting Russian team in an academic tournament ("The Russians are Coming, the Russians are Coming!"). In two later episodes, the IHP goes to Russia to compete ("Mission to Moscow 1 & 2").[8] In both tournaments, the IHP wins, proving their analytical skills. In another episode, Dennis gets to show off his smarts and his independence when he ends up in remedial history after Mr. Moore throws him out of IHP for too many practical jokes ("King of Reme-dial"). Dennis not only whips the remedial class in shape, he leads them in an academic meet against his former IHP classmates. In the episodes "The Bright Stuff 1 & 2," Dennis and Arvid's science project makes it to the NASA finals, once again showing that these students have "the right stuff."

The IHP students have a much harder time demonstrating their creativ-ity and independence. They've been sheltered because of their intelligence and academic abilities and focused on their schoolwork, yet Moore believes that they need to broaden their horizons. The students catch on fairly quickly (it is TV, after all) and begin to develop other interests. In "Love at First Byte," after sensing that Mr. Moore has a computer phobia, the students program one of the computers in the classroom (the one named Wilma) to send love notes to him. Thinking that a student in his class is writing the notes, Moore talks with every female student before he learns that a computer sent the notes. In this same episode, Moore encourages the students to be creative when writing their personal entries for the yearbook even though Samuels wants basic, standard-ized information from each of them. The students are reluctant to try at first, but then become enthused with the project, and write some very interesting bios for themselves. As the series progresses, Arvid, who is an avid film buff, turns out to have quite an imagination. In "The Secret Life of Arvid," he has a fully realized reverie about a girl he has a crush on. He daydreams a vision of *High Noon* after he is challenged by a bully in "Exactly Twelve O'Clock," and Moore and Arvid discuss their misadventures in love during a Woody Allen marathon in "Play It Again, Woody." Other examples of the students' creativity include episodes in which Eric makes up a memoir ("The Write Stuff"), Den-nis organizes a sit-in for better cafeteria food ("Child of the 60s"), the class puts out a lampoon version of the school newspaper ("Trouble in Perfectville"), the students stage the musical *Grease* ("That'll Be the Day"), and they use the computer to find dates for themselves ("Don't Play With Matches").

Because the students have been sheltered in their academics, becoming more independent and thinking outside the classroom is often a challenge. The young genius Janice stretches her wings when she tries out for the school orchestra in "Cello Fever," and takes the plunge when she graduates from high school at fifteen and goes to Harvard University in "Back to School." Several students end up taking part time jobs: Arvid works in a nightclub in "Privi-lege" and in a pet store in "The Importance of Being Alex," Dennis gets a job as a waiter in "Get a Job," Sarah babysits in "Be My Baby . . . Sitter," and Alex teaches dancing in "Dancing Fools."

The characters on *Head of the Class* face little discrimination in the areas of gender, race, age, sexual orientation, religion, mental or physical disability, socioeconomic status, and appearance. The students are evenly mixed males and females, with a wide variety of ethnicities—White, African American, Indian-American, Hispanic, Jewish. The show is utopian in its colorblindness. These students are validated because they are smart. They are seen as having earned their rightful places of privilege because of their intellect. Nevertheless, a few instances of discrimination are shown for other reasons.

Moore is discriminated against in the first episode because he is not seen as being educated enough to teach the IHP students. As mentioned above, in "Pilot," Dr. Samuels tell him to, "Just babysit, Mr. Moore, babysit." Ultimately, he proves he is smart enough to teach the students in the IHP class. When the class takes standardized personality tests, they worry that the results will make them discriminate against each other in "Psyched Out at Fillmore." In "Arvid's Sure Thing," the biggest nerd in the class decides to go out with Rhonda Giel-gud, a girl who wears short skirts, has bleached blonde hair, and is known as the school's sexiest and "most popular" girl. Arvid hopes he is going to have sex with her because he has heard about her reputation. Later, after talking with Mr. Moore, Arvid decides to go on a date with Rhonda but not to have sex. In this case, Arvid has been discriminated against because of his nerdi-ness, and Rhonda has been discriminated against because of her reputation. In "Tough Guys Don't Sew," Viki breaks gender roles when she teaches Eric to sew. Arvid's father substitutes for the class's calculus teacher in "Engen and Son," and it turns out that even though he is a brilliant mathematician, he can't teach. At first he receives preferential treatment because he is a math genius; later he is discriminated against because he can't teach. He just wanted to teach the class so he could spend time with Arvid. He tells Arvid, "Ever since you got into IHP, you're so darn popular I never see you anymore." This episode debunks two stereotypes: that any smart person can teach and that if you're in IHP you're not popular.

Another episode that tweaks stereotypes is "Revenge of the Liberal" in which Dennis has a little fun with his classmates' perceptions of him. After he writes a very disrespectful, confrontational letter of application, he is chosen to appear on the provocative, right-wing television show *Open Forum* (based on William F. Buckley's show *Firing Line*). Even though Alan had written an adoring letter applying to be on his hero's show, Dennis is chosen. The rest of the IHP students are horrified that Dennis will be representing the IHP on the show because they think he is a comical loose cannon (not to mention looking a little disheveled) and will embarrass them and their school program. Samuels urges Moore to talk to Dennis, "misfit to misfit" to keep him from appearing on the show. Dennis chastises his classmates, accusing them of having little faith in him. When asked by his classmates what he will tell the host of the show, he says:

> There are two point five million gifted students in the country and many of them will drop out of school because they can't get into classes like ours. And why? Because there's not enough money. Or at least not for education. Maybe then I'd remind him of something that Thomas Jefferson said, "That this country's greatness depends on an aristocracy of achievement arising out of a democracy of opportunity."

He had been acting like a clown because all his classmates expected him to. The class apologizes, and he tells Alan to go on the show instead. (Ultimately, Darlene represents the class on the show because Alan gets the measles!)

One area of discrimination dealt with is lookism, the privileged treatment that people receive because of their attractive appearance. On *Head of the Class* lookism occurs, but so does reverse-lookism, when one of the characters is discriminated against because of the way s/he looks. Unlike *Facts of Life* (and most of television), not all the characters on *Head of the Class* are physically attractive. Although Arvid is charming in a shy, self-deprecating way, he is one of the least attractive students in the class, and several stories involve his looks. In "Will the Real Arvid Engen Please Stand Up?" he sends Eric's picture to his pen pal, and in "Arvid Nose Best," he considers having a nose job. In "The Outsider," Janice experiences ageism when she feels left out in class because she is so much younger than the other students and she looks it. In all three instances, they seem to understand that how a person looks can influence their place in the world. Several episodes involve one of the students dating someone who is better looking than s/he is. Maria dates a very good looking student in "Partners" and hides her intelligence because she's afraid he won't like her if he thinks she's smarter than he is. In "Politics of Love," Alan thinks he's dating a rich, fashion model, but learns that she is using him as a dog sitter. Arvid goes out with the gorgeous Viki in "The Heartbreak Nerd," and Simone agrees to date Dennis after he saves her from drowning in "Simone Goes Overboard." In all these instances, people get what they want (or not) because of their appearance. It could be that because of the privilege of their intelligence their looks are less critical, but the show puts forth competing messages in this area. Lookism plays a lesser role on *Head of the Class* than on *Facts of Life* in the promulgation of the myth of meritocracy.

In an episode that plays on a different type of lookism, Dennis is asked to be on the football team because of the way he looks—like a football player—

in "The Refrigerator of Fillmore High." He decides to go out for the team because he needs more outside activities to help him get into college, but the other players give him the cold shoulder because he doesn't know how to play football. When he complains to Moore that the other players have something that he doesn't and that he is a wimp, Moore tells him that he has a different kind of courage. Dennis decides to play football to prove to himself (and the other players) that he can do it, but quits the team after playing one game.

Many of the episodes are devoted to demonstrating that the students of the IHP all deserve to be in the honors program. The underlying privilege of how they got there takes a back seat to their accomplishments. They are all smart; their analytical skills are impeccable; and with their teacher's help, they become more creative and independent. Although they may face some discrimination, they work through the issues raised and, because they are bright, they readily learn how to navigate these obstacles. On *Head of the Class*, the students love to learn, no matter what the topic, but their right to be in the IHP is not challenged.

Conclusion

Facts of Life and *Head of the Class* aired in the 1980s when the divide between the rich and the poor was increasing, but both shows reinforce the myth of meritocracy. Clearly, a culture that demands the sorting of "winners" from "losers" and limits the number of winners cannot accommodate *everyone* who follows the rules and works hard. The perpetuation of the very idea of meritocracy demands a certain scarcity for the idea of privilege to keep its meaning. The shows want us to believe that the students at Eastland School and Fillmore High have earned their rightful places of privilege, and in both instances Mrs. Garrett and Mr. Moore help perpetuate the meritocracy. In actuality, there are many students who never get the educational advantages that these students have, no matter how hard they try nor how smart they are. In the 1990s, teacher shows tried to be a little more realistic, but during the 1980s, we needed to believe there was hope.

SIX

1990s Gaining Ground from Margin to Center

Hangin' with Mr. Cooper and *My So Called Life*

The 1990s were bookmarked by the Persian Gulf War under President George Herbert Walker Bush near its beginning and the impeachment of President William Jefferson Clinton by the House of Representatives and acquittal by the Senate at its close. Widely considered a time of economic prosperity, teacher salaries continued to lag, however, and the average teacher salary in the U.S. during the 1997–98 school year was $39,347 ("Survey & Analysis of Teacher Salary Trends"). Globalization became more than a buzzword with the passage of the North American Free Trade Agreement (NAFTA), AIDS awareness and treatments greatly expanded worldwide, and technological advances included tremendous growth of the Internet and much wider availability of personal computers in the developed world.

Television was also influenced by advancements in technology. From 1990 to 2000, census figures indicate that the population in the United States grew from almost 250 million to a bit over 280 million, and a large portion of those Americans had access to cable television, which grew from a 56.4 percent household penetration in 1990 to a penetration of 67.5 percent by 1999 ("Cable and VCR Households"). In 1990, the documentary *Civil War* ran for five nights and became the highest rated series in PBS history. Two years later, Johnny Carson's retirement led to a battle between David Letterman and Jay Leno for late night viewers. The following year, 1993, closed captioning was required on all television sets. In 1995, coverage of the O.J. Simpson trial brought large audiences to cable television, one of several landmarks in television history during the decade. In 1997, over 33 million U.S. homes tuned in to live coverage of Princess Diana's funeral, and Tiger Woods' win at the Masters set a record rating for the golf tournament. According to Nielsen, computer usage topped 58 million in the U.S. and Canada that same year. The PAX TV network launched in 1998, and that same year 76 million viewers watched the series finale of *Seinfeld* on NBC, compared to 25 million viewers who watched Mark McGwire hit his then record-breaking sixty-second home run that same year.

It was a great decade for sitcoms. Highly rated shows included family sitcoms such as *The Cosby Show* (which revitalized the genre with its success in the 1980s), *Roseanne* (which introduced a blue collar perspective sorely missed since *The Honeymooners*), *Full House*, *Family Matters*, and *Home Improvement*. Work-family sitcoms, a few of which included biological family members, also remained popular. Shows such as *Cheers*, *Designing Women*, *Murphy Brown*, *Frazier*, and *Friends* regularly landed in the top ten. *The Golden Girls* brought senior citizens into primetime, and *Coach* showed a man curtailing his career to help his wife build hers. One unconventional sitcom, often referred to as the "show about nothing," *Seinfeld*, emerged as a television phenomenon.

Of course, sitcoms were not all the networks programmed. *Monday Night Football* and *60 Minutes* remained ratings stalwarts, and the newsmagazine genre expanded from CBS to other networks throughout the 1990s with the introduction of *20/20* and *Dateline NBC*, both of which were among the top-rated shows. There were also some successful dramas introduced, such as *ER* and *N.Y.P.D. Blue*, and the decade ended with the introduction of a hugely successful quiz show: *Who Wants to Be a Millionaire*. The Tuesday, Thursday, and Sunday installments of that popular program finished first, second, and third in the ratings for the 1999–2000 season.

Focusing on shows that populated the top ten during the 1990s only tells part of the story, however. Conventional genre shows, for the most part, led in the ratings, but cable television made serious inroads into primetime, long dominated by the major networks, which by then also included relative newcomer FOX. Ratings for even the top shows eroded over the period, and by the end of the 1990s, cable programs were eating into network ratings. The starkest contrast in ratings over the decade occurred at the lower end of the top 30 list where ratings went from 14.2 for *The Wonder Years* during the 1990–91 season to a single-digit 8.8 for the shows tied for number 30 in the 1999–2000 season, *Law & Order: Special Victims Unit* and the *CBS Wednesday Movie*.

It was cable shows like *Sex and the City* (HBO, 1998–2004) and *The Sopranos* (HBO, 1999–2007) that combined high production values, strong writing and performances, and mature subject matter to lure viewers away from conventional network fare to HBO at the end of the decade. Cable also allowed new networks to carve out niche audiences such as The WB, which catered to African American viewers interested in seeing programs featuring Black characters. Television network executives tried to compete with cable by offering more sophisticated programs and mature themes but, as in the case of *My So-Called Life* (ABC, 1994–95) and *Freaks and Geeks* (NBC, 1999–2000), failed to stick with such programs long enough for them to develop a wider audience. Apparently, America was more comfortable with the gay characters presented in comedic broad strokes like Will and Jack on *Will & Grace* (NBC, 1998–2006), than with an openly gay high school student and the closeted gay teacher in *My So-Called Life*. Other strong network programs, such as *Homicide: Life on the Streets* (NBC, 1993–1999), did present complex characters and narrative arcs that dealt directly with racial issues, but only once did this program land in the top thirty when the show claimed the number twenty-four slot during its first season.

While changes in technology led to changes in viewing habits and diluted the power of the major networks, teachers seemed more in vogue than ever. A survey of television shows featuring significant educator characters in the 1990s almost doubles the total for any previous decade. While many of these programs were short-lived and, in at least some measure, an indicator of the multiplicity of new outlets such as FOX, Nickelodeon, the USA Network, FOX Sci-Fi, The WB, UPN, MTV, and Comedy Central producing shows in addition to NBC, CBS, and ABC, the total number of programs featuring educators is still worth noting.

A survey of these series will follow, but the sheer number of programs produced is not the most groundbreaking aspect of teachers on TV during the 1990s. We see this decade as one of tremendous change in a progressive mode, a move from margin to center for two teacher characters. Mark Cooper, the eponymous character of *Hangin' with Mr. Cooper*, is the most popular teacher of the decade and, in terms of ratings success, one of the most popular teacher characters in television history. This is a significant cultural marker. The visibility and sustained popularity of this role represent prominent placement that is unprecedented for an African American teacher character. Perhaps the most remarkable teacher on television is featured only briefly, however. English teacher Richard Katimski moves from the wings to center stage in a single episode. Katimski is gay and mentors Rickie Vasquez, a gay Hispanic/Black fifteen-year-old, who is being raised by a physically abusive uncle. Katimski and his partner take Rickie off the streets and into the safety of their home, which is an extraordinary transition for a teacher to make, especially a teacher on primetime network television. While this portrayal does not have the sustained visibility of Mark Cooper's role, creating a recurring gay teacher character and putting him in the classroom to express both passion for teaching and compassion for students still seems a bold move over ten years after the fact.

Teachers on TV: 1990s

Two long-running programs, *Coach* and *The Simpsons*, are included in this section even though they premiered in 1989 because *Coach* ran through most of the 1990s and *The Simpsons* is still on the air as we go to press. *Coach* (ABC, 1989–97) is included in this survey because of the long tradition of coach characters functioning as teachers in film and television. In this popular series, Craig T. Nelson stars as Coach Hayden Fox, head football coach of the Minnesota State University Screaming Eagles. The show focuses on his life off the field with his bumbling assistant Luther Van Dam (Jerry Van Dyke), dim player Dauber Dybinski (Bill Fagerbakke), girlfriend and eventual wife Christine Armstrong Fox (Shelley Fabares who played daughter Mary Stone for the first five seasons on *The Donna Reed Show* on ABC, 1958–66), and daughter from a previous marriage Kelly Fox (Clare Carey).

Family members on *The Simpsons* (FOX, 1989–) are the most recognizable (not to mention iconic) characters on this long-running animated program, and there are a number of recurring teacher characters on the show: fourth grade teacher Edna Krabappel, second grade teacher Elizabeth Hoover, music teacher Dewey Largo, and gym teachers Mrs. Pommelhorst and Coach Krupt. Alhough most of these teachers appear in multiple episodes, Edna Krabappel is featured most prominently. She is portrayed as a sexually frustrated divorcée who often smokes cigarettes in class. In "Bart the Lover," Bart answers one of her personal ads using the name Woodrow then stands her up for a date. Over the course of that episode, the teacher discusses her love life openly with Bart and cries in front of him. In "Grade School Confidential," she begins a romantic relationship with the school principal, Seymour Skinner. They are fired when the relationship is discovered but get their jobs back when Principal Skinner reveals that he is a virgin. The couple then tells Bart they have broken up to keep their ongoing relationship a secret. One consistent impediment to the relationship is Skinner's strong connection to his mother who, according to Krabappel, does not "let him out to play." In typical fashion, *The Simpsons* takes liberties not only with conventional ideas about proper teacher behavior, but it also toys with the Hollywood Model. As cable networks exploded in the 1990s and 2000s, the number of shows increased dramatically, including those featuring educators. It makes sense in this chapter and the next to break those series out by the year in which they premiered.

1990

Eight programs featuring teacher characters premiered in 1990. *The Bradys* (CBS, 1990–90), the fourth incarnation of the TV family that started out as *The Brady Bunch*, features Jan's (Eve Plumb) college professor husband, Phillip Covington III (Ron Kuhlman). Because they had been unable to conceive a child, the Covingtons have just adopted a Korean girl when the series begins. *Parenthood* (NBC 1990–90), based on the 1989 Steve Martin movie of the same title, focuses on an extended family raising the next generation. Brooks and Marsh describe Susan Buckman-Merrick (Susan Norman) as "a free-spirited high school teacher" supporting her "fastidious husband Nathan, who was working on his Ph.D. while exploring 'alternative' parenting procedures for their gifted four-year-old, Patty" (1052).

In *Ferris Bueller* (NBC, 1990–91), Charlie Schlatter plays the title role created by Matthew Broderick in the 1986 movie *Ferris Bueller's Day Off*, and his older sister Jeannie is played by Jennifer Aniston four years before the debut of *Friends*. In "Scenes from a Grandma," Ferris' grandmother (Cloris Leachman) gets a job as a counselor at Ocean Park High School in Santa Monica, California, but the educator with the most screen time is Ferris' nemesis, Principal Ed Rooney (Richard Riehle). Like *Ferris Bueller*, *Parker Lewis Can't Lose* (FOX, 1990–93) was based on the film *Ferris Bueller's Day Off*, but *Parker Lewis* fared better than *Ferris Bueller* did, probably because FOX had lower expectations as a newer network. Despite some recurring teacher characters in peripheral roles, the main educator featured is Principal Grace Musso (Melanie Chartoff), who is Parker Lewis' (Corin Nemec) foil. Musso, whom Parker calls "Mussolini," is known for breaking the glass in her office door and being irritated when Parker does things like repeatedly use her parking space. He refers to her office as the "gates of hell."

The Fresh Prince of Bel Air (NBC, 1990–96), which preceded *Ferris Bueller* on Monday nights, is best remembered as a launching pad for superstar Will Smith, who plays a rapper from a tough neighborhood uprooted to live on the West Coast with wealthy relatives. In the episode "The Ethnic Tip," Will's Aunt Vivian (played then by Janet Hubert-Whitten and later by Daphne Maxwell Reid), appears at Bel Air Academy to teach a Black history class. Race is also an issue on *True Colors* (FOX, 1990–92), a sitcom about a blended family with a Black father and White mother who both bring children from previous marriages into the household. The focus is domestic, but it is worth noting that the mother, Ellen Davis Freeman (Stephanie Faracy) is a kindergarten teacher. The sitcom *Evening Shade* (CBS, 1990–94) features Burt Reynolds[1] as Wood Newton, coach of the Evening Shade Mules football team, and Michael Jeter as Herman Stiles, his assistant, who is also a math teacher at the school. Most of the activity on the series takes place away from the school.

The drama *Beverly Hills 90210* (FOX, 1990–2000), focuses mainly on the social lives of privileged high school, then college students, who live within the boundaries of America's most famous zip code, but two high school educators and three college professors have recurring roles. Assistant Principal Yvonne Teasley (Denise Dowse), who appears in twenty-four episodes, is tough but caring. Gil Meyers (Mark Kiely) is faculty advisor to the high school newspaper. This young, friendly, handsome teacher is featured in thirteen episodes and usually appears in the hallway or in the newspaper classroom with students. Professor Corey Randall (Scott Paulin) is included in a narrative arc in which his wife is having an affair with another character, but Professor Haywood (Mark Shera) and Professor Patrick Finley (Alan Toy) are portrayed negatively. In "Violated," Haywood sexually harasses a student, and in "Little Monsters," Finley convinces a student to join a cult he has formed.

1991

Five programs were introduced in 1991 that feature teacher characters. Phil Lewis appears as Teech Gibson, a token Black teacher at elite Winthrop Academy in the short-lived—one month—sitcom *Teech* (CBS, 1991–91). The drama *Sons & Daughters* (CBS, 1991–91) outlasted *Teech* by a month. This series tells the story of the sprawling Hammersmith family in Portland, Oregon and includes a son-in-law, Spud Lincoln (Rick Rossovich), who is a football coach. There is no heart of gold hiding beneath the crusty exterior of Dabney Coleman's many movie villains and television characters such as *Buffalo Bill* (NBC, 1983–84). On *Drexell's Class*, Coleman plays Otis Drexell, who becomes a fifth grade teacher to avoid going to jail for his failure to pay back taxes and alimony. Still, Drexell apparently gets along better with his students at Grantwood Elementary School in Cedar Bluffs, Iowa than he does with his colleague, a teacher named Roscoe Davis (Dakin Matthews), who insults Drexell and works to make his class better than Drexell's, or with his principal, Francine E. Itkin (Randy Graff), who has a nervous breakdown two months into the series and is replaced by Principal Marilyn Ridge (Edie McClurg). To this point, most of the episodes are set in the school and classroom, but after Principal Itkin leaves the show, the focus shifts to the domestic front. Although the sitcom *Sibs* (ABC, 1991–92) focuses on the relationship among three sisters, one of them is married to Howie Ruscio (Alex Rocco), a long-suffering school teacher who must put up with his wife, Nora's (Marsha Mason, nominated for an Oscar for Best Actress in a Leading Role for four films including *The Goodbye Girl*, 1977), zany single sisters (played by Margaret Colin and Jami Gertz). The final entry in 1991 is *Welcome Freshmen* (Nickelodeon, 1991–93). While the only educator character featured prominently is Mr. Elliott Lippman (Mike Speller), we mention this show because it was inspired by the success of the high school sitcom *Saved by the Bell* (NBC, 1989–93), and it demonstrates the rise in importance of cable networks in primetime programming.

1992-93

Hangin' with Mr. Cooper (ABC, 1992–97) will be discussed later, and four other new shows premiered in 1993. The drama *Angel Falls* (CBS, 1993–93) aired a little over a month and featured high school basketball coach Luke Larson (James Brolin, starred on *Marcus Welby, M.D.,* ABC, 1969–76, and *Hotel,* ABC, 1983–88) and his wife Hadley Larson (Peggy Lipton formerly of *The Mod Squad* on ABC, 1968–73 and *Twin Peaks* on ABC, 1990–91), who are trying to deal with the death of their baby. George Foreman stars as ex-heavyweight boxing champ George Foster in the sitcom *George* (ABC, 1993–94), and his wife Maggie Foster (Sheryl Lee Ralph) is an outgoing guidance counselor at urban Monroe High School. The final two shows introduced in 1993, *Saved by the Bell: The College Years* and *Boy Meets World* merit a bit more comment.

 Saved by the Bell: The College Years (NBC, 1993–94) is one of two spin-offs of *Saved by the Bell*, a thirty-minute, school-based situation comedy. The show was inspired by then-president of NBC Brandon Tartikoff's memories of teachers of his past. The program follows the primary conventions of a situation comedy, except for the fact that *Saved by the Bell* aired not during primetime but rather on Saturday mornings. In her unpublished paper "*Is It All Right Because It's Saved by the Bell?*: An Examination of the Social Curriculum of Hollywood as Depicted in *Saved by the Bell* and *Good Morning Miss Bliss*," Kaitlyn Ranney argues that the original programs play out the conventional bifurca-

Figure 6.1. (clockwise from left) Danielle Fishel as Topanga Lawrence-Mat-
thews, Will Friedle as Eric Matthews, Anthony Tyler Quinn as Jonathan
Turner, William Daniels as George Feeny, Rider Strong as Shawn Hunter, and
Ben Savage as Cory Matthews in *Boy Meets World* (ABC, 1993–2000). Photo
courtesy of Photofest. Used by permission.

tion of acceptable behavior for educators in terms of gender: women educators like Miss Carrie Bliss (Hayley Mills, star of many Disney films including *Pollyanna*,1960, and *That Darn Cat!*, 1985) are not allowed to have romantic involvement, and men educators like Mr. Richard Belding (Dennis Haskins) are able to have a personal life without apparent impairment of their ability to do their job. The primetime show *Saved by the Bell: The College Years* follows four of the Bayside High School students to their freshman year at California University where, naturally, they room together in a suite in a coed residence hall, and the narrative focus is on the students' personal lives. The series does not extend past the freshman year (though *Saved by the Bell: The New Class* joined the NBC Saturday morning lineup at virtually the same time *The College Years* premiered in primetime), but it does feature two educator characters: Professor Lasky (Patrick Fabian), who teaches anthropology, and Dean Susan McMann (Holland Taylor), a formidable administrator.

Boy Meets World (ABC, 1993–2000) was a popular sitcom that features a teacher in a significant role. Though the show focuses on Cory Matthews (Ben Savage) from the age of eleven through college and his marriage to childhood sweetheart Topanga Lawrence (Danielle Fishel), his nemesis-turned-mentor is George Feeny (William Daniels), his teacher and next-door neighbor. Feeny follows Cory and his friends from junior high school, to high school (where Feeny is the new acting principal), and to college (where he begins to date their academic dean). Although Cory never especially likes Mr. Feeny because the teacher wants the student to achieve at a higher level, their relationship is complex and develops over time. In "I Dream of Feeny" from season one, for example, Cory wishes that Feeny would be sick just once so that he could get out of his geography test and is overjoyed when his wish is granted. When he finds out that Feeny is in the hospital with appendicitis, however, Cory has guilty nightmares about Mr. Feeny and is moved to visit him in the hospital where he thanks Feeny for being such a great teacher. The episode ends with Cory helping Mr. Feeny plant the geranium Cory gave him in the hospital. When they reach high school, Cory and his friends have a new, cool teacher who reads poetry in English class, wears a leather jacket, and rides a motorcycle. This teacher, Mr. Turner (Anthony Tyler Quinn), employs an unorthodox teaching style and, predictably, often butts heads with Mr. Feeny.

1994

My So-Called Life, which is among the programs launched in 1994, will be discussed separately, but five other series with teacher characters were also introduced that season. Lasting all of two and half months, the sitcom *The*

Good Life (NBC, 1994–94) focuses on the home life of the Bowman family in the Chicago suburbs and on dad John Bowman's (John Caponera) job as the co-manager of a loading dock. Maureen Bowman (Eve Bowman) is wife, mother, and a grade-school tutor who aspires to be an avant-garde playwright. In another short-lived show, family drama *Byrds of Paradise* (ABC, 1994–94), Timothy Busfield plays Professor Sam Byrd, a Yale professor who has moved his family to Hawaii to escape his memories after his wife's death. In the series, Professor Bryd becomes headmaster of the private Palmer School. Kellie Martin is engaging as Christy Huddleston on the drama *Christy* (CBS, 1994–95), which is adapted from the novel of the same name by Catherine Marshall. Set in 1912, Christy leaves a comfortable life in Asheville, North Carolina, to teach in a mission schoolhouse in the remote and impoverished Great Smoky Mountains of Tennessee. She is confronted by numerous challenges inside and outside of the classroom but perseveres.

Weird Science (USA, 1994–98) is based on the 1985 John Hughes movie of the same title. As in the movie, two best friends use a computer to create their perfect woman, Lisa (Vanessa Angel). Lisa is a teacher in the sense that the wishes she grants the main characters usually teach them life lessons because her "magic" often backfires or results in unintended consequences, and in "Sex Ed," she is a literal teacher when she comes to Farber High School to conduct sex education class. Principal Scampi (Bruce Jarchow) is a recurring character, Coach Armstrong (Lyman Ward) is featured in one episode about basketball tryouts, and in "School Spirits," a number of old Farber High faculty haunt the school because they do not want the new library built over the teacher's lounge.

The drama *Party of Five* (FOX, 1994–2000), centers on the five Salinger siblings, who pull together to take care of the family after their parents die in an automobile accident. Kirsten Bennett (Paula Devicq) is an attractive, young nanny, who cares for the baby in the family while in graduate school at Berkeley where she is studying child psychology. She begins dating the oldest sibling and moves into the house. They will eventually marry but not until after Kirsten loses a teaching job when her advisor finds out she inadvertently plagiarized something in her dissertation.

1995

Four television shows with teacher characters premiered in 1995. In *The Preston Episodes* (FOX, 1995–95), David Alan Grier (formerly of *In Living Color*) plays David Preston, a divorced, thirty-seven-year-old English professor, who leaves the relative security of the campus to become a famous author but instead ends up in a job as a photo caption writer for a middlebrow magazine. Robert Townsend, a versatile producer, director, and actor, stars as New York University professor of communication Robert Peterson in *The Parent 'Hood* (WB, 1995–99), a family sitcom that focuses on the domestic sphere. The CBS horror program *American Gothic* (CBS, 1995–96) features Selena Coombs (Brenda Baake), a sexy teacher having an affair with the evil sheriff of Trinity, South Carolina. Professor Maximilian Arturo (John Rhys-Davies) appears on the science fiction program *Sliders* (FOX, 1995–97, Sci-Fi 1998–2000). Arturo is a physics professor who follows his brilliant graduate student, the student's friend, and a soul singer who just happens by (how improbable is this?), on a test trip into a worm hole. This begins a series of journeys into an infinite number of parallel universes where history has played out differently than in our known universe. Arturo dies at the end of the 1996–97 season.

1996

The year in which the largest number of teacher characters debuted was 1996. Although one of the programs was offered only in syndication, several of them went on to successful runs on different networks. The range of these series in terms of format and genre is broad, but many are sitcoms.

According to Brooks and Marsh, the sitcom *The Faculty* (ABC, 1996–96) was set in the office and faculty lounge of Hamilton Middle School and, in addition to Vice Principal Flynn Sullivan (Meredith Baxter) and Principal Herb Adams (Peter Michael Goetz), features the following:

> [B]est friend Shelly [Constance Shulman] was the drawling, acerbic English teacher; Amanda [Jenica Bergere] the flighty young math teacher, a '60s type; Clark [Peter Mackenzie] the milquetoast history teacher; Daisy [Nancy Lenehan] the snippy secretary; and Luis [Miguel A. Nunez, Jr.] the young school nurse. The students were dumb and the laugh track loud. Or was it the other way around? (442)

The sitcom *Boston Common* (NBC, 1996–96) centers on an enthusiastic freshman from a small town in Virginia who goes to Boston to study at Randolph Harrington College. This series features a self-absorbed young professor, Jack Reed (Vincent Ventresca). Though it, too, lasted only a season, the sitcom *Pearl* (CBS, 1996–97) features three dynamic actors and an education-related theme: as Pearl, Rhea Perlman (best known as Carla Tortelli on *Cheers*, NBC, 1982–93) is a woman who works a blue collar job during the day and attends a prestigious university by night; Carol Kane (known for quirky roles on television and films, including *Annie Hall*, 1977, *The Princess Bride*, 1987, and *Addams Family Values*, 1993) as her sister-in-law, co-worker, and best friend who is afraid Pearl will desert her roots after going to college; and Malcolm McDowell (despite his numerous roles on television and in films, McDowell remains best known as Alex in *A Clockwork Orange*, 1971) as Professor Stephen Pyncheon, a stuffed-shirt intellectual who belittles Pearl regularly but generally reconciles with her by the end of the episode.

Clueless (ABC, 1996–97; UPN, 1997–98) is based on the 1995 film of the same name, which was based loosely on the Jane Austen novel *Emma*. Cher Horowitz (Rachel Blanchard) goes to high school at Bronson Alcott High School in Beverly Hills and shops on Rodeo Drive. In between her antics with friends and family, she finds time to fix up guidance counselor Miss Geist (Twink Caplin) with debate coach Mr. Hall (Wallace Shawn, a recognizable character actor best known for playing the writer in *My Dinner with Andre*, 1981). The sitcom *Nick Freno: Licensed Teacher* (WB, 1996–98) features the title character (Mitch Mullany) as an aspiring actor who makes a living as a substitute English teacher at Gerald R. Ford Middle School during the first season; the school is transformed without explanation into a high school for the second season. Brooks and Marsh offer the following description:

> Nick, whose frenetic teaching style included running question and answer sessions like game shows, was attracted to Elana [Portia de Rossi], the perky, dedicated social studies teacher. Other teachers on staff were Mezz [Reggie Hayes], his childhood friend, now a science teacher; Al [Charles Cyphers], the cynical shop teacher who had seen it all; and Kurt [Stuart Pankin], the obnoxious gym teacher who eventually became assistant principal. (986)

Something So Right (NBC, 1996–97; ABC, 1998–98) is a blended family sitcom with the focus on the series squarely on the domestic sphere, but dad Jack Jarrell (Jere Burns) is an English teacher. The focus on the sitcom *Moesha* (UPN, 1996–2001) is the teenage star Moesha "Mo" Mitchell (Brandy [Norwood]), but her stepmother, Dee Mitchell (Sheryl Lee Ralph), is a teacher at Moesha's school, Crenshaw High. Later, she becomes the faculty advisor for the school newspaper and, eventually, vice principal. Similarly, the focus is off the classroom in the sitcom *3rd Rock from the Sun* (NBC, 1996–2001). In the series, four aliens have come to Earth to learn about human behavior. The High Commander of the contingent is Dr. Dick Solomon (John Lithgow, nominated for Best Actor in a Supporting Role twice—for *The World According to Garp*, 1982, and *Terms of Endearment*, 1983—but best known to younger viewers as the voice of Lord Farquaard in the *Shrek* films), a physics professor at Pendelton University in Rutherford, Ohio. His colleague and love interest is Dr. Mary

Albright (Jane Curtin, one of the original cast members of *Saturday Night Live* and co-star of the sitcom *Kate & Allie*, CBS, 1984–89), Dick's officemate. She is eventually promoted to dean, which makes her Dick's supervisor.

Figure 6.2. (clockwise from bottom left) Cedric the Entertainer as Cedric Jackie Robinson, Terri J. Vaughn as Lovita Jenkins, Merlin Santana as Romeo Santana, William Lee Scott as Stanley "Bullethead" Kuznocki, Wendy Raquel Robinson as Regina "Piggy" Grier, Steve Harvey as Steve Hightower, and Netfa Perry as Sara in *The Steve Harvey Show* (WB, 1996–02). Photo courtesy of Photofest. Used by permission.

The Steve Harvey Show (WB, 1996–2002) has Steve Harvey playing Steve Hightower, once lead singer in a soul group known as Steve Hightower and the Hightops turned music teacher and eventually acting principal of Booker

T. Washington High School in Chicago. Like so many teachers in the movies (including music teachers in *Mr. Holland's Opus*, *School of Rock*, and *Music of the Heart*), teaching is something for Harvey to "fall back on" when other options don't work out. In the first episode, Hightower laments the difference between how he thought teaching would be (informed, of course, by popular culture and mythology) and what it turns out to be: "When Sidney Portier had this gig, all the little white kids held hands and sang him a song." This line refers, of course, to the classic school-centered film *To Sir, with Love* (1967) and is good for a typical sitcom chuckle. Hightower quickly develops a connection with his students, and that closeness is demonstrated in episodes in which the teacher dances with some of them when he has to supervise detention, when he brings his depression to class after a close friend dies, and as he manages common lessons like how to handle a bully and how to handle lovesick students who get crushes on teachers and administrators. Comedic storylines often revolve around romantic mix-ups fueled by Hightower's interest in Principal Regina Grier (Wendy Raquel Robinson) and the courtship of sports coach Cedric Robinson (Cedric The Entertainer) and school secretary Lovita Jenkins (Terri J. Vaughn). Hightower's background as a musician is incorporated into the show with many storylines about talent shows and school dances and special appearances by guest hip-hop stars such as Snoop Doggy Dogg, Sean "Puffy" Combs (as he was known then), and Lil' Bow Wow.

Malibu Shores (NBC, 1996–96) is a teenage soap opera that centers on conflicts between wealthy students at Pacific Coast High School in upscale Malibu, California and a group of lower class students from the San Fernando Valley transferred to the Malibu school after their high school is destroyed by an earthquake. Teachers featured during the one-year run include Mr. Morrison (Ernie Lively), who teaches an upper level English class, and an unnamed art teacher (J. Downing), who sexually harasses a female student.

In the drama *Matt Waters* (CBS, 1996–96), Montel Williams plays a character who has retired from the Navy and moved into the classroom as a science teacher at Bayview High School in Bayonne, New Jersey. He finds the school he attended twenty-five years before very different, a change signified by armed security guards and metal detectors that are now part of the school campus. Other teachers included during the single season are gym teacher Charlie Sweet (Sam McMurray) and African studies teacher Nicole Moore (Kristen Wilson). The television show *Dangerous Minds* (ABC, 1996–97), like the 1995 biopic starring Michelle Pfeiffer, was based on the memoirs of Louanne Johnson, *My Posse Don't Do Homework*. In the TV drama, Annie Potts (best known for her role as Mary Jo Shively on the sitcom *Designing Women*, CBS, 1986–93) plays Johnson, a former Marine who takes on students who have already run off three English teachers in a single academic year. As in the movie, Johnson fits squarely in the Good Teacher Model and gets personally involved in the lives of her urban high school students in East Palo Alto, California. Other teachers on *Dangerous Minds* include the gang services counselor, Jerome Griffin (Michael Jace), and a burned-out computer teacher, Bud Bartkus (Stanley Anderson).

Two other short-lived series are a bit more unusual than those mentioned previously in this section. *Space Cases* (Nickelodeon, 1996–96) is a science fiction program in which young cadets from Staracademy are trapped in a wandering spacecraft with characters including Miss T. J. Davenport (Cary Lawrence), a British teacher. The twenty-four episodes of the drama *Two* (Syndicated, 1996–97) deserve mentioning for unusual premise and might come under the heading, "Don't Teachers Have Enough to Worry About?" An assistant English professor at a Seattle college, Gus McCain (Michael Easton) has an evil twin he never knew about who comes to town and ruins the teacher's life by killing Gus' wife and others then framing the professor for the crimes.

1997

Of the programs introduced in 1997, two are still on the air and going strong, and both are animated sitcoms. *King of the Hill* (FOX, 1997–) is a staple of the FOX Sunday night line up, and *South Park* (Comedy Central, 1997–) has transcended Comedy Central to become a popular culture powerhouse, inspiring a myriad of products featuring the cut-out characters portrayed on the show.

As we go to press, Peggy Hill, the mother on *King of the Hill*, is selling real estate in Arlen, Texas, and before that she was a columnist for the *Arlen Bystander*, but for most of the run of *King of the Hill*, Peggy has been a substitute Spanish teacher. She means well and has a high opinion of her abilities in the classroom, but the more complete perspective presented to viewers depicts her skills as uneven, a condition complicated by her lack of fluency in Spanish. Notable episodes include (but are not limited to): "Square Peg," in which Peggy must overcome her prudishness to teach sex education only to have her husband pull their son out of the class; "To Spank with Love," in which Peggy is fired for spanking a challenging student then, when reinstated, capitalizes on her reputation for violence; "Little Horrors of Shop," in which Hank Hill substitutes as shop teacher at Tom Landry Middle School and is so popular that he might beat Peggy as "Substitute Teacher of the Year"; and, "Lupe's Revenge," in which Peggy takes her class on a field trip to Mexico and mistakes a little Mexican girl for one of her students.

Figure 6.3. Mr. Garrison in *South Park* (Comedy Central, 1997–). Photo courtesy of Photofest. Used by permission.

Like *King of the Hill*, the long-running *South Park* series has a loyal following. The main characters are four third grade students, but the program regularly features teacher characters Mr./Mrs. Garrison, Mr. Mackey, and Ms.

Choksondik. Other teachers move in and out of the series, but many would argue that the person who teaches the boys the most practical and meaningful lessons is Chef, the school lunchroom supervisor. Ms. Choksondik replaces Mr. Garrison as the boy's teacher for a period of time, but once Mr. Garrison comes to terms with the fact he is gay, he returns to the school to teach kindergarten. Originally, Mr. Garrison is an odd man who relies on a hand puppet in the classroom to teach. Then he has a sex change operation and eventually becomes a lesbian. (The show is nothing if not provocative.) Mr. Mackey is a counselor on the series, but he is involved in the teaching of sex education to the students in an episode called "Proper Condom Use."[2] In an earlier episode, "Ike's Wee Wee," Mackey deals with his drug addiction.

Although teachers are only peripheral characters on animated show *Daria* (MTV, 1997–2002), the title character is a sarcastic loner. Daria's world includes a self-esteem teacher who can't remember Daria's name, a science teacher who hates men following her bitter divorce, an encouraging English teacher, and an authoritarian principal.

Most of the live action series for the year were less successful than the animated sitcoms. *Social Studies* (UPN, 1997–97), features Frances Harmon (Julia Duffy, best known as Stephanie Vanderkellen on the sitcom *Newhart*, CBS, 1983–90) as the rigid headmistress of a coed boarding school in Manhattan, history teacher Katherine "Kit" Weaver (Bonnie McFarlane), and gym teacher Dan Rossini (Adam Ferrara). One of the four main characters of the sitcom *Between Brothers* (FOX, 1997–98; UPN, 1998–99) is a junior high school teacher, Mitchell Ford (Tommy Davidson), who moves into an apartment with friends after his second wife throws him out. While the focus is not limited to school in the supernatural show *Buffy the Vampire Slayer* (WB, 1997–2001; UPN, 2001–03), Sunnydale High is an important setting for the series since Sunnydale, California happens to sit over the gates of Hell. It's up to sophomore Buffy Summers (Sarah Michelle Geller) to protect the world from demonic vampires. Other important characters include nasty Principal Snyder (Armin Shimerman) and librarian Rupert Giles (Anthony Stewart Head), a "watcher" who trains Buffy to fight the creatures. Buffy becomes a guidance counselor in the final season. The series was adapted from a 1992 movie of the same name that starred Kristy Swanson in the title role.

1998

Six shows featuring teachers emerged in the 1998 season; four of them were short-lived. According to Brooks and Marsh, *Kelly, Kelly* (WB, 1998–98), a sitcom featured Shelley Long (best known as Diane Chambers on the sitcom *Cheers*, NBC, 1982–93, she left the series after the fifth season) in the title role as Kelly Novak, "a fluttery, status-conscious college professor who, while trying to keep her suicidal teaching assistant from ending it all, falls (literally and figuratively) for the handsome fireman who was trying to rescue him" (732). The focus of the show settles on the domestic sphere. The professor and firefighter court and quickly marry, despite the misgivings of his four children. In *Brother's Keeper* (ABC, 1998–99), the focus is also on the home as history professor Porter Waide (William Ragsdale) tries to raise his young son after the death of his wife, and his NFL star brother Bobby Waide (Sean O'Bryan) moves in for adult supervision as a condition of his contract. Apparently, widowed professors were popular in 1998. The sitcom *Two of a Kind* (ABC, 1998–99) features Kevin Burke (Christopher Sieber) as a science professor in Chicago raising twins (played by Mary-Kate and Ashley Olsen, initially famous for playing Michele Tanner on the sitcom *Full House*, ABC, 1987–95) with assistance from one of his students who becomes the girls' nanny. Yes, dad eventually dates the nanny, Carrie Moore (Sally Wheeler). Unlike the previous three shows with shorter runs, *Little Men* (PAX, 1998–2000) was adapted from the novel by Louisa May Alcott. Jo Bhaer (Michelle Rene Thomas) is Headmistress of Plumfield School, a boarding school in Massachusetts in 1871. As in the previous two series mentioned, she has lost a spouse.

Two dramas, *Felicity* and *Dawson's Creek*, were more successful with viewers. For four seasons, *Felicity* (WB, 1998–2002) follows Felicity Porter (Keri Russell) as she moves across country to attend college in New York City. Although a number of professors and administrators make appearances on the series, three characters have particularly significant roles: two male teachers prove to be both sneaky and dishonest while the female professor is proven to be even-handed in her dealings with the title character. Dr. McGrath (Chris Sarandon) sleeps with a smart student in the first season and gives her an undeserved A on her exam. In the third season, Dr. McGrath returns after a student files sexual harassment charges against him. The original student realizes that her undeserved A paved the way for her to take advanced classes that benefited her, but she decides to testify against him, which leads to his firing. Professor Hodges (Jim Ortlieb) gives an organic chemistry midterm that includes a section that he specifically stated would not be included. The professor's dishonesty is further exposed when he is arrested on shoplifting charges, and Felicity, the teacher's assistant for the course in season four, must take over some classes. During the second season, Art Professor Sherman (Sally Kirkland) encourages Felicity to start dating her son, insisting they will get along. After the professor walks in on Felicity kissing a guy other than her son, the student worries about her grade on the final art project. Later, however, the professor offers Felicity an internship, which demonstrates the teacher's ultimate fairness.

Dawson's Creek (WB, 1998–2003) plays a bit like a teenage soap opera, and the focus is squarely on the teenagers, who are in their sophomore year at Capeside High School in Massachusetts when the series begins. The most significant teacher featured is Tamara Jacobs (Leann Hunley), a very attractive English teacher who has an affair with one of the four teens (who are the main characters), then leaves town before a scandal breaks out. It might seem odd that an adult teacher's affair with a 15-year-old student would attract little attention, but sex seems to be on everyone's mind in Capeside most of the time. As the characters go off to college, they encounter several professors, and by the end of the series, one of the student characters added in Fall 1998, Jack McPhee (Kerr Smith), has returned to Capeside High School as an English teacher.

1999

The 1990s ended with the introduction of three series featuring teacher characters. The protagonist in the sitcom *Strangers with Candy* (Comedy Central, 1999–2000) is a non-traditional student (a middle-aged ex-con) played by Amy Sedaris, who returns to high school. There she encounters "the clueless geography teacher" Mr. Noblet (Stephen Colbert, best known for *The Colbert Report*, Comedy Central, 2005–), "the somewhat hipper art teacher" Mr Jellineck (Paul Dinello), and "the deep-voiced, narcissistic principal of Flatpoint High" Principal Onyx Blackman (Greg Hollimon) in what Brooks and Marsh term a "sickcom" (1315).

The critically acclaimed dramedy *Freaks and Geeks* (NBC, 1999–2000) never found an audience commensurate with its reviews. The show depicts the conflicts between burnouts and nerds[3] (freaks and geeks) at William McKinley High School in Michigan, and it focuses on groups of students to whom teachers seem annoying and irrelevant even when the adults have good intentions. The primary educator character is Jeff Rosso (Dave Allen), a guidance counselor who wants to steer students toward healthy life choices. Although this long-haired former hippie means well, he is not taken very seriously by the students. An authoritarian math teacher, Mr. Kowchevski (Steve Bannos), is the other main educator character on *Freaks and Geeks*.

The WB series *Popular* (WB, 1999–2000) examines the pressure high school students feel to be accepted and the hierarchical scheme that determines popularity. The focus of the series is a group of students, originally sophomores, at Jacqueline Kennedy High School. Several teacher and administrator characters come and go, but parents are more important adult characters in this series. One teacher appears in all forty-three episodes, however; biology teacher Bobbi Glass (Diane Delano) is portrayed as loud, mean, and unfeminine.

The decade drew to a close with the presentation of a teacher character who foreshadows the educational policy discussions in shows on the horizon like *Boston Public*. Mallory O'Brien (Allison Smith) is not a recurring character on *The West Wing* (NBC, 1999–2006), but the elementary school teacher is introduced in the series pilot as Chief of Staff Leo McGarry's (John Spencer) daughter when she brings her class to the White House to visit. Later, in the episode "Enemies," she discusses the education system with Deputy Communications Director Sam Seaborn (Rob Lowe), whom she ends up dating.

Clearly, from their sheer numbers, the 1990s was a boom time for teachers on television. There is more to consider, however, than the quantity of these characterizations; the decade introduces a different type of teacher character than previously seen, moving beyond the reductive "good" or "bad" teacher archetypes. These teachers represent a range of complexity that will only intensify in the subsequent decade. As for the 1990s, it is a time when teachers who had been marginalized previously—because of race—or been invisible altogether—because of sexuality—move from margin to center on the small screen.

Hangin' with Mr. Cooper

One of the most popular teacher sitcoms, *Hangin' with Mr. Cooper* (ABC, 1992–97), reached #16 in the Nielsen ratings (a tie with *Fresh Prince of Bel Air* and *The Jackie Thomas Show*) for 1992–93, making it one of only five sitcoms featuring teachers in major roles to break the top thirty shows in a given season. In addition to starring in the program, Mark Curry is credited as Executive Consultant on twenty-two episodes beginning in 1995. In the series, Curry plays Mark Cooper, a basketball player who played briefly for the Golden State Warriors before being cut from the team. In the pilot episode of the series, Cooper gets a job as a substitute teacher for a high school science class. Later on, he becomes a physical education teacher, a history teacher, and a basketball coach. Much of the action of the program is set in Cooper's home that he shares with Vanessa Russell (Holly Robinson Peete, previously Officer Judy Hoffs on *21 Jump Street*, FOX 1987–90) and Robin Dumars (Dawnn Lewis, better remembered as Jaleesa Vinson on *A Different World*, NBC, 1987–93), who appears in six episodes during the first season. In the second season, the show becomes more family oriented when it became part of ABC's TGIF block that included the popular family sitcoms *Family Matters* (ABC, 1989–98; CBS, 1998–98) and *Step by Step* (ABC, 1991–97; CBS, 1997–98). For two and a half seasons starting in 1993, *Hangin' with Mr. Cooper* filled the last half hour of the block leading into the news magazine *20/20*. During those seasons, Mark purchases the house he shares with his roommates, and his cousin Geneva Lee (Saundra Quarterman) and her daughter Nicole (Raven-Symone) move in to replace Robin. Geneva takes over teaching music at Mark's school, Oakridge High School, a job previously held by Robin. Nell Carter also joins the cast as P.J. Moore, Mark's childhood babysitter, who has become the school principal, a job Geneva will take over in the fourth season. The series plays off the sexual tension between Mark and Vanessa, and the two ultimately end up together and plan to marry but do not exchange vows in the series. The final season of the series had only thirteen episodes, about half the length of most contemporary television seasons, and the episodes aired during the summer when most other shows were in reruns. Furthermore, during the final season, episodes aired on Saturday nights rather than the customary Friday TGIF slot. Ultimately, there were 101 episodes of the series produced.

Many episodes of the series are split between the domestic sphere of Mark's home and the public sphere of the high school, though there is generally more time spent at home (after all, Vanessa is there), and over time the show focuses even less on the school setting. Regardless of setting, Mark Curry, with his athletic build, is so much taller and bigger than the other actors that he dominates the frame. He looms large in every sense of the word, towering over others at home and at school. He even commands attention when there are cute kids competing in the scene. He is a "nice" guy, who would probably seem a bit dull if he didn't engage in so much physical comedy—dancing, dribbling, flopping around the house and the school spaces—that he comes across as a bit goofy. Curiously, Vanessa, a pampered, rich girl cut off by her family and regularly losing jobs, is a bit of a mirror of Mark's physicality. Though she is much smaller than Cooper, their physicality in these roles links them in ways that suggest their ultimate compatibility.

As a coach, Mark works with neighborhood kids who play basketball in the summer, represented in composite by Tyler (Marquise Wilson) who follows him home, and Mark eventually coaches the high school team. As a teacher, we see Mr. Cooper interact with individual students, especially Earvin Rodman (Omar Gooding[4]), much more than with an entire class. His teaching is restricted to very short scenes that are usually transitions into or out of other scenes. As in most sitcoms, the stories are familiar and generally come to predictable conclusions with comfortable moral lessons. The episode "Here Comes the Groom" serves as a good example. Earvin and his girlfriend Lisa are kissing at school and P.J. sends him off to "take a cold shower." When the students run off to Reno to elope, Mrs. Rodman (Jenifer Lewis) shows up at Mr. Cooper's house to get him to go with her to stop them because the student respects his teacher even if he has misinterpreted earlier advice about the relationship with Lisa. The two have already married when the adults arrive in Reno, but Mark talks to Earvin with more luck than the first time. During their previous conversation, Mr. Cooper had advised him to "cool things off for awhile" to see if the relationship was serious. Earvin said that he followed Mr. Cooper's advice because he and his girlfriend stayed away from one another for three hours and found it very difficult. This time, the teacher does a better job. He asks Earvin a series of questions about Lisa to convince the student that he doesn't know his girlfriend as well as he thinks he does. Mr. Cooper advises Earvin to have the marriage annulled, and everyone returns home to Oakland.

Figure 6.4. Nell Carter as P.J. Moore, Mark Curry as Mark Cooper, and Saundra Quarterman as Geneva Lee in *Hangin' with Mr. Cooper* (ABC, 1992–97). Photo courtesy of Photofest. Used by permission.

Considerable time in the same episode concerns Nicole getting glasses and hating them to the point that she refuses to take them to school. Consequently,

Geneva puts on an equally unattractive pair of frames and convinces Mark and Vanessa to follow suit to make Nicole feel more comfortable. The fact that magnifying glasses are all that's available for the three adults is played broadly for humor by Mark and Vanessa. Eventually, this thread resolves in the final scene of the episode when Nicole comes to breakfast wearing her glasses—she's happy to wear them now because a boy in her class at school told her they looked good on her. These two narrative threads, one played out at home and another played out either at school or with other characters from school, are common to many episodes.

Even when the show tackles a serious issue, such as gang violence, the hard edges of real life are smoothed out by the conventions of the sitcom. Mark Cooper is a Black man living in Oakland, California, yet race is not overtly addressed on the series. All of the major characters are African American, and Oakland is a largely non-White city, but the television school seems to be more racially mixed than an actual school in Oakland is likely to be. The setting is even more incongruous and looks more like a set representing a 1950s suburban high school than an urban school of the 1990s. Mr. Cooper represents the progress of an African American male from margin to center, but just as 1970s and 1980s shows blunted the effects of social class and so-called meritocracy, this series does not establish race as an issue, which is disingenuous and clearly a nod to the "dead-centering" principle that dominated television programming for decades as a strategy to appeal to the widest possible mainstream audience. Black characters could be replaced by White characters in this series without actually retooling the show. In an ideal world, this might not be a problem, but the failure to acknowledge race as an issue becomes problematic when the reference becomes a larger, more complex world where problems associated with race emerge.

An example is the episode "Increase the Peace" in which gang violence is the major narrative thread. Once again, Earvin has met a girl who catches his attention. Monica Carson (Karan Ashley) is in the front office to receive a letter notifying her that she has achieved the highest SAT score of any student in the history of Oakridge High School. Earvin starts talking with her and soon the two of them become a couple. When Earvin bumps into a gang member in the hall, the marginally aggrieved party and his two friends make things look bad for Earvin until Monica steps forward and it is revealed that the big guy behind the shades and beneath the bandana is Eddie (Bumper Robinson), her brother. At first, Eddie wants to give Earvin a "beatdown," but Monica tells him to back off. On a later day when Monica is not present, the two guys are talking in the hall—Earvin is relieved that Eddie isn't going to rough him up since the tension has dissipated—then Earvin pulls out a green handkerchief, which is apparently the color of one of Eddie's rival gangs. Eddie pulls a gun on Earvin in the eerily clean and quiet hall, but Mr. Cooper comes up just in time to diffuse the situation. He also, improbably, sends Earvin to the office to report the matter and follows Eddie out the side door. The next day, there is a brief classroom scene in which a White student gives Earvin a hard time for having Eddie expelled. Before they can really have an exchange, Mr. Cooper comes to the classroom and calls Earvin to the hallway to let him know that Eddie got into a gang fight the previous day, that members of the rival gang went to his house and fired shots, and that Monica was killed by a stray bullet. The teacher and student embrace in the empty hallway as the loudspeaker makes an announcement about Monica's death. This traumatic event allows the show to conveniently sidestep the racial tensions.

The idea of the episode is well-intended, of course, but the lack of attentiveness to issues of race, social class, and violence in previous episodes along with the fact that the school set and the characters feel much more suburban and "middle America" than urban, make it difficult for a viewer to feel any real threat from Eddie or his gang. This episode has the artificial feeling of a play that stands out from the other episodes because it is staged in a way that deviates from the formula of the sitcom. It isn't that others aren't equally artificial, relying heavily on broad physical comedy, for example, but "Increase the Peace" is artificial in a different way that depends on the establishment of race as an issue for it to be credible. In the final analysis, this lack of social relevance relegates *Hangin' with Mr. Cooper* to the category of mildly entertaining but anything but transformative. Perhaps that is precisely what it means to go from margin to center and stay there—becoming lodged intractably in the mainstream.

My So-Called Life

Before discussing *My So-Called Life* (ABC, 1994–95), it is helpful to look at the larger context by examining film and television representations of gay teachers. It bears repeating here that women teachers in popular culture lead bifurcated lives that require them to bracket or deny sexual expression (or face dire consequences), and we must underscore the fact that this is true of both straight and lesbian teachers. For the most part, lesbian teachers have been invisible in popular culture or presented as "troubled" in films like *The Children's Hour* (1961) and *Rachel, Rachel* (1968). For men, the history of gay teachers in popular culture is shorter, but it does offer a richer range of representations.

In *The Prime Time Closet: A History of Gays and Lesbians on TV*, Stephen

Tropiano cites three "issue of the week" episodes dealing with gay teachers on social relevancy sitcoms of the 1970s. In a 1977 episode of *All in the Family* (CBS, 1971–83) entitled "Cousin Liz," Archie Bunker (Carroll O'Connor) finds out that his wife Edith's (Jean Stapleton) deceased cousin and her "roommate," both teachers, were lovers. Tropiano notes that Archie's statement to Edith that "people like that" do not belong in the classroom coincided with a larger cultural discussion: "At the time, gays in the classroom was a national issue, thanks to homophobic crusaders like Anita Bryant, who successfully led the fight to overturn the anti-gay discrimination ordinance in Dade County, Florida in June of 1977" (232). About that same time, the "Out of the Closet" episode of *Carter Country* (ABC, 1977–79) aired. Local high school teacher Bill Peterson (Richard Jaeckel) is fired when he comes out of the closet, and most of the episode is devoted to how his friend Sheriff Roy (Victor French) deals with this revelation about his friend's sexuality. In 1978 on the Norman Lear sitcom *The Baxters* (Syndicated, 1979–81), the Baxter family learns that fourteen-year-old Jonah's favorite teacher is gay. Through various characters, the show presents several points of view about whether homosexuality is "normal" and whether a gay teacher should be allowed in the classroom, but the episode does not present a conventional resolution in the narrative. "After presenting both sides of the issues," Tropiano writes, "the remainder of the half-hour is devoted to a town hall meeting-style discussion with a studio audience, who, immediately after watching the vignette on tape, are invited to share their views. The series was syndicated around the country, so the discussion portion was produced locally within each TV market" (234).

Those three episodes comprise Tropiano's section called "The Gay Teacher." Other than a recurring role on *Doctor, Doctor* (1989–91) in which Tony Carreiro plays Richard Stratford, a gay college English professor who is the brother of the sitcom's star, Dr. Mike Stratford (Matt Frewer), there are no other representations of gay teachers in regular primetime roles. Not until 1994 would a gay teacher emerge in primetime in a story where his sexuality gives the character the sensitivity and perspective to work with television's first gay teenager without making the teacher's sexuality just another "issue of the week" (Tropiano 177). One of the most fundamental precepts of the politics of representation is based on looking at who is included and who is left out of the frame as a measure of power and powerlessness. For most of the history of moving images, gay teachers have been omitted from the picture, just as gay teachers in real life have been closeted. It is worth noting that television presented a healthy, mainstream image of a gay teacher several years before the safe (unrealistic), affirming (but comedic) portrayals in Hollywood films such as *In & Out* (1997) and *Object of My Affection* (1998).

Brooks and Marsh call *My So-Called Life* a "teenage version of *thirtysomething*" while noting that Marshall Herskovitz and Edward Zwick produced both series (945). Ginia Bellafante gets much closer to the (lasting) emotional resonance of the series in an analytical essay published in the *New York Times*. She writes:

> To claim that "My So-Called Life" is great, watershed television is to say something so firmly ingrained in the conventional wisdom that it hardly bears repeating. The series brought us the experience of adolescence outside the bounds of artifice, peril and pathology that had provided the context for nearly every other depiction of teenagers on television. Here what it meant to be 15 was not to discover that you suddenly had to raise your 6-year-old sister or that you might be pregnant with twins but merely that you suffered everyday indignities: overhearing people talk behind your back, the plop of a grim-looking lump of mashed potatoes on a pallid cafeteria tray.

In her essay, Bellafanta also contextualizes *My So-Called Life* with salient comparisons to two other critically acclaimed shows with marginal ratings discussed in this book: *Freaks and Geeks* and *Friday Night Lights*.

The ABC drama *My So-Called Life* was introduced in August 1994 and cancelled after 19 episodes, but it became a cult hit and, after its untimely cancellation, MTV aired re-runs, and the show was also distributed on DVD—twice. As Bellafante notes in her essay, there are many active fan web sites for the high school drama. The show stars Claire Danes as Angela Chase, a fifteen-year-old student at Liberty High School in a Pittsburgh suburb who is bright but, as Mr. Katimski tells her parents in one episode, doesn't work up to her potential. Angela is a nice girl from a stable family who begins to move away from the kids she used to hang out with to join a wilder crowd, including: new best friend Rayanne Graff (A.J. Langer), who uses drugs and engages in sex with little discrimination; intermittent boyfriend Jordan Catalano (Jared Leto), who is rebellious and nearly illiterate (it turns out to be due to dyslexia) but gorgeous; and, androgynous Rickie Vasquez (Wilson Cruz), who is gentle and insightful. The show focuses on Angela and regularly includes her reflections as voiceovers, but all of the characters are carefully written, well-developed, and nuanced. One such character is teacher Richard Katimski (Jeff Perry), who appears in four episodes of the series but has a substantial role in only two: "Self Esteem" and "Resolutions."

The introduction of Mr. Katimski as a new teacher is one of the major storylines in "Self Esteem," the twelfth episode of the series (he will not appear again until the sixteenth episode). One middle-aged, female teacher flirts openly with the new teacher as she shows him to his classroom. A viewer might assume that this nondescript man with graying hair, khakis, and a gray

Figure 6.5. Jeff Perry as Richard Katimski and Wilson Cruz as Rickie Vasquez in *My So-Called Life* (ABC, 1994–95).

sweater vest over a blue oxford cloth shirt is just shy, but careful viewers will discern that he is not open to her interest, a disposition that is presented in marked contrast to the first teacher and her friend giggling about Mr. Katimski in the hallway more like schoolgirls than like teachers.

In the classroom, Mr. Katimski is more animated. As the students look at their desks to avoid his gaze, he chooses one to read aloud the teacher's favorite Shakespearean sonnet, and he happens to call on Enrique Vasquez from the roll. When Rickie stands up, his pink shirt and vest constructed of bold blocks of different colors make a stark contrast to the colors worn by the other students. The earring—that at first glance appears to be a cross but closer inspection is revealed to be an ankh—swings back and forth, and his beautiful face is enhanced with the subtle use of cosmetics. While Rickie wears bold colors, his clothing—especially the sweater vest—is in some ways a brighter variation of the teacher's muted garb. Both males wear trousers and sweater vests, which sets them apart from the jean-clad students in the classroom and creates, simultaneously, a visual link and a contrast. In a later scene, Rickie is imitating Mr. Katimski's mannerisms for his best friend Rayanne when the teacher comes up to the students and asks Rickie to join the drama club. Seeing the student's impression of the teacher once again links them visually and suggests that, despite his protestations that the teacher is annoying, Rickie is paying close attention.

Of course, the female colleague with a romantic interest in Mr. Katimski is paying attention, too; in one scene she comes into his empty classroom wearing a skintight gray sweater dress (a variation on Mr. Katimski's sweater vest) and positions herself in what seems intended as a seductive pose. Mr. Katimski, who has forgotten her name, is wearing a pullover sweater this day, a sweater with patterned blocks that recall the blocks of color on Rickie's vest the first day of the English class, but the teacher's sweater is knit in muted tones of gray and brown, suggesting yet again a link between the teacher and student that will be reinforced in the next scene. As the female teacher flirts haplessly with Richard Katimski, the teacher catches a glance of Rickie walking past the door and jumps up to follow the student with a quick request to be excused. He leaves his colleague stretched across his desk with first her mouth hanging open in surprise and then in a look of acute disappointment.

Now, in the busy school hallway flanked by lockers, Rickie is wearing a cardigan sweater with bold stripes over a flowered shirt. Despite Mr. Katimski's gray and brown palette, they are the only two characters wearing sweaters yet again. Mr. Katimski makes another attempt to connect with this student.

Katimski: See ya, Enrique.

Rickie, who had been walking away, turns and steps in toward the teacher.

Rickie: Uh . . . people don't call me "Enrique" except, like, my grandmother, and she's dead.
Katimski: Oh, okay. I'll try to . . . boy . . . imagine having a name like Enrique and not using it. Gee whiz. I'm an Enrique, too. Well, sort of . . . well . . . Richard. It's not quite the same thing.
Rickie: No. Richard would be Ricardo.

The teacher then indicates the drama club sign up sheet and tries unsuccessfully to get Rickie to sign up.

Mr. Katimski does not give up easily, however. At the end of the episode, Rayanne and Rickie see Mr. Katimski standing in the hall beside the sign-up sheet, and they try to duck out of sight quickly. It's hard for Rickie to keep a low profile because he's wearing a bright, yellow vest over a cobalt blue shirt, and there is a jaunty beret perched atop his head.

Katimski: Enrique!

Rayanne: (to Rickie) Later.

Rickie: Rayanne, wait!

Katimski: Gee whiz, I was just thinking about you.

Rickie: Why are you doing this?

Katimski: Pardon?

Rickie: This is not something I'm going to do. I'm just not the type of person who joins things, okay?

Katimski: I'm really sorry, but no! That's not okay.

Rickie: What?

Katimski: Well, I mean, come on. I'm a teacher. How do you expect me to react to a ridiculous statement like that? You don't join things. Who are you? Groucho Marx? You'd never belong to any club that would have you as a member?

Rickie: What?

Katimski: Look, what is holding you back here? That I'm not cool enough? Don't let the fact that your English teacher is a dork stop you from fulfilling your potential. Just pretend that I'm a track coach. I happen to notice that you can run fast. I need you on my team! It's as simple as that, Enrique.

Rickie: Stop calling me that! Why are you calling me that?

Katimski: I'm sorry, I'm sorry. I keep forgetting. It's just . . . oh, gee whiz. It's such a great name. When I was in high school, I hated my name. I hated it.

Rickie: I don't hate my name. I just . . .

Katimski: Oh, well . . . good. I'm really glad. Nobody should . . . hate who they are.

Mr. Katimski smiles and walks away.

The teacher sees something in this student and understands something about him that other adults either do not recognize or do not broach in a help-ful way because his androgyny confounds them. After Rickie watches Mr. Ka-timski walk away, he puts his name on the sign-up sheet for the drama club.

Episode 16, "Resolutions," is the second episode featuring Mr. Katimski, and the only other episode in which he plays a major role. It has previously been established that Rickie lives with an abusive uncle, and he leaves his home after being beaten. At first, he stays with Angela's family, but he leaves after hearing Mrs. Chase (Bess Armstrong) tell her husband that the boy can't stay there forever. Throughout this episode, Rickie is wearing muted colors, earth tones closer to the wardrobe selected for Mr. Katimski's character, which is not incidental. After noting that Rickie does not have an assignment and is sleep-ing in class, the teacher figures out that he does not have a place to live. In one scene in which the teacher talks with the student and tries to find him a place-ment in a group home called "Pride House," they are both wearing wardrobe based on muted colors and plaids with a single reversal—Rickie wears a plaid shirt unbuttoned over a solid beige one while Mr. Katimski wears a blue plaid shirt under the previously seen gray sweater vest—which establishes another visual unity between the two characters. Because there is a waitlist for "Pride House," the school counselor indicates that Rickie will have to go to a "facility" (shelter) temporarily, but it turns out to be a grim, threatening place that sends Rickie out into the streets once again.

The next day, Rickie is missing, but that night he places a call to Mr. Katimski from a phone booth sheltering the young man from the pouring rain. Not incidentally, he uses the name the teacher calls him when Mr. Katimski answers the phone, "It's me, Enrique." It is clear that the teacher wants to offer shelter and the student wants to ask for it, but something holds both of them back. When Rickie hangs up the phone, he begins to cry. The teacher, equally distraught, begins to flip the lamp on the table beside him on and off absent-mindedly. His partner (John Proskey) walks into the frame, and it becomes clear to the audience why the teacher is reluctant to merge his private life and his public life at school. Katimski admits to his partner that he is afraid to take Rickie in because information about his living situation might be revealed.

> **Katimski:** Well . . . what could happen if . . . if we did take him in? If it got out? You realize what people could make of it? I'd lose my job. I'd be crucified.[5]
> **Partner:** I didn't say anything.
> **Katimski:** What am I supposed to do? Just decide like that that I'm the solution to some kid's life? How egotistical is that? I hate myself, but I can't.
> **Partner:** (leaning in to touch Katimski's leg) Don't hate yourself.

Richard Katimski receives the same affirmation from his partner that the teacher has already given to Rickie—don't hate yourself. This is a message that bears reinforcing even for the teacher, whose private life, previously invisible, has now been revealed to the audience. Later, when the two men are eating dinner, there is a tap at the door. Katimski opens the door to find Rickie there crying and shivering.

> **Rickie:** Your address was in the phone book. I'm sorry. It just got so hard to be alone.

The teacher hugs the student, and his partner stands in the background. The door of the apartment closes, revealing the number "3," which suggests that these three belong together. Mr. Katimski is a Good Teacher; he cares and tries to help his students.

Mr. Katimski appears in two other episodes in short scenes related to the drama club and to try-outs and rehearsals for the Liberty High School production of *Our Town*. In the final episode of the series, "In Dreams Begin Responsibilities," a bunch of the students involved in the play decide to pick up tickets to sell and to have pizza at the teacher's apartment. Rickie discusses the plan with other students as coming over to "our place. I mean, Mr. Katimski's." He seems happily at home while the students are at the apartment filled with antiques and emitting warmth that is not entirely related to the rich patinas of wood and the earth tones throughout. Rickie goes with Mr. Katimski to take some of the other students to their homes afterward, and it is clear that Rickie is thriving in his new home.

After decades of invisibility or severely limited roles, a gay teacher finally emerges from off screen and beyond the margins when Mr. Katimski arrives at Liberty High School (the name seems significant). Just as the representation of television's first gay teenager in Rickie Vasquez is surely significant, Richard Katimski also breaks new ground. With Katimski, the creators of *My So-Called Life* introduce a fully realized and indelible character while claiming a significant "first" in television history for a gay teacher.

Conclusion

The movement of an African American teacher and a gay teacher from margin to center on the television screen in the 1990s does not seem remarkable until we look at patterns of representation in the movies, a form reinforced by FCC constraints and the need to attract a wide, mainstream audience to stay on the air. Of course, *My So-Called Life* did not attract that audience and, for that reason, we'll never know whether or not Mr. Katimski would have been a continuing character. Still, even his appearance in the few episodes we have discussed is a more complex, positive, and realistic representation than had been seen in movies or TV to that point.

While very little has been written about gay teachers in the movies,[6] there has been discussion among scholars of the problems Hollywood has in dealing with race and teaching. As discussed in Chapter One, Chennault, Lowe, and Giroux each note that the White teacher's experience in *Dangerous Minds* becomes normative for her students without consideration of the racist implications of this standard. The same narrative assumptions are true for virtually all of the movies that depict a White teacher, a "savior" character, going to teach in an inner-city school that is filled almost exclusively with students of color. Television offers a different set of stories. Initially, television depictions of race in the classroom were nonexistent, then careful ("tamed" as Keroes would put it), and now these characters and stories are sometimes surprisingly complex. *Hangin' with Mr. Cooper* appears in the continuum somewhere between careful and complex. Even the sitcom's lack of direct acknowledgment of or reflection on race *is* a discourse on race, and audiences know that despite a wish by some people that race "not matter," it does. Race and ethnicity and other identities, such as sexuality, do matter in ways that may be played out as positive or negative depending on the context and the values of the people and groups involved.

All texts (from media texts to personal narratives) are ideological because they are informed by value frameworks, which may be implicit or explicit but are never completely neutral. Texts are also defined not only by what they contain, as we have demonstrated by the relatively recent depictions of teachers of color in main roles and gay teachers in any roles at all, but texts are also defined by what is omitted. It is, perhaps, counterintuitive to believe that television would offer a more progressive set of depictions of teachers than film, but the lower production costs of some series compared to major motion pictures and, more importantly, the episodic nature of the television narrative without the constraint of a self-contained narrative arc limited to roughly two hours of running time create a set of possibilities for television and cable series that are not shared by commercial Hollywood films.[7] In the 2000s, the richness of television narratives featuring educator characters will demonstrate that the medium is maturing and offering viewers some smart, challenging programs in addition to the standard fare.

SEVEN

2000s Embracing Multiculturalism

Boston Public

Without the perspective and context afforded by time, we find it harder to write about this decade than those that have preceded it. Actually, it has become more difficult, in many ways, to write about all of the decades as they have come closer and closer to where we are with less and less of a filter provided by time. With this chapter on the 2000s, it's even hard to know what to call it since there is no clear consensus, but we have decided on 2000s for writing about the decade and "the aughts" when talking about it. Difficulty in parsing the terms to use is emblematic in many ways of the difficult and sweeping issues facing the world as the decade comes to a close. Climate change and fuel overuse threaten the Earth, economies once thought stable have weakened and become increasingly unjust in terms of the distribution of wealth, and wars and the threat of additional violence around the globe persist. Maybe the problems of contemporary life always seem bigger than those that have come before because of their present nature, but the technological progress enjoyed in the modern and postmodern ages seems to have caused as many problems as it has solved when the broad view is taken.

The 2000s began with extensive coverage of the Y2K phenomenon and speculation about whether or not computer systems would crash worldwide. Fortunately, the rupture predicted by some media sources turned out to be a barely a ripple. At 8:46 A.M. on September 11, 2001, television sets relayed images of the first of the two attacks on the World Trade Center. The next year, *American Idol* became a sensation and helped mark the reality boom on television that would rock the industry throughout the decade. These two events—one tragic and the other a bit of fluff—exemplify the contrasts of contemporary life in the United States; sometimes it seems that the defining problems of the era are so large and complex that many people would rather vote for their favorite contestant than become politically active and work for change. By 2003, television newscasts relied on reports from embedded journalists, and many Americans believed the president when he said the wars in Iraq and Afghanistan would be short. By 2006, direct broadcast satellite (DBS) delivery was estimated at nearly 25 percent of US households while cable penetration fell to about 62 percent ("Satellite TV Subscriptions"). Despite the multiplicity of options available on satellite and cable systems, critics and viewers expressed dissatisfaction with the glut of reality programming, cable 24-hour news programming that lowers the level of political discourse, and the feeling that there are hundreds of channels available and hardly anything worth watching on them.

The 2000s are a perfect example of how far television has come in specific instances but how little most advances matter in the majority of shows. Teachers on television during the decade are more visible and on more networks than ever before. Yet, most of the representations fail to engage the imagination or suggest a progressive agenda that expands on the depictions cited from the 1990s as moving marginalized groups to center frame. This is true for most but not all of the series introduced thus far in the 2000s. There are a few notable exceptions: series that introduce a realistic high school landscape different from those regularly seen in primetime, an urban landscape on *The Wire* and a rural landscape on *Friday Night Lights*; a show that offers a bleak revisionism more common to films than to television on the shocking cable series *Breaking Bad*; and one program that offers a refreshing multiculturalism that is as novel for television as it is for motion pictures on the well-regarded FOX series *Boston Public*. It is unclear as we go to press in 2008 what the final seasons of the decade will provide, but based on the popularity of teacher characters in the first eight years of the decade, it seems a safe bet that teachers will have a place in the programming lineup.

Teachers on TV: The 2000s

2000

Of the eight shows introduced in 2000 featuring teacher characters, *Boston Public* will be discussed in detail later in this chapter, three of the shows lasted a single season, and the other four have enjoyed varying degrees of success. About the only thing *Higher Ground*, *Young Americans*, and *American High* have in common is their lack of longevity in primetime. The drama *Higher Ground* (Fox Family, 2000–00) was set at a wilderness camp for troubled teens called Mount Horizon High School (which seems a bit contradictory as if students are supposed to simultaneously climb toward the peak and gaze across the horizon). Brooks and Marsh offer a clever description of the series and adult characters:

> Although they could not bring many personal belongings, everyone arrived at the remote camp with a ton of emotional baggage. Peter, the ruggedly handsome headmaster, was a former Wall Street executive and recovering drug addict; Sophie, his concerned assistant director (they met in rehab); and Frank, the fatherly, white-bearded founder of Mount Horizon, who had opened the camp after his own son died of a heroin overdose. (613)

In the finale of the 22 episodes, Peter Scarbrow (Joe Lando) and Sophie Becker (Anne Marie Loder) decide to get married. The WB drama *Young Americans* (2000) features Ed Quinn as Finn, the crew coach and literature teacher at Rawley Academy, who overlooks the fact that a local student from a disadvantaged family cheated on the entrance exam to get in because the teacher is convinced the student has talent as a writer and belongs at the elite boarding school. The documentary *American High* (FOX , 2000–00) ran for two weeks before it was pulled and later picked up by PBS, which aired the entire series the next year and won a Emmy for Outstanding Nonfiction Program. While the focus was on fourteen students at Highland Park High School in Illinois, they were shown at school as well as at home.

The remaining four series introduced in 2000 include an animated sitcom, two dramedies, a live action sitcom, and a drama. That's quite a range. The Nickelodeon cartoon *As Told by Ginger* (Nickelodeon, 2000–04) and focused on a Lucky Junior High School student with bright red hair named Ginger. While many of the situations involve Ginger, her friends, and family, there are several teacher characters in recurring roles: Ms. Korski is a homeroom and English teacher who encourages Ginger's writing talent, organizes school plays and art fairs, and stays in touch with Ginger even after she moves on to another grade; Principal Milty tries to enforce rules and discipline but is generally walked over by the students; Mr. Cilia is a tough science teacher loved by students with an affinity for science and feared by those without such leanings; and, Mr. Hepper is a jazz musician and cool music teacher at Lucky Elementary School where Ginger's brother attends.

The first of the two dramedies, *That's Life* (CBS, 2000–02) centers on Lydia DeLucca (Heather Paige Kent), who is steps away from her working class roots when she starts college as a freshman at age 32, she encounters a psychology professor with a drinking problem. Dr. Victor Leski (Peter Firth) impregnates one of Lydia's friends, Jackie O'Grady (Debra Mazar), then dies in a freak accident in the first episode of the second season after proposing to Jackie. *Ed* (NBC, 2000–04) centers on an attorney, Ed Stevens (Tom Cavanagh), who leaves his life in New York after learning his wife is cheating on him. He returns to his hometown, Stuckeyville, Ohio, where he buys a local bowling alley and begins to pursue the girl he liked in high school. Carol Vessey (Julie Bowen) is a teacher and aspiring writer, and her friend Molly Hudson (Leslie Boone) is also a teacher. Principal Dennis Martino (John Slattery) is featured in the second season. More episodes involve the school and student characters as the series progresses, and ultimately Ed and Carol marry and return to New York when she is offered the opportunity to write for a magazine.

The sitcom *Malcolm in the Middle* (FOX, 2000–06) focuses on a bright eleven-year-old (he graduates and is headed to Harvard when the series ends) stuck in a wacky family of underachievers and less capable characters. Malcolm Wilkerson (Frankie Muniz) excels at school and faces challenges at home, but few teacher characters appear in the series except the rigidly authoritarian commander of the Alabama military academy where Malcolm's older brother Francis (Christopher Kennedy Masterson) is sent after wrecking the family car. Francis is always competitive with Commandant Edwin Spangler (Daniel von Bargen), and during the first season he seeks legal emancipation to leave school and get a job in Alaska.

Of the series that premiered in 2000, *Gilmore Girls* (WB 2000–06, CW 2006–07) was the longest running. The main characters of the series are Lorelai Gilmore (Lauren Graham), a single mom in rural Stars Hollow, Connecticut, and her daughter, Rory Gilmore (Alexis Bledel). The main teacher character in the series appears in thirteen episodes between 2000 and 2003. Max Medina (Scott Cohen) is Rory's English teacher at Chilton Preparatory Academy and Lorelai's love interest. He almost loses his job when he is seen kissing Lorelai at the school parents' day, and they put the relationship on hold. In the series, he is mostly presented as Lorelai's love interest, but he is also depicted assigning papers and projects and teaching in the classroom. Medina is portrayed as a challenging but fair teacher, honest and bright but also kind. Three other prep school teachers featured in occasional episodes do not have character names, but they are played by Carol Hickey, Julia Silverman, and Jill Matson. When Rory begins applying to colleges, Harvard Professor (Karl T. Wright) is featured in two episodes, and when she ultimately enrolls at Yale University, there are three Yale professors featured: Professor Anderson (Lorna Raver), Professor Gilbert (Thomas Redding), and Professor Asher Fleming (Michael York).

2001

Only three series featuring teachers premiered in 2001, and all of them were short-lived. The sitcom *What About Joan?* (ABC, 2001–01) features Joan Cusack[1] as an English teacher who is depicted in her apartment and in the teacher's lounge but not actively engaged in teaching. The focus is on Joan's romantic life, as it is for co-workers Betsy Morgan (Jessica Hecht) and Mark Ludlow (Wallace Langham), who are having an off-again/on-again relationship before abruptly getting married.

The CBS drama *The Education of Max Bickford* (CBS, 2001–02), which stars Richard Dreyfuss (his long, successful career includes an Oscar nomination for playing a teacher in *Mr. Holland's Opus*, 1995 and a win for *The Goodbye Girl*, 1977) in the title role, offers a more substantive depiction of actual teaching (which is to say, it offers some representation of teaching!). Dreyfuss plays a passionate yet uncompromising history professor who is a recovering alcoholic. Ever since his wife's death, he feels lost and finds that even though he thought he knew everything, he still has a lot to learn—from his colleagues, his students, and his children. And, did Max Bickford ever learn a lot during this single season! The show follows teachers at all-female Chadwick College in New Jersey and between classes and dealing with his two children, he has his hands full with colleagues and with his own issues as a recovering alcoholic. He expects a promotion, which goes to a new professor, Andrea Haskell (Marcia Gay Harden won an Oscar for Best Actress in a Supporting Role for *Pollock*, 2000, and was nominated in the same category for *Mystic River*, 2003), who is a former student and ex-lover of Bickford's, specializing in popular culture, which traditionalist Bickford disdains. College President Judith Hackett Bryant (Regina Taylor) is an old friend of Bickford's, but that doesn't keep her from passing him over for the promotion and hiring Haskell. Other history professors featured include Josh Howlett (Patrick Fabian), Rose Quinley (Natalie Venetia Belcon), Walter Thornhill (David McCallum, of *Man from U.N.C.L.E.* fame), and Rex Pinsker (Stephen Spinella). The most important teacher character other than Bickford and Haskell comes from the Anthropology Department rather than the History Department, however. Bickford's friend Steve Bettis returns from sabbatical as Erica Bettis (Helen Shaver) following a sex-change operation. As occasionally happens with TV teachers of English or history, the discipline offers a mechanism for teachers to make links between the subject matter in the classes and real life situations involving the teachers and students.

The drama *Undeclared* (FOX, 2001–02), from the creators of *Freaks and Geeks*, focuses on a group of college freshmen at the University of North Eastern California. While several professor characters are listed among the guest stars, the focus of the series is clearly on Steven Karp (Jay Baruchel), his friends, and his father (played by noted musician Loudon Wainwright, Rufus Wainwright's father), who spends a lot of time around the dorm as a result of his impending divorce.

2002

Four series featuring teachers premiered in 2002, and two of them are cartoons. The animated sitcom *3-South* (MTV, 2002–02) features a couple of dense slackers who have managed to enroll at Barder College where they room with a studious pre-med student. The series, of which thirteen episodes were produced, features a pompous administrator, Dean Earhart (voiced by Jeffrey Tambor, widely cast as a character actor and known for such live action shows as *Arrested Development*). *Whatever Happened to Robot Jones?* (Cartoon Network, 2002–02) follows Robot Jones, a small robot with a boxy head topped by a glass dome, that has been sent by his parents to Polyneux Junior High School to study humans. In addition to his friends, he interacts with Principal Madman (the name is telling) and gym teacher Mr. Rucoat.

More significant is the drama *The Wire* (HBO, 2002–08). Each season of the show follows Baltimore police officers, politicians, and drug dealers, but there are also storylines that look specifically at various institutions in the city. The fourth season includes an emphasis on the school system. Detective Roland "Prez" Pryzbylewski (Jim True-Frost) is great with paperwork but not ultimately cut out to be a police officer. The fact that he shot and killed a Black man holding a gun who turned out to be a police officer in season three (this following a brutal beating he gave a suspect in the first season) leads to his departure from the police department and paves the way for him to land in the profession where he always figured he would end up—teaching. In season four, he becomes a teacher at Edward Tillman Middle School where he has great difficulty maintaining order. Prez joins a few other White teachers and administrators in what otherwise appears to be a school populated entirely by African American students, faculty, and staff. Notably, the Principal is a Black man who is not a visible presence in the hallways or the classrooms , and the Assistant Principal is a no-nonsense White woman. Prez, known to the students as "Prezbo," is able to make some tentative connections to some of the troubled eighth graders, but the oppressive conditions of their homes and neighborhood ultimately prove too onerous to make his efforts to teach and to help successful.

8 Simple Rules for Dating My Teenage Daughter (ABC, 2002–05) is remarkable for the way it handled the death of its star, John Ritter, in 2003. The show began as a nuclear family sitcom with realistic dialogue and enough angst from teenagers *and* parents to go around. Most of the action takes place in the domestic setting during the first season, but two early episodes involve Principal Connelly (Mo Gaffney). In one, Kerry is suspended for skipping school and in the second, she draws a cartoon of the principal as The Incredible Boring Woman that ends up in the school newspaper. When Ritter dies unexpectedly, the show producers have his character, Paul Hennessy, die suddenly, leaving his widow, Cate (Katey Sagal, formerly of *Married . . . with Children*, FOX, 1987–97), teenage daughters Bridget and Kerry (Kaley Cuoco and Amy Davidson), and preteen son, Rory (Martin Spanjers). Added to the cast is Kate's father, Jim Egan (James Garner[2]), and a year later her adult nephew, C.J. Barnes (comedian David Spade previously of *Just Shoot Me*, NBC, 1997–2003). During the last season, Cate becomes the nurse at her children's high school, and C.J. becomes a substitute teacher and then a full-time teacher at the school. Additional educator characters include cold Japanese calculus teacher Mrs. Krupp (Suzy Nakamura), and big, brawny home economics teacher and bully Marion Edwards (Michael Milhoan). A former high school boyfriend of Cate's, Principal Ed Gibb (Adam Arkin) is a kind, understanding, and sympathetic character who has been divorced for several years. By the series finale, he and Cate are dating. One interesting episode, "Ditch Day," revolves around a day at school when no teaching occurs. The teachers take attendance, the students leave, and the teachers have a party for the rest of the day. Rory describes it as having something to do with keeping their federal funding. After the students leave (except for Kerry, who *wants* to attend classes), Cate and the other teachers drink margaritas and play poker in the teacher's lounge. Cate wins thirty dollars.

2003

The single series featuring educator characters to premier in 2003 is the animated show *Clone High, USA* (MTV, 2003–03). According to Brooks and Marsh, thirteen episodes of the series were produced in Canada, but not all were broadcast before it was pulled in response to protests by activists in India over a "disrespectful" depiction of Mahatma Gandhi (262). The series is set in Clone High where all the students are teenage clones of famous historical figures, and the four main characters are clones of Abraham Lincoln, Mahatma Gandhi, Joan of Arc, and JFK. There are three major educator characters in the series: Principal Scudworth; the Vice Principal, Mr. Lynn Butlertron (Mr. B.); and, a history teacher, Mr. Sheepman. Principal Scudworth (voiced by Phil Lord) has evil plans for the cloned students. In theory, the clones are a military experiment with the ultimate goal of harnessing the greatness of the historical figures to gain advantage in battle. Scudworth has other plans, however; he wants to use them to staff a clone-themed amusement park called Cloney Island. He is selfish, has no regard for the students, and is continually plotting against the clones on the series. Mr. B., a robot that serves as Scudworth's "vice principal/butler/dehumidifier" is both a parody of Mr. Belvedere (played by Christopher Hewett on the ABC sitcom of the same name) and emblematic of the robotic administrative style of vice principal characters in many teen-orientated television shows. Mr. Sheepman (voiced by comedian Andy Dick as a combination of Don Knotts and a sheep) is a kind but easily excited history teacher. He was the first (mostly) human clone who ended up with some sheep DNA mixed into his genes. Clearly, this is one of the most unusual set of TV educators we have encountered in this survey of shows!

2004

Several different types of programs featuring teachers debuted in 2004, but none of those shows lasted on the primetime schedule past 2007. There was one reality show, one contest program, two cartoons, five sitcoms, and five dramas, including one detective drama. The reality show *My Big Fat Obnoxious Fiancé* (FOX, 2004–04) was billed as "the world's biggest practical joke," and the victim was a twenty-three-year-old first grade teacher named Randi Coy. As described by Brooks and Marsh, it's hard to imagine that the audience wasn't also victimized.

> She [Randi] had been told that she and Steve, the fake "fiancé" the producers had picked for her, had to convince their families that they were in love and getting married in 12 days. If they made it to the wedding ceremony they would win $1,000,000. What Randi didn't know was that Steve, his family and friends were all actors paid to be annoying as possible. (939)

At the altar Steve balked, but Randi and her family ended up with a bundle of money for participating. The competition show *The Real Gilligan's Island* (TBS, 2004–05) was a cross between *Gilligan's Island* and *Survivor*, and—true to the 1960s sitcom *Gilligan's Island*—includes real-life professors reminiscent of the original sitcom character.

The two cartoons that premiered in 2004 were *Danny Phantom* (Nickelodeon, 2004–) and *Fatherhood* (Nick at Nite, 2004–05). In the first, fourteen-year-old Danny turns into a "half-ghost" when a machine his dad has built to fight ghosts has unintended consequences. Characters at Caspar High School include Vice Principal Lancer, who is keen to enforce the school rules. *Fatherhood* was created by Bill Cosby, perhaps best known for his live action family sitcom *The Cosby Show* (NBC, 1984–92). The show focuses on daily life in the Bindlebeep household, and characters include high school teacher Dr. Arthur Bindlebeep. The character, voiced by Blair Underwood (Jonathan Rollins on *L.A. Law*, NBC, 1987–1994), is the patriarch of this conventional, middle-class Black family.

Three sitcoms were launched in 2004: *Ned's Declassified School Survival Guide*, *Unfabulous*, and *Phil of the Future*. Ned (Devon Werkheiser) is a smart, cheerful student at James K. Polk Middle School who compiles helpful tips in *Ned's Declassified School Survival Guide* (Nickelodeon, 2004–). According to Brooks and Marsh, the staff in this series includes "weird shop teacher Mr. Chopsaw (Dave Florek), evil science teacher Mr. Sweeney (Don Creech) and lazy janitor Gordy (Daran Norris)" (957). One educator has a recurring role in *Phil of the Future* (Disney, 2004–06). When the Diffy family tries to take a vacation in 2121, the time machine malfunctions and deposits the family back in the year 2004 where Phil (Ricky Ullman) tries to blend in at H.G. Wells Junior/Senior High School and escape detection of his ruse by Vice Principal Neal Hackett (J.P. Mannoux). In *Unfabulous* (Nickelodeon, 2004–), the focus is on Addie (Emma Roberts), a chirpy seventh grader at Rocky Road Middle School—chirpy because she is so cheerful that she often breaks out into song and accompanies herself on the guitar. Recurring educator characters include Principal Brandywine (Mildred Dumas) and Coach Pearson (Sean Whalen).

Five dramas were released this year, *Clubhouse*, *Jack & Bobby*, *Life as We Know It*, *Summerland*, and *Veronica Mars*. A detective drama, *Veronica Mars*

(UPN, 2004–05; CBS, 2005–05; UPN, 2006–06; CW, 2006–07), features the title character (Kristen Bell) as a high school senior and then college student who solves individual crimes and mysteries while working on unraveling those more complex storylines over the better part of each season as the show was broadcast first on UPN, then on CBS, then back to UPN before ending up on the CW. Professor Hank Landry (Patrick Fabian) is a major character in the second season who accidentally kills his lover when she accuses him of murdering her husband (a murder actually committed by the professor's teaching assistant—whatever happened to grading papers?). The remaining four dramas are more conventional, if also more short-lived. Pete Young (Jeremy Sumpter) has just landed the dream job of batboy for the fictional New York Empires baseball team on *The Clubhouse* (CBS, 2004–04). While the job will let him help his single mom, Lynne Young (Mare Winningham), financially, he still has to balance the new job with his studies at a strict Catholic high school, the domain of Sister Marie (Cherry Jones). *Jack & Bobby* (The WB, 2004–05) follows a future president, Bobby McCallister (Logan Lerman), and his brother, Jack (Matthew Long), during their formative years with their mother, Grace (Christine Lahti, also known for her portrayal of Dr. Kathryn Austin on *Chicago Hope*, on CBS from 1994–2000), a divorced history professor at Plains State University in Missouri who is outspoken and unwavering in her liberal ideology. Sex is central to the ten episodes of *Life as We Know It* (ABC, 2004–05). Most of the storylines focus on three high school stock characters, a cool jock, a brain, and a socially awkward guy, and their love interests. The smart student, Ben Connor (Jon Foster) has an affair with his attractive teacher, Monica Young (Marguerite Moreau). Finally, *Summerland* (WB, 2004–05) features a single fashion designer with a beach-front home in California and cool friends who inherits her two nephews and niece when her sister and brother-in-law are killed in a flood. Aunt Ava Gregory's (Lori Loughlin) glamorous California lifestyle is quite different from the Kansas farm life they have left behind. Ava begins a serious relationship with her niece's principal, Simon O'Keefe (Jay Harrington). She proposes to him, but he ultimately quits his job and moves away.

2005

There was an even wider variety of television genres featuring educators among the series launched in 2005, even though a smaller number of shows with teachers debuted. In the reality show *Tommy Lee Goes to College* (NBC, 2005–05), rock star Tommy Lee, drummer for Mötley Crüe, encounters a number of students and some professors at the University of Nebraska at Lincoln. The supernatural *Ghost Whisperer* (CBS, 2005–), centers on Melinda Gordon (Jennifer Love Hewitt), who can communicate with the spirits of people who have died but not yet left Earth. Professor Rick Payne (Jay Mohr) is a university psychology professor who specializes in the study of the paranormal. He has always given Melinda the advice and information she seeks, but it has taken him awhile to actually believe in her ability to talk with the dead. The police drama *Numb3rs* (CBS, 2005–) draws heavily on the ability of applied mathematics professor Charlie Eppes (David Krumholtz) to help his FBI agent brother Don (Rob Morrow, who played Dr. Joel Fleischman on *Northern Exposure* on CBS, 1990–95) solve crimes. Charlie is not pictured in the classroom very often, but he does draw on the expertise of his mentor and former professor Larry Fleinhardt (Peter MacNicol) and the graduate student whose work he is supervising, Amita Ramanujan (Navi Rawat). Amita earns her Ph.D. and turns down a professorship at Harvard to take a position at California Institute of Science and remain with Charlie. Another in a long line of professors who date their students, Charlie and Amita become a romantic item.

Two cartoons, *My Gym Partner's a Monkey* and *American Dragon: Jake Long*, premiered in 2005. Despite the tired stereotypes of teachers and administrators on many series over the years, we don't recall another show that goes so far as to cast animals as educators. The series *My Gym Partner's a Monkey* (Cartoon Network, 2005–) follows Adam Lyon to Charles Darwin Middle School after a clerical error in which someone believes his last name is "Lion." Since this is a school for the offspring of zoo animals, Adam is the only human enrolled. There are no humans among the faculty and staff either: "The principal was a small frog, while other staff included Coach Gills (a goldfish in a tank), Miss Chameleon the art teacher, Mr. Hornbill (a rhinoceros), lunch lady Mrs. Tusk (who served wormy joes), band director Mr. Mandrill and teacher Mr. Blowhole (a killer whale . . .)" (Brooks and Marsh, 942). Adam also develops a menagerie of friends on this series. *American Dragon: Jake Long* (Disney Channel, 2005–) features a Chinese American boy living in New York City who is descended from dragons. Professor Hans Rotwood is a suspicious but ineffective teacher.

Three sitcoms, *Naturally Sadie, Everybody Hates Chris*, and *How I Met Your Mother*, also premiered during the 2005 season. *Naturally Sadie* (2005–) is a Canadian-produced television show airing on various networks around the world and the Disney Channel in the United States. Sadie Hawkins (Charlotte Arnold) is an aspiring naturalist, and she's fascinated with animals—the kind she finds in the wild as well as the types she finds in at R. B. Bennett High School. The cast includes Principal Alberta Mann (Alison Sealy-Smith).

Everybody Hates Chris (UPN 2005–06, CW 2006–) is comedian Chris Rock's semiautobiographical look at his childhood. The character Chris Rock (Tyler James Williams) is pulled from the school in his Bedford-Stuyvesant neighborhood by his father in order to attend Corleone Junior High School where he is the only Black student. Ms. Morello (Jacqueline Mazarella) is featured as a racist math teacher. Mrs. Milone (Lynda Scarlino) monitors the school hallways and disciplines Chris whether or not he breaks school rules. Principal Edwards (Jason Alexander is perhaps best known as George Constanza on *Seinfeld* on NBC, 1990–98), gets Chris to confront the school bully in "Everybody Hates the Buddy System" and, in the episode "Everybody Hates Snow Day," the principal and Chris spend the day together when he's the only student to show up for school. In addition to narrating the series he has created, Chris Rock also appears as Mr. Abbott, a guidance counselor who is less helpful than one would hope. The premise of *How I Met Your Mother* (CBS, 2005–), a father in 2030 explaining to his two kids how he met their mother, is a novel idea. The show features a group of friends in their late twenties and early thirties who are all looking for love and includes Ted Moseby (Josh Radnor), Marshall Eriksen (Jason Segal), and Lily Aldrin (Alyson Hannigan), who share an apartment. School teacher Lily and Marshall marry during the second season while Ted continues his search for his future children's mother.

2006

Sitcoms remained popular in 2006 when five of them relevant to this survey were introduced. *Just for Kicks*, *Teachers*, *Twenty Good Years*, *'Til Death*, and *The Class*. Another in a long line of series featuring coach characters, *Just for Kicks* (Nickelodeon, 2006–) centers on a multicultural girls' soccer team at elite Brookwell prep school in New York City, and the team coach is Brit Leslie Moore (Craig Robert Young). Lasting just over a month, *Teachers* (NBC, 2006–06) focuses mainly on the personal lives of teachers at New Jersey's Filmore High School even though the teacher's lounge is the main set. Justin Bartha stars as Jeff Cahill, an English teacher who cultivates a veneer of cynicism and pretends to be slack on the job while actually feeling some passion for the profession and demonstrating a level of proficiency. Jeff's best friend is drama teacher Calvin Babbitt (Deon Richmond), and he has a crush on history teacher Alice Fletcher (Sarah Alexander), who is British, until sexy substitute Tina Torres (Sarah Shahi) arrives on the scene. Other cast members include biology teacher Dick Green (Phil Hendrie) and wimpy principal Emma Wiggins (Kali Rocha). *Twenty Good Years* (NBC, 2006–06) focuses on two long-time friends who plan to make the most of their retirement. John Lithgow plays Dr. John Mason, whose daughter Stella (Heather Burns) is a grade school teacher who has decided to become a mother with the aid of a sperm bank. Jeffrey Tambor plays Mason's friend, Judge Jeffrey Pyne. Ostensibly a comedy comparing the married lives of two couples, *'Til Death* (FOX 2006–) makes great use of Winston Churchill High School in Abbington, Pennsylvania where the two husbands work. Eddie Stark (Brad Garrett) is a crusty, cynical history teacher married to Joy Stark (Joely Fisher, a regular on *Ellen*, ABC, 1994–98), a travel agent. Their neighbor Jeff Woodcock (Eddie Kaye Thomas) is vice principal at the high school and is enjoying wedded bliss with his new bride, Steph Woodcock (Kat Foster), who is working on a Ph.D. in European history. The contrast between the two couples—one seasoned and bickering and the other new and gushy—is echoed in the contrast between the two friends who carpool together and talk in the teacher's lounge. *The Class* (CBS, 2006–07) focuses on Dr. Ethan Haas (Jason Ritter), who throws a reunion party for members of his third-grade class (from 1986). When Ethan's fiancée dumps him at the party, he embarks on a series of dramatic situations with the assorted former classmates, including gay Kyle Lendo (Sean Maguire), a first-grade teacher at a private school.

Dramas are the second most popular genre featuring teachers in 2006. *Friday Night Lights*, *The Bedford Diaries*, and the war drama, *Jericho* all make their debut this year. Loved by critics and a small, but devoted fan base, *Friday Night Lights* (NBC, 2006–) is based on the 1990 book and 2004 feature film of the same name. Set in rural Dillon, Texas where football still reigns supreme, the Taylor family—Coach Eric Taylor (Kyle Chandler), guidance counselor Tami Taylor (Connie Britton), and teenage daughter Julie (Aimee Teegarden)—anchor the series. The adults provide a caring but no-nonsense approach to helping the students at Dillon High School sort through assorted obstacles on the field, in the classroom, and at their homes. Several additional teacher characters were added in the second season, notably Noah Barnett (Austin Nichols), Julie's writing teacher, who gets a little too friendly with her to suit Tami. As we go to press, it has been announced that the series will return for a short third season. Filmed at Barnard College, *The Bedford Diaries* (WB, 2006–06) was a short-lived show focused on a seminar course called Sexual Behavior in the Human Condition taught by Professor Jake Macklin (Matthew Modine) at Bedford College in Manhattan. Students are given video cameras to record their life experiences. While the professor sees all tapes, the students can decide which of their tapes will be made available to other classmates. Other faculty include Professor Sean Dixon (Paul Fitzgerald), a married man involved with

Figure 7.1. (left to right) Connie Britton as Tami Taylor, Kyle Chandler as Eric Taylor, and Aimee Teegarden as Julie Taylor in *Friday Night Lights* (NBC, 2006–). Photo courtesy of Photofest. Used by permission.

one of his students, and Professor Carla Bonatella (Audra McDonald), who is charged with dealing with Dixon in her capacity as Chair of the Ethics Committee at the college. *Jericho* (CBS, 2006–) is set in the aftermath of a nuclear attack that leaves residents of rural Jericho, Kansas to fend for themselves. One of the series regulars, Emily Sullivan (Ashley Scott), is a teacher.

Two documentaries, *Cheerleader Nation* (Lifetime, 2006–06) and *Two-a-days* (MTV, 2006–), feature coaches. One sports competition show *Knight School* (ESPN, 2006–06)—featuring one of the most colorful and controversial sports figures of all time, basketball coach Bobby Knight—put 16 high school students through their paces over six episodes as they tried to earn a chance to play for his Texas Tech Red Raiders. Clearly, 2006 was a boom year for coaches on television.

Two series present other types of teacher characters. The animated *Class of 3000* (Cartoon Network, 2006–) features hip-hop star André Benjamin, better known as André 3000 of the duo Outkast. Benjamin voices the character Sunny Bridges, a music star tired of the competitive music scene and ready to return to a simpler life in Atlanta, Georgia. Once there, a young fan talks him into becoming the music teacher at Westley School of Performing Arts. Finally, the popular science fiction show *Heroes* (NBC, 2006–) features Mohinder Suresh (Sendhil Ramamurthy) as a genetics professor from Madras, India, who is trying to assemble a collection of people with special powers that may have been given to them to help avert a disaster that threatens the world.

2007

The increasing profile of quiz shows and so-called reality shows—as a result of the economic realities imposed by lower ratings for television, lower production costs for these shows, and uncertainties caused by guild strikes—can be noted in a survey of teachers on TV in 2007. On a set, designed to look like a classroom, actual teachers compete on the quiz show *Are You Smarter Than a 5th Grader?* (FOX, 2007–) It is worth noting, as the fine print at the end of episodes reveals, that the students have an advantage because they are given study materials about the subjects before taping. On *Flavor of Love Girls: Charm School* (VH1, 2007-), thirteen contestants move into an ivy-covered mansion dubbed the "Charm School" to compete under the supervision of headmistress Mo'Nique for a $50,000 prize and the title "Charm School Queen." It might be a little dubious to call actress and comic Mo'Nique a teacher, but she does function in that category—at least in a broad sense—on this series.

The other four series launched in 2007 are more conventional venues for teachers in primetime. The sitcom *Notes from the Underbelly* (ABC, 2007–) is based on a novel of the same title by Risa Green. Lauren (Jennifer Westfeldt) and her husband Andrew (Peter Cambor) are expecting a baby, and while most of the storylines focus on their relationship and the impending pregnancy, several episodes do focus on her job as a high school guidance counselor. Specifically, in "Million Dollar Baby," Lauren questions whether or not she should continue to work, and in "Oleander," her "pregnancy breasts" attract the attention of some of the students she counsels. Two dramas also premiered in 2007. Educator characters on the drama *Lincoln Heights* (ABC Family, 2007–) include Principal Jeffers (Gary Carlos Cervantes) and Vice Principal Omar Caffey (Terrell Tilford). The drama/melodrama *October Road* (ABC, 2007–) features successful novelist Nick Garrett (Bryan Greenberg), who has returned to his hometown, Knights Ridge, Massachusetts, to teach at local Dufresne College. The sitcom *Aliens in America* (CW, 2007–) mainly focuses on high school student Justin (Dan Byrd) and the Pakistani exchange student living in his home, Raja (Adhir Kalyan), but principal Mr. Matthews (Christopher B. Duncan) also makes appearances at school. There isn't much character development of this African American administrator who is almost—but not quite—a jerk.

2008

One of the most recent television shows with a teacher as the central character is the dark revisionist series *Breaking Bad* (AMC, 2008–). Despite the black comedy that erupts on the series, there is a complexity to the characterization of high school chemistry teacher Walter White (Bryan Cranston, best known as the bumbling father on *Malcolm in the Middle*) that rivals Dan Dunne (Ryan Gosling) in the 2006 independent film *Half Nelson*. In that feature, Dunne is a gifted teacher with a vision for social justice who is hampered by his addiction to drugs while in the television show, White discovers he has terminal cancer and decides to put his chemistry skills to work cooking meth to make money that he can leave to his pregnant wife and their teenage son, who has cerebral palsy. In the classroom, White seems passionate about his subject and eager to engage students with classroom experiments. Watching him deal with the realities of low teacher pay and a growing family by working a part time job at a car wash that demeans him is painful. Watching him face his imminent death when his family gives him so much to live for is tragic. It is unclear at the time of this writing whether or not *Breaking Bad* will return for a second season. Tim Goodman points out that the surprising thing is that the show, which was originally developed by FX, aired at all on American Movie Classics. There was some concern about the show because the subject matter is so dark. Some wondered whether anyone would want to advertise on a show that features a high school teacher making drugs in his underwear in a trailer in the desert. In its quest to enter the arena of original dramas, AMC apparently overcame any trepidation it may have (Goodman). Whatever the future holds for *Breaking Bad*, Walter White is surely one of the most indelible and complex teacher characters to appear on television.

In March 2008, *Miss/Guided* (ABC, 2008–) debuted. Becky Freeley (Judy Greer, Kitty Sanchez in *Arrested Development*, FOX 2003–06) returns to her old high school as a guidance counselor. High school was awkward for her, which makes her sensitive to her troubled students. She is attracted to hunky mechanic-turned-Spanish teacher Tim (Kristoffer Polaha). Just as things are falling into place for her at work, Becky's high school nemesis Lisa Germain (Brooke Burns) is hired as an English teacher, which causes Brooke to relive some high school traumas and compete for Tim's attention. Executive producer Ashton Kutcher (best known as Michael Kelso on *That '70s Show*, FOX, 1998–2006) appears in the pilot episode as a guest star playing a gorgeous, cool substitute teacher who temporarily turns Becky's head, but he is exposed as a fraud who does not have a college degree. Lisa does not realize this when the two of them leave with him driving her classic Mustang convertible. The series also includes an African American principal (Earl Billings as Principal Huffy), who speaks in a monotone but occasionally makes inappropriate comments to females, and creepy Vice Principal Bruce Terry (Chris Parnell), who seems more like a security officer.

Boston Public

If *Hangin' with Mr. Cooper* lacks authenticity because it softens all the hard edges of life in urban Oakland, *Boston Public* risks sacrificing a certain realism by moving from edgy to quirky in ways that seem too overblown with actors, dialogue, and staging that is more glossy than edgy. Despite these observations, scholars J. Casey Hurley, Alvin C. Proffit, Elizabeth M. Vihnanek, and Gayle Moller argue that the series strikes just the right note. They write:

> At a time when educational policy makers see a need to improve student test scores, this show suggests that other issues are more important in the lives of modern high school students, teachers, and administrators. *BP* does a service to all who care about the education of our youth by exposing this reality gap—the gap between focusing on accountability for student test scores when those who inhabit today's high schools are increasingly embroiled in youth issues that have been ignored by families and communities. (7)

Figure 7.2. (clockwise from top left) Fyvush Finkel as Harvey Lipschultz, Loretta Devine as Marla Hendricks, Anthony Heald as Scott Guber, Bianca Kajlich as Lisa Grier, Joey Slotnick as Milton Buttle, Sharon Leal as Marilyn Sudor, Scott Vickaryous as Daniel Evans, Nicky Katt as Harry Senate, Chi McBride as Steven Harper, Jessalyn Gilsig as Lauren Davis in *Boston Public* (FOX, 2000–04). Photo courtesy of Photofest. Used by permission.

These researchers might well be on to something in terms of the depiction of youth issues and the people who must manage them. In *Daily Variety*, Pamela McClintock cites a study by the Partnership for Trust in Government that said teachers were portrayed more negatively than any other government-related occupation during the 1998–2001 television seasons. The study made special mention of *Boston Public* and concludes that "the complexity and sophistication" of the show could be one reason why the favorable rating of teachers had declined because the series "portrays teachers as human beings with failings, as opposed to vessels of perfection" (27). In this case, a negative rating of teachers certainly reflects the difficulty and dissatisfaction confronting teachers daily at *Boston Public*'s Winslow High School.

Quirky might be a benign way to describe some of the truly bizarre storylines incorporated into *Boston Public* (FOX, 2000–04),[3] and imposing principal, Steven Harper (Chi McBride) is the man charged with trying to ride herd over the "loopy troops," as Mike Flaherty calls the cast in an *Entertainment Weekly* review titled "Hot for Teachers." Flaherty quotes McBride as describing the Winslow principal thus: "He's like the guy on the old *Ed Sullivan Show* spinning the plates on the sticks. There's no time to say, 'Oh, I gotta get this one spinning real good,' because the rest of them are going to be on the ground in pieces." Against the odds, he keeps the plates spinning more often than not. It would be difficult to overstate the sorts of challenges Harper faces, and a litany of some of the various storylines explored on *Boston Public* seems almost outlandish. Clearly, this administrator spends his days putting out fires instead of pushing papers. Over the course of the series, Harper has to deal with multiple lawsuits and uprisings of students and faculty. He calls the FBI on a student who accesses a terrorist recruitment web site from the school library; he decides to allow a gay student to compete for the prom queen's crown despite the opposition of some students; he wants a straight-A student transferred to a continuation school because of her pregnancy, even though a teacher tries to help her get into Princeton; and he cancels a cheerleading competition after judging the routine to be too sexual. He fires teachers for their involvement with students, intercedes in a hostage situation before the SWAT team arrives, and tries to protect teacher jobs by cancelling athletic programs. In one case, his job is threatened by the school board and superintendent, and in another, he is jailed on manslaughter charges. Sometimes he has to deal with issues closer to home, such as when his daughter gets involved with illegal drugs and inappropriate men while trying to get her parents to reconcile. In even more personal issues, Harper dates a teacher in his employ, and another asks him to donate sperm for her in vitro fertilization. Finally, Harper is even faced with having to deal with death when his close friend and a popular teacher, Mr.

McMahon, dies, and when a former student has dies while on military duty in Iraq.

Steven is very supportive of his teachers. He supports Harry after he fires a gun, supports Marla after she leaves her class, and supports Lauren after she teaches about cannibalism. He gives the superintendent Marsha Shinn (Debbi Morgan) a reason to cite him as a poor example and bring him before the school board for possible firing in "Chapter Three." Steven defends his teachers:

> Harry Senate was wrong to fire a gun in his classroom. Marla Hendricks is frustrated. Show me a faculty member who isn't, and I'd question his or her commitment. The reason I didn't fire Marla Hendricks, the reason I didn't fire Harry Senate: they're gifted teachers. Lauren Davis allows her class to digress into cannibalism because she saw a spark. What Marsha Shinn left out when she went into Lauren's class, she saw a room full of students participating, engaged. When Harry Senate fired off that gun, I know the motivation behind it, and he will get to those kids even if he has to do it one by one, he'll do it. He'll break through to each and every one of them. Those people over there, they're teachers. It's in their hearts. You think they're easy to find? Here's a flash. Kids don't go to college today wanting to become high school faculty members, not when they can make over a million dollars on Wall Street. The top salary for a teacher is under $50,000. Over half the people who get into our profession quit within the first five years, either because it isn't in them or because they can't continue to keep it in them. Those people sitting there, it's in them. I've seen it. They're teachers, and when a school is lucky enough to get people like that, you don't let go. You live through their mistakes. You get in their faces. You stand in front of them. Tonight I stand behind them. I may have made my mistakes, but keeping Harry Senate isn't one of them. You want to get rid of me, do it, but don't you be touching them.

Scott stands up and says that if they get rid of Steven, he'll resign. Coach Kevin Riley (Thomas McCarthy) stands, then Lauren Davis (Jessalyn Gilsig), then Milton Buttle (Joey Slotnick), then Marla Hendricks (Loretta Devine), and they all say that they will leave if Steven is fired. Harry Senate (Nicky Katt) stands and says, "I'll stay forever." The school board chair says the board will not be held hostage, but the meeting was to address concerns, which have now been addressed. The meeting is adjourned with Steven still intact as principal of Winslow High.

Boston Public was abruptly pulled from the schedule before completing its final season, or Harper might have faced even more dramatic dilemmas. He is not perfect. Sometimes he errs in judgment, and sometimes he loses his cool, but more often than not this principal is a solid citizen and functions as the glue that holds everything at Winslow High School together if just barely. He is also a straight-talker who deals as openly as he is able with issues including, but not limited to, race. Steven Harper is African American, but his racial identity is neither ignored nor dwelled upon in the series. This is one way in which the smoothly produced series gains some authenticity.

To frame our discussion of *Boston Public* as a multicultural text that transcends Steven Harper's towering stature, signature circle moustache, and direct way of dealing with a myriad of issues, we want to draw on Douglas Kellner's approach to critical cultural studies. For Kellner, critical media studies is "not merely interested in providing clever readings of cultural texts" but also "interested in advancing a critique of structures and practices of domination and advancing forces of resistance struggling for a more democratic and egalitarian society" (95). Kellner advocates interrogating texts with attention to what is included as well as what is left out and employing a wide range of critical perspectives to understand and interpret cultural phenomena because "gender, race, class, and other key cultural constructs are interconnected and reproduced in cultural forms and representations" (97). His general approach to analyzing texts—with attention to these constructs and using various theoretical frameworks to explicate them—has shaped the way we have viewed all of the series considered in depth thus far and influenced our topical explorations of gender, race, social class, meritocracy, and sexual orientation. Now we will look again at many of these constructs as well as others that emerge under the larger rubric of multiculturalism in *Boston Public*. Rather than arrange this analysis by issue, and many of the storylines of the series do include an "issue of the week" structure, we will look at some of the central educator characters and examine how these teachers and administrators both reveal and interact with significant cultural issues over time.

Lauren Davis. The episodes of *Boston Public* are presented as chapters rather than episodes, and History Department Chair Lauren Davis (Jessalyn Gilsig) is one of the main characters introduced in "Chapter One" and remains important to the series for the first two seasons.[4] The first time we see her, she wears a nondescript outfit comprised of a white blouse and brown slacks. Her long, light brown hair is pulled back into a ponytail, but she looks pretty. It is hard to tell from the outset whether or not Davis will be another in a long line of women teachers who must deny their sexuality to uphold some outmoded ideal repeated endlessly in films and on television. In "Chapter One," Lauren encounters student Dana Poole (Sarah Thompson) in the hallway after she has been ejected from class for not wearing a bra. During their exchange, the student says, "I like you as a teacher and stuff, but are you a nun on weekends?" Davis is clearly uncomfortable and mumbles, "I'm not a nun." It's hard to tell, however, just how the wholesome-looking teacher does spend her weekends so early in the series. When straitlaced vice principal Scott Guber (Anthony Heald) asks her to join him on a date to hear the Boston Philharmonic, she looks like a deer trapped in headlights. It's clear that she does not want to go, but it will be several chapters before viewers will know whether Lauren's objection is to dating in general or dating Scott in particular.

It turns out that Lauren can let her hair down with the right partner. She shares a kiss with colleague Harry Senate in "Chapter Six" that is captured on video by a student and posted on the student's web site. In the next episode they discuss the video and accompanying gossip, and Harry reassures her, "It shows that I'm attracted to a grown-up and you're not a nun." They decide to date exclusively, and by "Chapter Ten," there are two scenes of them in bed, which adds a greatly missed look at the private life of a woman teacher in popular culture. In the first such scene, they are stretched out talking during the day, and in the second they are getting ready to go to sleep (or to make love) when he says "I think I'm starting to love you." Although their relationship is not lasting (he has dated another teacher before her and will date yet another after), there is nothing inherently unhealthy about their relationship. Lauren is not so lucky in her interactions with a student and a former student, however. In "Chapter Four," a disturbed student, John LeBlonde (Travis Wester) tells Lauren he's in love with her. He's academically gifted but filled with anxiety and depressed after losing an academic award he thought should have been awarded to him. At the end of the episode, he takes a drug overdose and dies.

Unlike the commonplace storyline in which a student gets a "harmless" crush on a teacher, there is nothing innocent about this situation, and the students at Winslow High School are presented as sexual beings whose interactions are not limited to their peers. Lauren confides in Harry, "Sometimes I feel so clueless about how to do this job," and this is just the beginning. Lauren and Harry break up in "Chapter Sixteen," and three episodes later she encounters former student, Daniel Evans (Scott Vickaryous) when her car breaks down. The failure of her old car is an indication of the constraints on her finances. He shows her a history textbook he's written, invites her out for a drink, and they spend the night together at her place. Two episodes later, when she finds out Daniel is stalking her, she buys a gun. In "Chapter 22," Lauren brings the loaded gun to campus and draws it on someone. When Principal Harper confronts her, she tells him that she's being stalked but goes on to say that most teachers are scared. "We're all a little more fragile than we used to be, Steven." Harper is not unsympathetic, but he does tell her that the odds of a teacher being attacked are very slim and suspends her for two months. When Lauren tells him that she wants a hearing, he fixes his gaze on her and lets her know that a hearing will make her situation worse.

Ongoing storylines make Lauren question her own attitudes about race: she protects colleague Harvey Lipschultz (Fyvush Finkel), hires three White teachers in a row into the history department, has higher test scores for White students, does not change a Black football player's grade but does change a White hockey player's grade, insists that a Black student who spits on her be expelled while a White student who hits her with a breast implant is not expelled, and seems to have discipline problems with Black students. Steven points these things out to Lauren. Later, Harry asks Steven about calling Lauren a racist.

Steven:	I did no such thing. I simply asked the question.
Harry:	Why you even do that?
Steven:	Harry, when there's a conflict between two people and one of them's White and the other one's Black, there's always that question.

Later, Lauren and Harry sit on the steps inside the school. He asks if she's wondering if she's a bigot, and she replies that she's just gone through all her test scores and is questioning herself.

Character arcs like Lauren's, presented in an overarching narrative context that treats complex issues as ongoing, are a welcome relief from simplistic stories where issues are either ignored or neatly resolved at the end of an episode. Lauren has a good relationship for awhile with Harry, a misfire with Daniel, and she avoids becoming involved with Scott. While one might read the stalking incident with Daniel as punishment for engaging in a sexual relationship, we prefer to focus on Lauren's relationship with Harry. It may not be the Hollywood happily ever after ending some viewers prefer, but it is a companionable relationship while it lasts and remains friendly after Lauren and Harry break up; they sit together at graduation in the season's final episode. Just as Lauren must grapple with her attitudes about race, she must express her sexuality to try to find a suitable partner, and she must acknowledge when she can't get a loan (in "Chapter Eleven") for her "dream house" that she has chosen a profession that does not pay well. These are not situations and issues with easy solutions, and rather than simplify them, *Boston Public* presents them as the complicated issues they are.

Harvey Lipschultz.
Harvey Lipschultz (Fyvush Finkel) is an 80-year-old American history teacher who is constantly being accused of racism and sexism. Eventually, it is revealed (to the audience and to Harvey) that he fathered a son from a brief encounter with a Black woman years before, and the widower has a hard time overcoming his loneliness to join them at Christmas

because he is an observant Jew. Although his age is an issue in a few episodes, and he also makes an inept attempt to get the football team to accept a team-mate who may be gay by making a link between the fact that Jackie Robinson improved the Brooklyn Dodgers and homosexuals may improve football if a "team of courage" invites them to play. He urges the team to "welcome the gay linebacker into your shower." Harvey actually means well, but he incites students in various ways and, in "Chapter Eight," almost dies after a student drops Ecstasy in his coffee. He is often unreasonable and intractable. Antici-pating a hearing over his racism in "Chapter Eight," Lauren advises Harvey to bring a union representative. Harvey asks Lauren, "I know I'm old-fashioned, but am I a racist?" Before she can answer, Marla Hendricks (Loretta Devine) replies, "Yes, you are an old-fashioned racist." Harvey continues that he doesn't notice students' skin color, and Marla later shows up at the hearing to argue that Harvey's bigotry doesn't come from hate. That is not, however, the final word. Steven points out that intent may not matter because bigotry fosters hate in any case. Marla will continue to call Harvey on things he says and does in subsequent episodes.

Scott Guber. Vice Principal Scott Guber (Anthony Heald) is unlucky in love and has sequential crushes on female teachers who are uncomfortable with his attention. He is passionate about classical music and conducts recorded music in his office when he gets upset and needs to unwind. While he is frequently the butt of student jokes, he wins an award at the graduation ceremony at the end of the first season and is nearly overcome with emotion at being recognized in a positive way, "I'm overwhelmed. This is wonderful. I'm overwhelmed." It is an interesting dramatic choice to have this socially awkward man who appears formal if not uptight take a firm stand for gay rights in "Chapter 58." Scott comes across a swim team hazing incident in the locker room before Trevor James (Richard Keith) is seriously injured. No one is around to protect Trevor when he is attacked in the parking lot that night, and police tell Scott and Steven that the student will not name his attackers. When Scott asks Steven, "Who do you think he's trying to protect?" the principal replies, "Maybe him-self." Scott holds himself responsible for not protecting Trevor and tells Steven he wants to start a Gay-Straight Alliance at Winslow and serve as faculty sponsor. The principal expects controversy but backs his assistant.

At the first meeting, only two students show up. Their only question of Scott is "Are you gay?" A half dozen or so parents show up to complain. Scott tells them that only two students showed up, "So go home. The world will stay unchanged, as you like it." When he turns on his heel and leaves, a parent says, "Is he gay?" Scott shows up at the hospital and finds the blinds drawn to Trevor's room. He walks in and finds Trevor holding hands with his teammate Devin Rickman (Matt Lutz). It turns out that Devin was there and watched while the others assaulted Trevor. In the hospital hallway, Devin tells the vice principal that he can't tell because then the other swimmers will find out that he is gay and that it would kill his parents. Scott tells him that not telling will be what ruins his life. What follows is a montage of Scott going class to class making a pitch for tolerance. He tells the students that ever since he proposed the alliance, everyone wants to know whether or not he's gay. "It's not about who you are," the vice principal tells them. "It's about who you have the right to be. Yourselves." He reminds the students that they are living in an atmosphere of fear and that is "the true hate crime." His pitch ends with the next meeting time of the Winslow Gay-Straight Alliance.

Later, at the next meeting, it appears that only the same two students from the first meeting are attending. The boy claims a dental appointment and leaves. The girl pops her gum. Then, one by one, students file in and take seats. It's a diverse group. Finally, Devin walks in and Scott addresses him: "Mr. Rickman, would you like to start this meeting?" Devin nods. Only on television would events unfold so conveniently! At the end of the episode, Steven comes to the office to tell Scott that all of the assailants have been identified, which wouldn't have happened if the vice principal had not gotten involved. The episode presents the relationship between Trevor and Devin in a non-judgmental, matter-of-fact way, which is in direct contrast to the actions of the other swimmers who participate in the hate crime. The fact that Scott is the champion of gay rights is a more powerful statement on *Boston Public* than if one of the more typically heroic, progressive teacher characters had sponsored the alliance.

Marla Hendricks. In the premiere episode of the series, Marla Hendricks (Loretta Devine) leaves her classroom with the note on the board "Gone home to kill myself, hope you're happy." When Steven finds her, he is not able to calm her down immediately. "They don't want to learn" she says. "They don't want to listen. I'm no parole officer. You got that? I'm a teacher. People don't respect me. I'm a teacher for god's sake." She walks away from Steven then, but eventually he is able to get her to go back on her anti-depressants. She is reluctant because she says she can't feel when she's on the medication. "What good is a teacher who can't feel?" Steven puts her on medical leave and says he'll have to fire her if she does not get help and go back on her pills. Marla is a substantially built African American woman who calls it like she sees it and delivers her verdicts in great one liners. She is frequently the character who charges racism or size-ism. Marla can seem unyielding at times, but she is ultimately a generous spirit.

Disappointed in romance and periodically struggling with her meds, Marla decides to try in vitro fertilization and asks Steven to donate sperm in "Chapter 73." Harvey turns the tables on Marla and lands a choice retort in the teacher's lounge when she announces that she's off her meds and will be more emotional while trying to get pregnant. Harvey replies, "More emotional? Will you be breathing fire?" Her experience in the waiting room at the fertility clinic is poignant. All of the other women have male partners with them. When she does get to see the doctor, Marla is reminded that she is 42, that there is a risk to the baby, and that the attempt will cost $12,000. She has already discussed with friends that she's going to have to make financial sacrifices for the procedure, but she is not prepared when the doctor tells her to be prepared to try up to six times to get pregnant. Steven finally declines Marla's request that he give her a sperm sample, and it appears that Marla has given up on her plans. That's the appearance, but in "Chapter 79," Marla miscarries and then decides to take in one of her students, a "goth" girl named Rainy Murphy (Natasha Melnick) who has been kicked out of her foster home. This storyline emerges near the abrupt end of the series, so it is difficult to project how the plot might have played out, but the implication is that families come in all shapes and sizes and by a design that is not always easily discernible. Rainy is White and has not had an easy time of things; Marla is Black and has endured her own set of challenges. These two could not look less like mother and daughter, but together they fill in gaps in one another's lives and seem poised to build a mutually sustaining family.

Harry Senate. When Harry Senate (Nicky Katt) is called to take over Marla's class in "Chapter One" after she walks out of "the dungeon" (where the most difficult students are housed), he is wearing a gun. The students get quiet right away. Harry asks them if they are quiet because they respect the gun. He shoots the gun, which has blanks, and the students hit the floor. Harry tells them to stay there until he says they can get up. Harper describes him as "a zealous teacher, who is overzealous on occasion." Harry is a complex character—moody, unorthodox, but unquestionably dedicated to teaching. He is blackmailed by student Dana Poole because they once shared a kiss. In "Chapter Seven," a student asks him to be faculty sponsor of a student NRA group as a result of the gun incident, and Harry speaks against the group while pretending to support their cause at the first meeting. This teacher really listens to his students, and they respond to him. When one student talks about how he thinks a lot about death, Harry takes the student to visit a friend of his who works at a morgue, and the student gets a part time job working there. Later he lets another student teach the class as a way to get him back in school. Of all of the teachers introduced in the first season of the series, Harry is probably the most outrageous, but he is left to practice his unorthodox pedagogy.

Ronnie Cooke. The first episode of the second season introduces corporate attorney Ronnie Cooke (Jeri Ryan), a college friend of Harry's, who comes to guest lecture in his class. Her day starts with a blaring alarm in her upscale apartment. The camera pulls back to reveal a handsome man in her bed, who joins her in the shower. It turns out that he is her "former" boyfriend and a colleague at her law firm. She wears elegant, white clothes that suit her lean body and complement her long, blonde locks. Scott can hardly take his eyes off her when she arrives at the school, and Ronnie looks like she belongs in a fashion magazine rather than a Boston public high school. Once in Harry's class, a student asks to see her breasts—she handles the inquiry deftly—and she is transfixed when a fight breaks out and Harry dashes in to break up the fight. Seeing how Harry handles the situation and hearing a parent come in to thank him for "saving his son's life" over a gang connection, impresses her. She tells him, "You used to laugh more, Harry. You used to laugh all the time." When he talks about how the job gets to him, she advises him to get help, but she is hooked. When she tells the ex-boyfriend—who is still hanging around—that she's thinking of quitting her job and teaching he can't believe that she'll throw away a six figure job to become a "minimum wage babysitter." Still, by the end of the episode, Ronnie shows up in Steven's office and says, "I want to be a teacher." Like Harry, she begins to get personally involved with her students and goes to great lengths in "Chapter 37" to help a homeless student and her mother. She has written a personal check to give them shelter and keep the girl from being sent to a foster home. In "Chapter 52," she begins a relationship with colleague Zach Fischer (Jon Abrahams) after he walks in her empty classroom and says that he wants to have sex with her within the next 24 hours. Though they have difficulty finding a spot for their rendezvous, they eventually have a passionate interlude at the empty school, but the relationship soon fizzles. A story arc begins in "Chapter 59" that will take Ronnie from the classroom to the front office as a second assistant principal for academics, and she will receive a lot of credit (and publicity) for raising test scores. When renegade art teacher Henry Preston (Phil Buckman) arrives on the scene in "Chapter 78," it is suggested that a romance might ensue between him and Ronnie, but the series ended before that storyline could develop. While Ronnie's character never feels as authentic on screen as Lauren's, she is an important character in the history of the gendered teacher in popular culture because she is able to express her sexuality without negative repercussions.

Danny Hanson. If Ronnie's character lacks some of the authenticity of the teachers introduced in the earlier episodes of the series, Danny Hanson (Michael Rapaport, who went on to star in *The War at Home*, FOX, 2005–) is remarkably—and sometimes infuriatingly—real. Part of the success of the character can be attributed to the writing, but much of that success must be credited to the outstanding performance of Michael Rapaport. Hanson has a confrontational style with students, colleagues, and administrators, yet he is completely guileless. When a student brings up masturbation in class, he says that "Guys do it all the time. Always have. Always will." But, when the student who initiated the conversations says that her boyfriend is thinking about one of their classmates when he masturbates, Danny cannot leave well enough alone. "I've thought about some of your nasty little classmates." When Marla is asked by a group of students to be the advisor to the "Fat Girls Club," something she is not happy about, he tells her to "get those tubs on a treadmill," if she wants to be a role model to the girls. Over time, he matures and advises the student television station, works well with a 12-year-old student who has skipped middle school, and gets married to provide a better home for his niece when his sister's addiction problems get out of control. In "Chapter 52," he helps a student, Joe Coolege (Jake Richardson), who has been molested, by revealing that he, too, was molested by the parish priest. After Joe tries to commit suicide and Danny starts drinking heavily and missing some classes, he admits to Steven what happened in his past and finds the strength to press charges against his molester.

Given his propensity for finding conflict and intensifying it, Danny can't stay out of a student fight over the "n word" in "Chapter 37." Before class, students Jordan Murphy (Stuart Stone) and J.T. (DeJuan Guy) are calling one another "nigga." Because Jordan is White, Andre (Aldis Hodge), who is Black, gets angry. Danny walks in just before a fight breaks out and decides to push back midterms so the class can talk about the situation. They talk about music, specifically rappers, and many students of color say it is all right for Black people to use the n-word but not for White people, though some students believe no one should use it. Danny suggests that if a word has so much power that it can make people want to fight then maybe they should all use it and take away its power. Danny uses the word "nigger," and Andre tells him that he doesn't like it when the teacher uses that word. Danny says they should all read

Randall Kennedy's book *Nigger: The Strange Career of a Troublesome Word*, and he uses a Chris Rock video in class to raise questions about who can use the word. When Marla sees the book, she is not happy about its title and says, "I think I'll take this directly to Steven." When Steven tells Danny that using the offensive word in class "pushes controversy to the point of being irresponsible," Danny says that being a teacher is about asking questions. That question—who can use the word "nigger"—is not acceptable to Steven. When Danny checks with his union representative (Troy Ruptash), he is told that if Danny is fired for using that word, that his firing will be upheld whatever the context because "Schools come down to politics." The representative advises Danny to choose something lighter "like the death penalty."

The next day, Danny fully intends to give the midterm and move on, but the students have read the book he gave them and want to discuss it. Andre offers that Professor Kennedy has it right that when Whites say it, it is oppressive, but Blacks take away the power of the word when they say it. Later, Steven is talking with Marilyn Sudor (Sharon Leal) and Marla about whether or not he should fire Danny. As *Boston Public* conveys so often—and generally so well—there are no easy answers to complex problems. Marilyn says Danny should not be fired because she thinks the word should be explored. Marla thinks he should be fired: "The word need to go and so does Danny Hanson for using it." Meanwhile, the students have signed a petition to try to keep Danny from being fired, and Steven's daughter Brooke (China Shavers), a student in the class, brings it to him with her own signature on it. Finally, Steven calls Danny in and tells him that he doesn't like the word nigger used in any context because it's too powerful. Danny tells the principal to read the book, and Steven says he does not need to read the book. "Do you really think you understand the word nigger, Danny?" he asks. "Do you really think you get it?" Steven ultimately resolves the situation by keeping Danny on staff but taking over the class himself that day for the discussion of the book.

Other Teachers. Certainly, there are other teachers on the faculty of Winslow High School. The school music teacher Marilyn Sudor (Sharon Leal), who finishes number one in the poll of which teacher the male students want to sleep with in "Chapter One." She dates a couple of teachers but ultimately ends up with Steven by the end of the series. She is continually trying to counsel students and consistently gets more involved in their personal lives than most of the other teachers. She is stunningly pretty but reticent. Even after they are dating, Steven does not know her political affiliation until a situation comes up at school involving affirmative action. Coach Kevin Riley is one of the teachers who wants to go out with Marilyn, but they decide to hold off to avoid hurting Marla, who mistakenly thought he wanted to date her. He is a kind person who tries to protect a gay football player from exposure so he won't lose a scholarship to Boston College (a Jesuit school), and he tries to help an overweight female student get some positive attention by joining the wrestling team and successfully competing. Another coach, Derek Williams (Boris Kodjoe) does go out with Marilyn, but he leaves the school (and the show) almost as soon as he appears in "Chapter 54" because of apparent conflict over recruiting a star basketball player. Williams, who played professional basketball for a time before coaching, takes Marilyn to an expensive restaurant and places their order in French because "I wanted to let you know that I'm more than a jock."

Several teachers have inappropriate affairs: students working for the TV station videotape nerdy (and married) Mr. Schiffer (Michael Monks) having sex with the much more attractive Miss Sofer (Anne Marie Howard) in her classroom; dull English teacher Milton Buttle dates the school secretary briefly but meets the college student of his dreams in "Chapter Nine" and continues to have sex with her even after learning that she's a high school student; and, English teacher Colin Flynn (Joey McIntyre) has an affair with a student's mother (played by Anne Archer). As in real life, some of these teachers lose their jobs, and some of them do not. In any case, the sexuality of teachers (and of students, for that matter) is explored on the series rather than facing artificial constraints.

Other teachers have other issues. Charlie Bixby (Dennis Miller) is an investment banker convicted of securities fraud who avoids jail by agreeing to teach. Scott refers to Charlie as "smug, sexist, appalling," which seems pretty accurate. Carmen Torres (Natalia Baron) gets so involved with a student who is struggling with addiction that she misses class and feels that she might fall off the wagon. Carmen meets with her sponsor. He reminds Carmen that teaching is her dream and that she cannot choose for this student but can lead her in the right direction. The rest is up to the student. Finally, Carmen tells Jenn Cardell (Lyndsy Fonseca) that she is a recovering alcoholic and that even though Jenn's lifestyle feels great now that she will end up broken and alone if Jenn stays on the path she is following. Carmen says that she is living proof anyone can start over but that she is letting go of Jenn now to save herself. It is unusual among teacher narratives for a teacher to make that kind of statement and to "let go." This is another example of the complexity of some of the storylines employed in *Boston Public*.

Conclusion

We want to close this chapter with a discussion of "Chapter 78" as an exemplar of how *Boston Public* provides a space for the interrogation of issues without giving clear indications of "right" and "wrong" except in clear-cut cases such as the episodes that feature the battery of a gay student on the swim team or the molestation of a student by his parish priest. By providing a public discursive space where characters can explore issues from various perspectives and viewers can follow along, *Boston Public* functions as an example of just how far television has come to present educators as human rather than heroic and positioning them in a multicultural landscape where life is not always harmonious, but it is honest. In this episode, teachers deal with divergent student (and faculty) views on affirmative action by holding a televised debate for the student body.

The show opens with Alex Buchanan (Taran Killam) holding a bake sale in the hallway to support a group called Winslow Young Conservatives. Alex, a White student, is selling cookies to Whites for $1.00, Asians for $.75, Latinos for $.50, and Blacks for $.25. When a Black student, Lawrence Sorrenson (Garikayi Mutambirwa) tries to buy up all the stock and put Alex out of business, a fight breaks out between the two students. Danny breaks up the fight and reminds Lawrence to stay out of trouble, or he will risk his early acceptance to Harvard. Marilyn is the faculty advisor for Alex's group, and when she expresses her anger at him, Alex maintains that he is merely demonstrating the inequities of affirmative action.

In a later conversation, Steven says that affirmative action "levels the playing field." Marilyn brings up that some people would argue that affirmative action is reverse discrimination sanctioned by the government, and Steven replies that there is no such thing as reverse discrimination, which is "a term created by racists." When he asks her view on affirmative action, Marilyn says, "Personally, I'm against it." He asks if she is a Republican, and his surprise is palpable when she replies that she is. Marilyn asks Steven if her party affiliation is a problem (implicitly referring to their dating relationship), and he says, "Not at all." It is not clear to the viewer, however, whether or not this is true.

Later a fight erupts in the hallway. Alex yelling while Lawrence stands by another student he has shackled and chained to the wall in a mock slave auction. While Marilyn characterizes the action as "completely rude and offensive," Danny Hanson says that he told Lawrence to use his head to handle the situation but that this is stupid. Lawrence accuses Alex of pursuing this because Lawrence, who is Black, got into Harvard and Alex, who is White, did not. Alex responds defensively by maintaining that his GPA is higher, and

Lawrence counters that the difference is a tenth of a point. Alex's frustration spills out—his SAT score is higher, he has more extra curricular activities, and he has been rejected because he is White. When Scott points out that he got into Yale, Alex says "So what? So did George W., and the man was a C student. I wanted to go to Harvard, and he took my spot." When she learns that Alex was motivated by jealousy rather than political conviction, Marilyn is disappointed. Steven tells the two students to stop making trouble.

It is not only the students who have a conflict, however. Marla is angry with Marilyn for supporting Alex, "This is either a 'for us' or 'against us' of kind of issue, and it hurts me to say it, girl, but right now you are against us." When Danny brings up the mock slave auction in his class "talk time," the students face off by race. Marilyn and Steven have a bit of a face-off as well. She detects that it makes a difference to him that her views diverge from his on affirmative action. When she asks that they talk it out, he says, "I already know your position." She walks out of his office.

After Scott breaks up a fight in Danny's class, the faculty and administration meet in the teacher's lounge to figure out how to address the situation. Marilyn suggests a workshop. Danny suggests a student debate on Winslow One (the student TV station). Steven determines that a debate is a good idea but that the faculty should be involved. As he puts it, "We need to be role models in this." Danny moderates the debate with Steven and Lawrence on one side while Alex and Marilyn are on the other side. Strong arguments are heard for both positions. Marilyn, who has not been able to articulate her position earlier in the episode, closes with the famous quote by Martin Luther King, Jr. that people should be judged by the "content of their character, not the color of their skin."

This is not how the episode ends, however. In the final scene, Marilyn and Steven are debating various issues over a pitcher of beer. They disagree on some topics and end up tossing pretzels at one another before sharing a kiss. Or, they almost share a kiss. The frame freezes as they each lean in halfway with lips nearly touching. Is this a perfect resolution? No. Some narratives—like some social policies—are better than others, and one could read this ending as a suggestion that meeting halfway and striking a compromise is best. We prefer to read this debate as a starting place. Out of the shouting match arises a forum for open, respectful discussion involving faculty, administration, and students. But, the discussion is not the resolution; it is the process.

At Winslow High School, teachers come and go in a rhythm that approximates real life with some staying for the duration while others are around for an episode or two. What is most distinctive about *Boston Public* among the shows we have studied is that it establishes a collective social space on the small screen that is both multicultural and filled with transformative possibilities. If it does not offer a singular resolution to complex issues, robust discussion at this school does challenge cultural constructs and offers the possibility of systemic changes at Winslow High that will advance the cause of social justice over time.

EIGHT

What About Students and Schools?

In Chapter One, we provided a context for this examination of television narratives featuring teachers by looking at the literature on educators in popular culture. Subsequent chapters have provided a survey of television shows featuring teachers and school administrators from the 1950s to the 2000s and have traced the evolution of Good Teacher characters on television in tandem with relevant cultural issues of each decade, making this book topical as well as chronological. Though some of these TV teachers are engaging and fun (and occasionally inspiring) to watch, these characters have tended toward a degree of predictability and simplicity up until the mid-1990s. When Richard Katimski opened the door of his apartment to reveal his male partner to the viewing audience and to take a homeless student in off the streets in *My So-Called Life*, a metaphorical door was opened in American households to allow a new generation of teachers inside living rooms and bedrooms across the country during the primetime hours. These complex characters, on shows as diverse as *South Park*, *Boston Public*, and *Breaking Bad*, blur the line between the public and private spheres and deal with issues in their work lives and private lives that would never have been confronted openly in previous decades.

But, what about the students TV educators teach and the schools where they work? Just as the teacher characters have grown in complexity over the decades, their students have become more authentic and multi-faceted at the same time their schools have been imbued with a verisimilitude heretofore unseen on television. This final chapter will look beyond the TV teachers to explore more fully the world in which they work, including larger issues related to the depictions of students, administrators, and schools. By the mid-1990s, the medium of television had expanded as a result of cable and satellite options, and the audience had matured at the same time it had become more fragmented—all factors that set the stage for multi-dimensional depictions of teachers, students, and schools.

Two recent programs have presented cultural landscapes that have thrilled critics—even if audiences have remained relatively small—and that speak to issues at two very different types of American schools. The cultural landscape explored on *Friday Night Lights* (NBC, 2006–) is rural and includes the importance of football, dating, and church to students at Dillon High School in the small Texas town of the same name. The cultural landscape explored during the fourth season of *The Wire* (HBO, 2002–08) links an urban middle school in Baltimore and the entrenched problems hampering the school system with similar problems that limit the effectiveness of the police department and City Hall politicians. These two cultural landscapes, one rural and the other urban, are infused with a realistic style that, even if it seems counterintuitive aesthetically, actually magnifies the drama of each episode.

The "issue of the week" approach of dramas or the occasional "very special episode" of select sitcoms featured in earlier decades suggests that problems are isolated rather than systemic and easily solved with more attention. Even the quirky multiculturalism of *Boston Public*, which represents a step forward from earlier school dramas, seems consciously polemical or, at times, didactic in ways that make the series more obviously constructed and less authentic than either *Friday Night Lights* or *The Wire*. On the newer series, it is as if the glossy veneer of *Boston Public* has been stripped away to reveal some of the same issues treated in the earlier series—racism, sexism, poverty, addiction, sexual abuse— but the more recent programs are less about the issues than they are about the systems that produce (or reproduce) these social problems. While *Friday Night Lights* focuses more on school activities outside of the classroom than on a formal curriculum, the second season of the series introduces more teacher characters and launches an implicit examination of Title IX when Tami Taylor begins to coach the women's volleyball team at Dillon High School. While *Friday Night Lights* is appealing and relevant, it is *The Wire* that must be singled out for special consideration. *The Wire* is worth looking at in depth because the series directly addresses the most pressing problems confronting teachers, students, and inner-city public schools in contemporary life and does so with astonishing insight and power. Issues we will examine in greater detail include race and poverty, the culture of testing, and dropping out.

Race and Poverty

The Wire was created, produced, and primarily written by author and former police reporter David Simon, who was also a producer and writer of *Homicide: Life on the Street* (NBC, 1993–99). Like the earlier show, *The Wire* is set in Baltimore. Season four, the only one to deal directly with the school system, starts with the episode "Boys of Summer" and introduces four boys from West Baltimore as they are about to enter the eighth grade: Duquan "Dukie" Weems (Jermaine Crawford), Michael Lee (Tristan Wilds), Randy Wagstaff (Maestro Harrell), and Namond Brice (Julito McCullum). Before the boys start school, a new teacher arrives at the front door without a school ID. Even though talk in the school's main office has been centered on all the teachers who are not returning, one of them because the students tore up her classroom, it is agreed that they should buzz the new guy in "before he changes his mind." From the grainy, black and white image of the surveillance camera to the buzzer that admits the waiting man, this facility seems more like a prison than a school. It's no wonder that Principal Claudell Withers (Richard Hidlebird) and Assistant Principal Marcia Donnelly (Susan Duvall) are happy to hear that the new teacher was "a police." In fact, Donnelly jumps up, pumps his hand enthusiastically, and says, "Welcome to Edward Tillman Middle."

The new teacher, Roland "Prez" Pryzbylewski (Jim True-Frost), will find his training as a former detective useful over the course of the season, but first he has to clean the classroom that looks like a tornado swept through it, leaving a few broken desks and assorted papers on the dirty floor. By the time the new students arrive in their khaki pants and burgundy polo shirts, it is clear that while some of the teachers and administrators (including Prez and Donnelly) are White, virtually all of the students in this school are Black. Social class also distinguishes teachers from students. While the teachers scrape out a middle class existence, the students are poor. Two of the four featured boys live with adults who are addicts, one lives with a foster mother before he is sent to a group home at the end of the season, and the fourth boy is sent out to sell drugs to support his mother, just as his father had before he was sent to prison. These situations are woven into the narrative arcs of episodes of *The Wire* without a lot of flash and fanfare; the hardship faced by these boys is simply part of the

Figure 8.1. Jim True-Frost as Roland "Prez" Pryzbylewski in *The Wire* (HBO, 2002–08). Photo courtesy of Photofest. Used by permission.

fabric of their everyday lives. While Prez frets over how to reach the students in his nice house with his nice wife, the students don't fret. They just try to figure out how to survive another day against difficult odds and how, just maybe, to get a little bit ahead. Duquan, called "Dukie" because of his poor hygiene, has only the clothes on his back because the addicts in his house sell everything he brings home to get money for drugs. Randy, who dreams of having a store one day, changes shirts to match the younger students' polo colors (different colors designate the various grades) and mingles with the students, selling them candy for a small profit. Michael is a vigilant guardian of his younger brother because his mother is an addict, and the younger boy's father—who returns mid-season—molested Michael when he was his brother's age. Namond has more material possessions than the other boys and a job selling drugs on one of the corners, but he is not cut out for the street life imposed on him by his greedy and manipulative mother.

There are teachers who care about students and about their subjects of instruction at Tillman Middle, but even a new teacher like Prez is soon overwhelmed by the demands of maintaining order in the classroom, of connecting with students whose life experiences are so vastly different from his, and by running up against the roadblocks put up by the nameless and faceless "system" that dictates what he must teach and how he must teach it to prepare his class for standardized testing. How does Tillman, as depicted on television, square with real schools in inner-city neighborhoods? In his 1991 book *Savage Inequalities: Children in America's Schools*, Jonathan Kozol exposes the gross inequities between public schools in wealthy neighborhoods and those in poor neighborhoods because of disparities in funding and needs, and he explores the racial segregation in many of these schools. His subsequent book *The Shame of the Nation: The Restoration of Apartheid Schooling in America*, published in 2005, takes an even closer look at the segregation and decline of inner-city schools, schools in which the "isolation" of Black and Hispanic children is "absolute" (8). Kozol uses site visits and individual narratives to put a personal face on a public problem of epic proportions and to call for a different sort of accountability *to* schools rather than *from* them. Kozol says:

> This nation can afford to give clean places and green spaces . . . to virtually every child in our public schools. That we refuse to do so, and continue to insist that our refusal can be justified by explanations such as insufficiency of funds and periodic 'fiscal crises' and the like, depends upon a claim to penury to which a nation with our economic superfluity is not entitled. (62)

The chase for dollars takes up time and energy at Tillman Middle School, but there is not much evidence that stopgap methods translate into lasting improvements.

Dennis "Cutty" Wise (Chad Coleman) is a boxing coach in the neighborhood who is trying to make a difference in the boys' lives after his release from prison. He gets a "custodian" job at the school for $12 an hour only to find out that he is really supposed to round up kids who have stopped attending school. There is no budget for truant officers, so Assistant Principal Donnelly keeps a couple of janitor jobs unfilled for this purpose. In "Refugees," Cutty learns that he has a list of students he must bring to school at least one day a month because the school gets a financial allotment per student based on how many attend in a given month—his job has nothing to do with pedagogy and everything to do with the money. A few episodes later, he quits because, as Cutty tells the assistant principal, it's not enough to bring them in for a day. "If you had something where I was working with these kids . . ." Cutty says and walks out of the school. Cutty returns to the gym where he can teach boys to box while trying to keep them off the streets and away from the drug trade. Ironically, he is able to help teenagers more when he is unaffiliated with the school than when he is employed there.

Mrs. Donnelly, the assistant principal, is not uncaring; she is practical. When Prez wants to get some board games for his class, she does not stop him. When she asks him if he is still teaching eighth grade math, he responds that he's trying. She then sighs and gets a key reminding him to "[s]tay on the curriculum, Mr. Pryzbylewski, or you'll have an area superintendent on our backs." When Prez and Duquan get inside the book room, they find a few old games with missing pieces and quickly collect the dice (to teach probability lessons in the classroom), along with new copies of the fifth edition of their textbook; students are using the third edition upstairs. They also find some brand new computers in sealed boxes. Prez brings new textbooks and a computer to his classroom for the students to use for special projects.

In time, Prez makes progress with his students. He is nothing like the heroic White teachers of the movies who come to inner-city schools to save the students; his progress is incremental and marked by serious setbacks. Given his experience with the problems permeating the police department, he does not presume that he has all the answers or that he represents the "right way" to do things. He personalizes the curriculum with the dice and other games, but the results are modest compared to the dramatic highs featured in the movies. In the end, Prez will lose more battles for his kids than he wins, and some of the losses are devastating while the wins are, at times, barely discernible. How much can a good teacher accomplish when the system and the neighborhood stack the deck against these children? There are, however, those small victories to keep him going. One day, the seasoned teacher on his team who has counseled Prez from the beginning of the term comes to the door of his room while the students are working in groups, rolling the dice, and playing for Monopoly money. This colleague, Grace Sampson (Dravon James) is African American and has a "tough love" way with the kids that Prez has not yet acquired, but on this day, they share a nice moment watching the busy, happy students. When Prez says, "Trick 'em into thinking they aren't learning, and they do," she says nothing but clearly understands and relishes her colleague's satisfaction. With so much to overcome outside of the classroom, it would be unrealistic to think that these students could shed that background when they walk into the classroom, and *The Wire* brilliantly conveys the tightrope many inner-city children walk to get through another challenging day without a reliable safety net.

The Culture of Testing

Rhetoric and policies of testing and "accountability" or "standards" or "outcomes" are not new, but recently they have been ratcheted up considerably. The No Child Left Behind Act of 2001 has as its goal proficiency in reading and mathematics for all public school students by 2014, and the legislation threatens schools with harsh penalties if they do not improve performance at mandated levels. The problems with the policy are many and include the fact that government mandates for academic improvement have been poorly defined and largely unfunded. Because states take a piecemeal approach to record keeping and use different metrics for measuring proficiency in math and reading and, so far, keeping records such as graduation rates, it is very difficult to make valid comparisons. Disputes between states and low performing school systems are increasingly common as each year passes.

In 2006, the Maryland school board used No Child Left Behind as justification for taking control of four Baltimore high schools and reassigning the operation of seven Baltimore middle schools to charter school groups and other entities. According to Diana Jean Schemo, who reported the story in the *New York Times*, this was the first time a state had moved to take over schools under the No Child Left Behind law, "the most drastic remedy" in the act "reserved for schools that have failed to show sufficient progress for at least five years." She quoted Jack Jennings, president of the Center on Education Policy, as crediting Maryland for "leading the way in terms of state actions in dealing with schools with low test scores" and characterized Baltimore city officials and community leaders as "enraged by the move, accusing the schools chief of bad faith, of failing to deliver needed resources and of playing politics." Looking beyond Baltimore and even beyond the specific constraints of No Child Left Behind, Kozol is critical of the larger culture of testing that measures the worth of a child by a set of scores and reduces teaching and learning to test preparation. Kozol writes in *Shame of the Nation*:

> Most Americans whose children aren't in public school have little sense of the inordinate authority that now is granted to these standardized exams and, especially within the inner-city schools, the time the tests subtract from actual instruction. (112)

Not to mention that regimenting the curriculum into blocks of test preparation and more test preparation—and focusing on reading and math to the exclusion of other subjects—strips the passion out of teaching and the joy out of learning.

Clearly, *The Wire* creator/writer David Simon paid attention to the local news in preparing season four. The students, teachers, and administrators are constantly aware of the power test scores have over them. In "Alliances," Prez is in the teacher's lounge sharing his frustration with colleagues about how ill-prepared his kids are for the test and how stressed they are about the testing process. More seasoned teachers remind Prez that he has to stick to the curriculum to which he replies, "I can't. It's absurd." Another teacher cautions him, "You have to. That test in April is the difference between the state taking over the school or not." Prez counters, "Maybe the state should." The teachers demur and bring out references to No Child Left Behind and spoon-feeding the curriculum. When Prez asks, "And, what do they learn?" No one has an answer. Finally, Mrs. Sampson tells him to strike a balance and teach some for the test each day and always "keep a unit problem on the board for Donnelly"; the rest of the time "do what you feel like you need to do." Prez is the only man among the five teachers gathered there. He and a young-looking woman are White, and the other three women are African American. The oldest of the Black teachers gives him a bit of advice as she leaves the lounge: "The first year isn't about the kids. It's about you surviving."

Part of surviving requires negotiating the culture of testing. In "Know Your Place," a group of teachers and administrators are meeting to discuss an upcoming test, the Maryland School Assessment, which had a passing rate of 22 percent the previous year.

> **Vice Principal:** . . . don't think they haven't noticed it down at the puzzle palace. They're looking for at least a 10% increase from all city middle schools this time around.

A teacher asks if they have to start teaching the test so early.

> **Principal:** This year, the preferred term is "curriculum alignment."
> **Vice Principal:** There's nothing wrong with emphasizing the skills necessary for the MSA . . .

Another teacher says that skill-sets are one thing but the booklet they have has them teaching test questions.

Vice Principal: Test questions that involve skills.

When Prez says he doesn't see math questions, Vice Principal Donnelly announces that for the time being all teachers will devote time to teaching language arts sample questions because the school's grade was "failing" the previous year.

Later, Prez asks Grace Sampson what exactly the tests are assessing in the students. She says, "Nothing. The tests assess the teachers. If the scores go up, they can say the school is improving. If the scores go down, then they can't." This is a paradigm the former detective has seen before.

Prez: Juking the stats.
Sampson: Excuse me?
Prez: Making robberies into larcenies and making rapes disappear. You juke the stats and majors become colonels. Been here before.
Sampson: Wherever you go, there you are.

Prez is not the only person questioning the validity and relevance of the tests. A university researcher in the school supervising a funded pilot program notes that the "test material don't exactly speak to their world." His assistant, another former police officer, agrees, "Don't speak too loud to mine, either." The culture of testing is pervasive in actual schools, and *The Wire* expertly presents views of how that culture affects each stratum of the system from students, to teachers, to local administrators, to system bureaucrats, and to politicians overseeing the system. There is no precedent on television or film for a narrative to present such effective and compelling analysis of the failure of standardized tests used for punitive rather than diagnostic purposes.

Trying Something New

If the standardized curriculum is not yielding the desired results, why not try something new? Of course, there are special programs for students in some districts, magnet schools for children interested in the arts or science and technology, special programs for advanced students located in colleges and universities, but—as Jean Anyon established in "Social Class and the Hidden Curriculum of Work," *Social Class, School Knowledge, and Retheorizing Reproduction* and confirmed in *Ghetto Schooling: A Political Economy of Urban Education*—the same public school options and programs that are available to students from elite and middle classes are not available to kids like Duquan, Randy, Michael, and Namond. Even when a program with the potential to improve teaching and learning at Tillman comes along, it is hard to challenge the status quo guarded by layers of professional bureaucrats. The complexity of these relationships and the reason educational reform is so difficult are brilliantly revealed in *The Wire.*

In "Refugees," a researcher from the University of Maryland, Professor David Parenti (Dan DeLuca) discusses his project with an administrator who is offended at first, believing that the professor thinks "the system has lost control of the school." Eventually, she authorizes the project (after all, Parenti has $200,000 in funding), but she cautions him that it's all right for him to proceed only so long as there's no upheaval because there is an election coming up. The target group is violent repeat offenders, but teachers see the project as "this year's band-aid." Parenti hires a former police officer, Howard "Bunny" Colven (Robert Wisdom) as his assistant, and Colven helps him make the distinction between "stoop kids," who stay there when their parents tell them to remain on the stoop, and "corner kids," who don't stay on the stoop as instructed. Parenti and Colven work with school officials to identify forty corner kids among the regular attendees at the middle school, and they start with ten, including Namond.

It is clear that the special class is helping the "corner kids" over time. Their teacher is a doctoral candidate from the psychology department of the College Park campus, and Colven and Parenti observe. Various pedagogic strategies are used in the class, many of them successfully, but the superintendent objects to the program after hearing that some members of the class went with Colven to dinner at an expensive steak house. He thinks the teachers aren't educating the students, just socializing them, failing to realize that socialization is a part of the educational process for these students. Socialization does not end in the classroom, however. Colven has become attached to Namond, and he and his wife will eventually become foster parents for the boy, but the pilot research program will be less successful over time than this particular relationship. Mrs. Donnelly sees Colven in the hall one day and mentions that the central office has cancelled the program. Another storyline during the season involves the race for mayor of Baltimore, and it is disclosed during one mayor's Cabinet meetings that a school audit has revealed a fifty-four million dollar deficit in the system. This sets the stage for a meeting Colven and Parenti have with school administrators

Colven uses a political connection to get a meeting with the mayor to try to overrule school administrators and let them resume the pilot program. It turns out that the mayor is not there; he's gone to beg the governor for money to cover the school system's budget shortfall. Colven and Parenti do not fare much better with the mayor's political staffers than they did with the school system administrators. One complains that the pilot program tracks students and, because they're not teaching the test curriculum, that the students will be "left behind." Colven responds that the system is leaving all the students behind anyway, and the meeting is over. Outside the office, Colven is furious. He's been dismissed for telling the bureaucrats something they didn't want to hear. The professor is more philosophical about the situation.

Parenti: It's not you. It's the process.
Colven: The process?"
Parenti: We get the grant. We study the problem. We propose solutions. If they listen, they listen. If they don't, it still makes for great research. What we publish on this is going to get a lot of attention.
Colven: From who?
Parenti: From other researchers, academics.
Colven: Academics? What, they going to study your study?

Colven is laughing bitterly as they enter the wood-paneled elevator.

Colven: When do this shit change?

Indeed. Although Colven has made a significant, and probably a life-saving, change in one student's life by fostering Namond, he is not in a position to create larger, systemic change without a collective force with the power to alter policy.

Dropping Out

Recent headlines have revealed great disparities between test results and graduation rates. In more bad news for inner-city schools in cities like Baltimore, the wide divide between the performance of minority students and White students on the SAT and the ACT has continued to show an achievement gap based on race. While no study has documented that low-scoring students have been encouraged to leave school by school administrators, some researchers are concerned that this may be happening. "Most troublesome to some experts was the way the No Child law's mandate to bring students to proficiency on tests, coupled with its lack of a requirement that they graduate, creates a perverse incentive to push students to drop out. If low-achieving students leave school early, a school's performance can rise," writes Sam Dillon in "States' Inflated

Data Obscure Epidemic of School Dropouts."

Clearly, a television series, even one as insightful as *The Wire*, cannot provide the answers to questions about drop-out rates; these answers that will have to come from statistical analysis and careful questioning. The program has, however, presented the heartbreaking story of one middle school drop out and the teacher who tries to retain him. When Prez meets Duquan, he quickly notices the boy's poor hygiene and the unkind nickname, "Dukie," that plays on his name and the fact that he never has clean clothes. Prez not only arranges for Duquan to take showers at school before classes and provides him with a locker and a toiletry kit, but he also takes the boy's other clothes home with him to launder then returns them to the locker daily. Prez takes Duquan under his wing, and the boy begins to blossom. He has an affinity for the computer that the teacher finds in the book room and quickly makes friends with girls who want him to look up jewelry online for them. Prez eats lunch at his desk and allows students, like Duquan and Michael, to eat lunch there and use the computer or play games so long as they are well-behaved. Prez also begins to bring extra food for Duquan after the first day when Prez offers him half a sandwich and sees the boy devour it hungrily.

The trust and friendship that develops between Prez and Duquan is beautiful to observe, but it grows slowly in little moments. Duquan is in the class after school one day playing a video game on the computer. Prez tells the student that he has to leave soon and looks over the boy's shoulder at the screen.

Prez: What level are you on?
Duquan: Twelve.
Prez: I never made it past ten.
Duquan: Want to see me make it to 40?

A cheat screen comes up on the computer.

Prez: That's cheating.
Duquan: Want me to show you how?

Duquan smiles, and the teacher leans in to learn from the student.

Duquan has made tentative but steady progress during the term, and Prez is devastated when the Assistant Principal tells him that Duquan has made enough progress to be promoted to high school. When the teacher argues that the student is not ready, Donnelly says Prez has "adopted" him. She advises him to have some kids. "The kids in this school aren't yours. You do your piece with them, and you let them go. Because there will be plenty more coming up behind Duquan, and they're going to need your help, too." Prez will undoubtedly try to help other students, too, risking the disappointment that often comes from becoming emotionally connected to teenagers in his classes because becoming personally involved with students is what good teachers do.

When he learns that he will have to go to the high school, Duquan asks if he did something wrong and that's why he's being forced to leave the middle school. Prez assures the boy that he can do the work and tells him to come back any time if he needs to use the showers or get clean laundry. The transition is too hard for Duquan. He walks toward the high school, but he is scared by the unfamiliar buildings. He stops on the sidewalk, and several other boys push past him then turn back and laugh. Slowly, Duquan turns and walks away rather than proceed to the school. Duquan no longer lives with the family members who sold the boy's clothes to get drugs and left him to scavenge the streets for food. Now he lives with Michael in a nice apartment provided by the local drug dealer who is taking Michael into his crew. Later, Duquan brings Prez a present (a pen and pencil set for his desk) in a Christmas bag. Prez notices that he doesn't have a bookbag with him even though the school day is about to begin. The teacher tells his former student to stop by any time, and it's clear that he longs to say and do more. When Prez drives away from the middle school at the end of the day, he sees Duquan on the corner selling drugs. With this narrative arc, *The Wire* provides an indelible story of how a boy—even with promise, intellectual curiosity, and the support of a good teacher—can become a drop-out statistic.

Conclusion

Good teachers can make *a* difference but not *the* difference. There are too many other interests involved inside the school and outside of it for teachers in *The Wire* to change their students' lives, and, certainly, they are in no position to rescue them or shift the entire culture in inner-city neighborhoods to protect them. For one thing, there are just too many children who need help and too few resources supplied by the current system to go around. The children know the score. As Michael says to Randy when the school year is beginning, "Teachers are like cops. They come at you like they got you by the ass, but they ain't nothing they can do. More times than not, they go away." Michael's little brother, Bug (Keenon Brice), who seldom speaks in the series, concurs, "Word on that." But, Prez's story is not one of failure, only one of disappointment that he cannot do more and of the realization that the system wants to sustain itself above all else. The following season of *The Wire* turns away from Tillman Middle School, but viewers know that Roland Pryzbylewski is back in his classroom. The story goes on as it has been established. Prez survives the first year, and he returns to Tillman with a skill-set that cannot be conveyed in a teacher training session but must be earned in practice. This character who feels more "real" than those who have come before him, will scan the faces of his burdened students to search for tentative breakthroughs and overlook on-going setbacks because he knows that some students will make progress and, eventually, he may help guide a student to the kind of success that will be an unmitigated victory.

All texts are intertextual and speak in some way to our lived experience, but teacher narratives have a particular resonance for those of us who are teachers . . . or students. We must first learn to recognize the patterns embedded in these television shows and puzzle over what these patterns might mean—that is the project of this book—but we should not stop with these interrogations of teachers on television. Recent years have brought us an ever-expanding range of educators on television. The journey from Mr. Peepers and Miss Brooks to Steven Harper and Mr. Garrison is a long one. Or, is it? Teachers on television today are more complex and more realistic in their failings both inside and outside of the classroom, but the students and bureaucracies TV teachers confront are more complicated, too. It might be tempting to yearn for simpler times when Miss Crump was trying to get Opie to study assigned history lessons or when Mr. Kotter just wanted the Sweathogs to laugh at his jokes and stay out of trouble, but Prez proves that television is ready for a more realistic vision of educators. Perhaps this is because audiences have become more aware and critical in their viewing over time as well. In any case, *The Wire* serves as an exemplar and demonstrates that a Good Teacher in the tradition of the Hollywood Model can exceed the parameters of that model, face insurmountable problems, and still become an iconic teacher on television. Because of the "leaky boundaries" between popular culture and lived experience, characters like Prez assume an importance that transcends the confines of the television screen. These characters can help raise awareness about problems in education, help viewers understand the personal implications of these problems, and help establish a climate that makes people receptive to change. It is up to us to think about the possibilities of new policies and practices that will create schools where social justice is more important than perpetuating the class system in America, and leading children to self-actualization and civic engagement is more important than preparing them to meet the wants and needs of business interests or, simply, score higher on the next standardized test. Our students deserve better . . . as do our teachers.

Notes

Chapter One

1. There are a number of methods that have been advanced for undertaking this type of analysis, but one of the most useful is Kellner's diagnostic critique introduced in *Media Culture: Cultural Studies, Identity, and Politics Between the Modern and the Postmodern.*
2. When we are referring to this particular category of film and television narratives, we refer to them as a group designated by the proper noun "Good Teacher."
3. Sandra Weber and Claudia Mitchell look beyond both film and television in *That's Funny, You Don't Look Like a Teacher! Interrogating Images and Identity in Popular Culture* to consider the importance of the "culture of childhood to teacher identity and teacher education" (5). They consider books, toys (including the student teacher Barbie), children's play, drawings, and people's memories.
4. Some of the most popular educator biopics released in the last twenty years include *Dangerous Minds* (1995), *Freedom Writers* (2007), *Lean on Me* (1989), *Mr. Holland's Opus* (1995), *Music of the Heart* (1999), and *Stand and Deliver* (1987).
5. Since the mid-2000s, the FCC has periodically cracked down on broadcast stations that cross lines of decency, but this effect is limited because cable and satellite penetration is at an all time high and cable networks do not fall under the purview of the FCC.

Chapter Two

1. Specific estimates vary by source but a surge in television set sales throughout the 1950s is constant across sources. These figures are from "Television," *The World Book Encyclopedia*. Chicago: World Book, Inc. 2003:119.
2. Beaver's favorite teacher Miss Canfield, an occasional character in the first season, handles her classroom with gentleness and grace. Since many episodes of *Leave It to Beaver* aired in the 1960s, however, there will be additional discussion of this series in Chapter Three.
3. Just as there are "leaky boundaries" among texts, so, too, are there connections the mind makes among the various roles and real life incidents of actors' lives. Putting these roles in a larger context is part of examining the iconography of stars, and since understanding this iconography is part of the critical viewing process, we will reference other roles some of these actors have played when it seems relevant.
4. The LexisNexis Statistical database, Table 240, Statistical Abstracts, for 2004 provides the following list of all public elementary-secondary school districts with 100 or more full-time employees: All classroom teachers, 608,000 male and 1,859,000 female. The numbers are more divided when broken down into elementary and secondary classification with 173,000 male and 1,073,000 female elementary school teachers and 374,000 male and 547,000 female secondary teachers.
5. Even in the latest of the iconic Good Teacher movies featuring a woman in the main role, *Freedom Writers*, Erin Gruwell (Hilary Swank) sacrifices her marriage for her students as she demonstrates that it is impossible for her to meet their myriad needs and have any time left over for her husband. At first it seemed that the recent film *Then She Found Me*, starring and directed by Helen Hunt, might break the mold. She and her husband (Matthew Broderick, another teacher) have sex early in the film, but he leaves her the next morning. When Hunt's character begins dating the father of one of her students (Colin Firth), she is never again depicted in the classroom. It is unclear whether or not she gives up her job, but at least for the purposes of the film, she ceases to exist in the public sphere when she begins to express her sexuality in the private sphere.
6. The episodes of *Mister Peepers* from season one have recently become available on DVD, but they do not carry episode titles only original air dates.
7. *Our Miss Brooks* peaked in the ratings at #14 during its second season.
8. This is the central argument of Dalton's essay, "*Our Miss Brooks*: Situating Gender in Teacher Sitcoms" in *The Sitcom Reader*.

Chapter Three

1. Andy Griffith also played Benjamin Matlock on *Matlock* (NBC, 1986–92; ABC, 1992–95) as well guest appearances and film roles. Ron Howard would later star in *Happy Days* (ABC, 1974–84) before becoming a highly successful film director of *The Da Vinci Code* (2006), *Cinderella Man* (2005), *The Missing* (2003), Oscar-winner *A Beautiful Mind* (2001), *How the Grinch Stole Christmas* (2000), *Edtv* (1999), *Ransom* (1996), *Apollo 13* (1995), *The Paper* (1994), *Far and Away* (1992), *Backdraft* (1991), *Parenthood* (1989), *Cocoon* (1985), and *Splash* (1984) among others.

2. Mr. Kincaid also tells students their grades in front of all the other students, something teachers wouldn't do today.

Chapter Four

1. This was a good decade for professional has-beens. Not only did *Lucas Tanner* feature an athlete becoming a teacher, so did *The White Shadow*, *The Waverly Wonders*, *Hanging In*, and *Dorothy*. In one of these, a former showgirl becomes a teacher!

2. This moniker dates from Ken Howard's basketball career at Manhasset High School on Long Island, New York, where, as the only White player, his nickname was "White Shadow" (Deveney).

3. According to the *Oxford English Dictionary*, the term "hidden curriculum" was first used in 1964 by W. C. Kvaraceus in *Negro Self-concept*.

4. Travolta was nominated for Oscars for *Saturday Night Fever* (1977) and *Pulp Fiction* (1994).

5. As the show continues, Julie is relieved of this tedious task, and other characters are commandeered to listen to Kotter's jokes. Ultimately, the jokes are eliminated altogether.

6. The debate/drama coach is played by a young James Woods, who would go on to have a serious career as a film actor and received Oscar nominations for Best Actor in a Supporting Role in *Ghosts of Mississippi* (1996) and Best Actor in a Leading Role in *Salvador* (1986).

7. It was reported that CBS president William Paley was one of its biggest fans (Harmetz "CBS" and Houseman 82).

8. Writers were challenged to find a new way to describe Kingsfield (See Blau, Brooks and Marsh, Buckley, Farber, Harmetz "*Paper Chase*" and "CBS," O'Connor "Old Friends" and "The Preakness," "Profile," Schneider "Odyssey.")

9. In the book and film the school is identified as Harvard University.

Chapter Five

1. Redgrave was nominated for Best Actress in a Supporting Role for *Gods and Monsters* (1998) and Best Actress in a Leading Role for *Georgy Girl* (1966).

2. The first show was *The Alvin Show* (Brooks and Marsh, 586).

3. Tim Reid and Daphne Maxwell Reid are also married and have been partners in several television ventures, most notably the half hour dramedy *Frank's Place* (CBS, 1987–88). Individually, Tim is better known as Venus Flytrap on *WKRP in Cincinnati* (CBS, 1978–82), Det. Marcel 'Downtown' Brown on *Simon & Simon* (CBS, 1981–88) from 1983–1987, and as Ray Campbell on *Sister, Sister* (ABC, 1994–95, WB, 1995–99). Daphne is better known for replacing Janet Hubert-Whitten as Aunt Vivian Banks on *The Fresh Prince of Bel Air* (NBC, 1990–96) from 1993–96.

4. Fox would go on to have a substantial film career, starring in all the *Back to the Future* films as well as many others, before returning to television situation comedy as Mike Flaherty on *Spin City* (ABC, 1996–2002) for five years. Fox's career was curtailed when he revealed in 1998 that he had been diagnosed with early-onset Parkinson's disease in 1991.

5.   Although there are a few other girls featured in the early episodes, these girls were written out of the show by the second season. The first season, a short 13 episodes in August and September of 1979, featured seven teenage girls (one of them played by Molly Ringwald, who would go on to fame in John Hughes' teenage films of the 1980s, most notably *Sixteen Candles* and *Pretty in Pink*).

6.   Leachman has had a long career as an actor (beginning in the 1940s). She portrayed Frau Blücher in the feature film *Young Frankenstein* (1974) but is best known for her work for five years as Mary's neighbor, friend and landlady, Phyllis Lindstrom, on the sitcom *The Mary Tyler Moore Show* (CBS, 1970–77) and its spin-off *Phyllis* (1975–77), and as Grandma Ida on *Malcolm in the Middle* (FOX, 2000–06) from 2003–06. She won an Oscar for Best Actress in a Supporting Role for *The Last Picture Show* (1971).

7.   His character is replaced in the classroom by Billy Connolly (comedian Billy MacGregor) for the final season.

8.   In 1988, *Head of the Class* was the first sitcom to be filmed in the Soviet Union. The episode was filmed entirely on location in Moscow.

Chapter Six

1.   Reynolds has been an actor for fifty years. He was nominated for an Oscar for Best Actor in a Supporting Role for *Boogie Nights* (1997). Other memorable films include *Citizen Ruth* (1996), *All Dogs Go to Heaven* (1989) (voice), *The Man Who Loved Women* (1983), *The Best Little Whorehouse in Texas* (1982), *Cannonball Run* (1981), *Starting Over* (1979), *Smokey and the Bandit* (1977), *At Long Last Love* (1975), *The Longest Yard* (1974), *Deliverance* (1972). On television, in addition to *Evening Shade*, he starred 1962–65 in *Gunsmoke* (CBS, 1955–75), *Dan August* (ABC, 1970–71; CBS, 1973–75), and *B.L. Stryker* (ABC, 1989–90).

2.   For an analysis of this episode, see Dalton's chapter "Making Condoms Transgressive: South Park and 'Proper Condom Use'" in *Culture and the Condom*.

3.   Linguistics scholar Mary Bucholz uses the term "superwhite" to describe the language of nerds. Writing about Bucholz's work, Benjamin says, "By cultivating an identity perceived as white to the point of excess, nerds deny themselves the aura of normality that is usually one of the perks of being white."

4.   Omar Gooding is the brother of Cuba Gooding, Jr. and the son of Cuba Gooding, Sr.

5.   The public outcry and job loss feared by Richard Katimski is, in a more complicated scenario, what happens to Bill Truitt (Martin Donovan) in Don Roos' wonderful film *The Opposite of Sex* (1998).

6.   See Chapter 6, "Here but Not Queer: The Mainstreaming of Gay Teachers in the Movies," in *The Hollywood Curriculum: Teachers in the Movies*.

7.   Obviously, there are some revisionist teacher films, such as *Blue Car* (2002) and *Half Nelson* (2006) that offer a contrast to commercial Hollywood cinema, but our point still holds that television in the 1990s and 2000s offers more complex representations of teachers for mainstream audiences than cinema.

Chapter Seven

1. Joan Cusack had a more successful turn as a teacher when she played the love interest of Kevin Kline's character in the successful Hollywood feature *In & Out*. That film was number 25 in box office rankings for 1997 and grossed over 65 million dollars.
2. Garner was nominated for Best Actor in a Leading Role for *Murphy's Romance* (1985), but is best known as the title characters in the television shows *Maverick* (ABC, 1957–62) and *The Rockford Files* (NBC, 1974–80).
3. Quirky also describes some of the other series developed by the show's creator David E. Kelley, including *Picket Fences* (CBS, 1992–96), *Ally McBeal* (FOX, 1997–02), *The Practice* (ABC, 1997–04), and *Boston Legal* (ABC, 2004–).
4. In *Entertainment Weekly*, Mike Flaherty calls her "the youthful head of the social studies department and the de facto liaison between the overheated staff and their pimply charges (a sort of post-Columbine Karen Valentine for all you *Room 222* fans)."

Bibliography

Allen, Robert C. "Introduction to the Second Ed.: More Talk about TV." *Channels of Discourse, Reassembled.* Ed. Robert C. Allen. Chapel Hill: University of North Carolina Press, 1992.

Anyon, Jean. *Ghetto Schooling: A Political Economy of Urban Education.* New York: Teachers College Press, 1997.

———. "Social Class and the Hidden Curriculum of Work." *Journal of Education* 162 (1980): 67–92. (Reprinted 15 times over 25 years!)

———. "Social Class, School Knowledge, and Retheorizing Reproduction." Ed. Greg Dimitriadis, Cameron McCarthy, Lois Weis. *Ideology, Curriculum, and the New Sociology of Education: Revisiting the Work of Michael Apple.* London: Taylor & Francis, 2006.

Ayers, William. "A Teacher Ain't Nothin' but a Hero: Teachers and Teaching in Film." *Images of Schoolteachers in America.* Ed. Pamela Bolotin Joseph and Gail E. Burnaford. 2nd. ed. Mahwah, NJ: Lawrence Erlbaum Associates, 2001.

Bauer, Dale M. "Indecent Proposals: Teachers in the Movies." *College English* 60.3 (1998): 301–317.

Bayles, Martha. "Television: New Kids on the Block." *Wall Street Journal* 8 Sept. 1986, Eastern ed.: 1.

Bellafante, Ginia. "A Teenager in Love (So-Called)." *New York Times* 28 Oct. 2007, NY East Coast late ed.: 2.20.

Beller, Emily, and Michael Hout. "Intergenerational Social Mobility: The United States in Comparative Perspective." *The Future of Children.* 16.2 (2006): 19–36.

Bindas, Kenneth J. and Kenneth J. Heineman. "Image Is Everything? Television and the Couter-culture Message in the 1960s." *Journal of Popular Film and Television* 22.1 (1994): 22–37.

Blau, Eleanor. "Television Week: 'Paper Chase' Returns." *New York Times* 29 Mar. 1981: D41.

Bogle, Donald. *Prime Time Blues: African Americans on Network Television.* New York: Farrar, Straus and Giroux, 2001.

Bradbury, Katharine, and Jane Katz. "Issues in Economics." *Regional Review: Federal Reserve Bank of Boston.* 12.4 (2002): 3–5.

Brittenham, Rebecca. "'Goodbye, Mr. Hip': Radical Teaching in 1960s Television." *College English* 68.2 (2005): 149–167.

Brooks, Tim, and Earle Marsh. *The Complete Directory to Prime Time Network and Cable TV Shows 1946–Present.* New York: Ballantine, 2007.

Buckley, Tom. "TV: 'Paper Chase' Stays." *New York Times* 9 Jan. 1979: C19.

Bulman, Robert C. *Hollywood Goes to High School: Cinema, Schools, and American Culture.* New York: Worth Publishers, 2005.

"Cable and VCR Households." *Media Info Center,* 2006. 1 Mar. 2008. http://www.mediainfo-center.org/television/size/cable_vcr.asp

Chennault, Ronald E. *Hollywood Films About Schools: Where Race, Politics, and Education Intersect.* New York: Palgrave Macmillan, 2006.

Color Adjustment. Director/Producer Marlon Riggs, Producer: Vivian Kleiman. Narrator, Ruby Dee. Perf. Hal Kanter, Norman Lear, Steve Bochco, David Wolper, Bruce Paltrow, Esther Rolle, Diahann Carroll, Tim Reid, Daphne Maxwell Reid, Henry Louis Gates, Jr., Herman Gray, Alvin Poussaint, and Pat Turner. California Newsreel, 1991.

Dalton, Mary M. *The Hollywood Curriculum: Teachers in the Movies.* Rev. ed. New York: Peter Lang Publishing, 2004.

———."Making Condoms Transgressive: South Park and 'Proper Condom Use'." *Culture and the Condom.* Ed. Karen Anijar and Thuy Dao Jensen. New York: Peter Lang Publishing, 2005.

———. "*Our Miss Brooks*: Situating Gender in Teacher Sitcoms." *The Sitcom Reader: America Viewed and Skewed.* Eds. Mary M. Dalton and Laura R. Linder. Albany, New York: State University of New York Press, 2005.

Deveney, Sean. "Sports Talk with . . . Ken Howard." *Sporting News* 2 Dec. 2005: 9.

Dillon, Sam. "States' Inflated Data Obscure Epidemic of School Dropouts." *New York Times* 20 Mar. 2008, East Coast late ed.: A1.

Duncan, Charles A., Joe Nolan, and Ralph Wood. "See You in the Movies? We Hope Not!" *Journal of Physical Education, Recreation & Dance* 73.8 (2002): 38–44.

Edelman, Rob. "Teachers in the Movies." *American Educator: The Professional Journal of the American Federation of Teachers.* 7.3 (1990): 26–31.

Farber, Stephen. "'Paper Chase' Canceled by Graduation." *New York Times* 18 Feb. 1986: C22.

———. "Time for Hollywood to Stop Playing It Safe." *New York Times* 4 Nov. 1973: 159.

Farhi, Adam. "Hollywood Goes to School: Recognizing the Superteacher Myth in Film." *The Clearing House.* 72.3 (1999): 157–159.

Feuer, Jane. "Genre Study and Television." *Channels of Discourse, Reassembled.* Chapel Hill and London: The University of North Carolina Press, 1992.

Fiske, John. *Understanding Popular Culture.* Boston: Unwin Hyman, 1989.

Fiske, John and John Hartley. *Reading Television.* London and New York: Routledge, 2003.

Flaherty, Mike. "Hot for Teachers." *Entertainment Weekly.* New York: 29 September 2000: 2.

Forman, Murray. "Freaks, Aliens, and the Social Other: Representations of Student Stratification in U.S. Television First Post-Columbine Season." 53 *Velvet Light Trap* (Spring 2004): 66–82.

Friedan, Betty. *The Feminine Mystique*. New York: Norton, 1963.

Giroux, Henry A. *Breaking in to the Movies: Film and the Culture of Politics*. Malden, Massachusetts and Oxford: Blackwell Publishers, 2002.

———. "Race, Pedagogy, and Whiteness in *Dangerous Minds*." *Cineaste* 22.4 (1996): 46–49

Gitlin, Todd. *Media Unlimited: How the Torrent of Images and Sounds Overwhelms Our Lives*. New York: Henry Holt and Company, LLC, 2002.

Glanz, Jeffrey. "From Mr. Wameke to Mr. Rivelle to Mr. Woodman: Images of Principals in Film and Television." American Educational Research Association. Chicago, Illinois, 25 March 1997.

Goodman, Tim. "Review: Teacher Turns into Meth Maker in *Breaking Bad*." *San Francisco Chronicle* 18 Jan. 2008: E1.

Harmetz, Aljean. "CBS Moves 'Paper Chase' in Effort to Raise Ratings." *New York Times* 16 Jan. 1979: C7.

———. "'Paper Chase' Is Shifting to Pay-Cable." *New York Times* 13 Oct.1982: C28.

Harper, Phillip Brian. "Extra-Special Effects: Televisual Representation and the Claims of 'the Black Experience.'" Ed. Sasha Torres. *Living Color: Race and Television in the United States*. Durham, NC: Duke University Press, 1998.

"Hidden curriculum." *Oxford English Dictionary*. Oxford, England: Oxford University Press, 1989.

Houseman, John. "Kingsfield's Folly: The Death of 'The Paper Chase'." *Harper's Magazine* Dec. 1979: 81–85.

Huber, Joan, and William Form. *Income and Ideology: An Analysis of the American Political Formula*. NY: Free Press, 1973.

Hurley, J. Casey, Alvin C. Proffit, Elizabeth M. Vihnanek, and Gayle Moller. "Exposing the Reality Gap: Public Expectations and Boston Public." *The High School Journal* 87.2 (2003–04): 7–13.

Jones, Gerard. *Honey, I'm Home! Sitcoms: Selling the American Dream*. New York: St. Martin's, 1992.

Kellner, Douglas. *Media Culture: Cultural Studies, Identity, and Politics Between the Modern and the Postmodern*. London: Routledge, 1994.

Keroes, Jo. *Tales Out of School: Gender, Longing, and the Teacher in Fiction and Film*. Carbondale and Edwardsville: Southern Illinois University Press, 1999.

Kluegel, James R. and Eliot R. Smith. *Beliefs about Inequality: American's Views of What Is and What Ought to Be*. New York: de Gruyter, 1986.

Kozol, Jonathan. *Savage Inequalities: Children in America's Schools*. New York: Crown Publishers, 1991.

———. *The Shame of the Nation: The Restoration of Apartheid Schooling in America*. New York: Crown Publishers, 2005.

Ladd, Everett Carll. *The American Ideology*. Storrs, CT: The Roper Center for Public Opinion Research, 1994.

Lowe, Robert. "Teachers as Saviors, Teachers Who Care." *Images of Schoolteachers in America*, 2nd ed. Ed. Pamela Bolotin Joseph and Gail E. Burnaford. Mahwah, NJ: Lawrence Erlbaum Associates, 2001.

Lubrano, Alfred. *Limbo: Blue-Collar Roots, White-Collar Dreams.* Hoboken, NJ: Wiley, 2004.

MacDonald, J. Fred. *Blacks and White TV: African Americans in Television Since 1948*, 2nd ed. Chicago: Nelson-Hall, 1992.

Maloney, Henry B. and Jack E. Neuman. "Mr. Novak: Man or Superman?" *Television Quarterly* 3.3 (Summer 1964): 8–21.

Marc, David, and Robert J. Thompson. *Prime Time, Prime Movers: From* I Love Lucy *to* L.A. Law—*America's Greatest TV Shows and the People Who Created Them.* New York: Little Brown, 1992.

McClintock, Pamela. "Pols Shine, Teachers Decline in Primetime." *Daily Variety Gotham* June 2001: 27.

McNamee, Stephen J. and Robert K. Miller, Jr. *The Meritocracy Myth.* Lanham, MD: Rowman & Littlefield, 2004.

Means Coleman, Robin R. and Charlton D. McIlwain. "The Hidden Truths in Black Sitcoms." *The Sitcom Reader: America Viewed and Skewed.* Ed. Mary M. Dalton and Laura R. Linder. Albany: State University of New York Press, 2005.

Mittell, Jason. "A Cultural Approach to Television Genre Theory." *The Television Studies Reader.* Ed. Robert C. Allen and Annette Hill. London and New York: Routledge, 2004.

"Naked Classroom." *Time* 4 Oct. 1963. 4 June 2007. http://www.time.com/time/magazine/article/0,9171,875277,00.html

Nelson, F. Howard, and Krista Schneider. *Survey & Analysis of Teacher Salary Trends 1998.* Washington: American Federation of Teachers, 1998.

Newcomb, Horace. "Television and the Present Climate of Criticism." *Television: The Critical View*, Ed. Horace Newcomb. New York and Oxford: Oxford University Press, 2000.

Nugent, Benjamin. "Who's a Nerd Anyway?" *New York Times Magazine*, 29 Jul 2007: 15.

O'Connor, John J. "TV: Four Premieres of Comedy and Adventure." *New York Times* 9 Sept. 1975: 76.

———. "TV Review: Hesseman in *Head of the Class.*" *New York Times* 17 Sept. 1986: C26.

———. "TV Weekend: Old Friends, New Start." *New York Times* 15 Apr. 1983: C30.

———. "TV Weekend: The Preakness; 'Paper Chase' Reruns." *New York Times* 15 May 1981: C30.

Oxford English Dictionary. Oxford, England: Oxford University Press, 1989.

Paul, Dierdre Glenn. "The Blackboard Jungle: Critically Interrogating Hollywood's Vision of the Urban Classroom." *MultiCultural Review* 10.1 (2001): 20–27, 58–60.

"Profile: John Jay Osborn's 'The Paper Chase' being reissued more than 30 years after its original publication." Narr. Laura Sydell. *Morning Edition.* Natl. Public Radio. 4 Mar. 2003. http://www.npr.org/templates/story/story.php?storyId=1182266

Ranney, Kaitlyn. "*Is* It All Right Because It's *Saved by the Bell?*: An Examination of the Social Curriculum of Hollywood as Depicted in *Saved by the Bell* and *Good Morning Miss Bliss.*" Unpublished paper. May 3, 2007, 1–13.

"Satellite TV Subscriptions Soar, Cable Penetration Hits 16-year Low." *Broadcast Engineering.* Television Bureau of Advertising (TVB). 18 Dec. 2006. http://broadcastengineering.com/news/satellite-tv-soar-1218/

Schemo, Diana Jean. "Maryland Acts to Take Over Failing Baltimore Schools." *New York Times* 30 Mar. 2006, East Coast late ed.: A16.

Schneider, Steve. "The 'Paper Chase' Odyssey Continues." *New York Times* 5 Aug. 1984: H22.

Scott, Janny and David Leonhardt. "Shadowy Lines That Still Divide." *New York Times* 15 May

2005, East Coast, late ed.: 1.1

Soetaert, Ronald, Andrew Mottart, and Ive Verdoodt. "Culture and Pedagogy in Teacher Education." *The Review of Education, Pedagogy, and Cultural Studies*. 26: 155–174, 2004.

"Still the Best Teacher Show Ever." User Comments. "Mr. Novak." 4 June 2002. 22 May 2007. http://www.imdb.com/title/tt0056774/

Tropiano, Stephen. *The Prime Time Closet: A History of Gays and Lesbians on TV*. New York: Applause Theatre & Cinema, 2002.

Troy, Gil. *Morning in America: How Ronald Reagan Invented the 1980s*. Princeton, NJ: Princeton University Press, 2005.

U.S. Bureau of the Census, Statistical Abstract of the U.S.: 1995 (115 ed.) Washington, DC, 1995.

Veblen, Thorstein. *The Theory of the Leisure Class: An Economic Study of Institutions*. New York: Macmillan, 1902.

Watson, Mary Ann. "Primetime Parables of the New Frontier." *Journal of Popular Film and Television* 16 (1988): 70–78.

Weber, Sandra, and Claudia Mitchell. *That's Funny, You Don't Look Like a Teacher! Interrogating Images and Identity in Popular Culture*. London: The Falmer Press, 1995.

Weems, Lisa. "Representations of Substitute Teachers and the Paradoxes of Professionalism." *Journal of Teacher Education* 54.3 (2003): 254–265.

Index

I

L

S

U

V

Y

Z

Studies in the Postmodern Theory of Education

General Editors
Joe L. Kincheloe & Shirley R. Steinberg

Counterpoints publishes the most compelling and imaginative books being written in education today. Grounded on the theoretical advances in criticalism, feminism, and postmodernism in the last two decades of the twentieth century, Counterpoints engages the meaning of these innovations in various forms of educational expression. Committed to the proposition that theoretical literature should be accessible to a variety of audiences, the series insists that its authors avoid esoteric and jargonistic languages that transform educational scholarship into an elite discourse for the initiated. Scholarly work matters only to the degree it affects consciousness and practice at multiple sites. Counterpoints' editorial policy is based on these principles and the ability of scholars to break new ground, to open new conversations, to go where educators have never gone before.

For additional information about this series or for the submission of manuscripts, please contact:

> Joe L. Kincheloe & Shirley R. Steinberg
> c/o Peter Lang Publishing, Inc.
> 29 Broadway, 18th floor
> New York, New York 10006

To order other books in this series, please contact our Customer Service Department:

> (800) 770-LANG (within the U.S.)
> (212) 647-7706 (outside the U.S.)
> (212) 647-7707 FAX

Or browse online by series:
> www.peterlang.com